MOTHER PHILIPPINE
DUCHESNE

NIHIL OBSTAT:

ARTHUR J. SCANLAN, S.T.D.

Censor Librorum

IMPRIMATUR:

PATRICK CARDINAL HAYES

Archbishop, New York

New York, November 5, 1926

In all statements concerning the holiness of life of the characters who come into this volume the writer wishes to acknowledge her humble submission to the judgment of our Holy Mother the Church and especially to the decrees of Urban VIII and other Sovereign Pontiffs.

Mother Philippine Duchesne

MOTHER PHILIPPINE DUCHESNE

by

MARJORY ERSKINE

With an Introduction by
MOST REVEREND JOHN J. GLENNON
Archbishop of St. Louis

LONGMANS, GREEN AND CO.
55 FIFTH AVENUE, NEW YORK
39 PATERNOSTER ROW, LONDON, E.C. 4
TORONTO, BOMBAY, CALCUTTA, MADRAS
1926

Copyright, 1926,
By LONGMANS, GREEN AND CO.

INTRODUCTION

A dominant characteristic of the Frenchman is his love for his native land. For his country he is prepared to live and, if necessary, to die. What though tears and blood at times dim its history's pages—what though craft and cruelty, lust of power, and hatred of God distinguish many of its rulers—what though he himself is made the victim of their cruelties—yet does he even in his agony absolve his country. Rulers and Revolutions come and go—blood-red clouds sweep her horizon. Yet in his sight his country's escutcheon remains ever stainless. His France remains with her lilies loved and fair—a land whose history is woven of culture, faith and chivalry—whose future is bright with promise, whose destiny is with God.

Even though other lands are also blessed, yet he feels for his France that *"non fecit taliter omni nationi."* Is she not the Eldest Daughter of the Faith? —and has she not her special mission—to teach and to help her sister nations in the family of Christendom?

And to this abiding love of his is added his determination in his homeland to live—there to die, and in the little cemetery to seek his rest. The great world outside may for the moment beckon him forth. It has gold to give and crowns to offer. He may yield—he may follow the phantom, but ever in his heart is the hope that soon, his exile ended, he can greet his native land once more.

And yet though that love be deep and abiding there is a force that can dethrone it; there is a voice, a call that is stronger than that of home or kindred—a voice that rises higher and strikes deeper than all others. It is the voice of God—it is His call to them to leave father and mother and home and country—to come out from them and these and follow Him. In answer to it his response is sudden and complete. Lo! Thy servant heareth! My country I love well, but my God more. Thy will be done. Behold, I come!

In obedience to the divine mandate to go forth and teach, the French have gone in such numbers and with such zeal that to-day it may well be said of them there is no region of the world that is not filled with their labors. For three hundred years this nation of home lovers has given to God an ever-increasing army of Apostles, whose feet shod with His Gospel of Peace have trod shores of distant lands, crossed the plains, scaled the mountains—bearing the glad tidings of the Gospel.

And it is furthermore to be remembered that the French lead the world not only in the numbers and devotion of their missionaries, but in the quality and extent of their individual sacrifice. The Frenchman never does anything by halves. If it is God's will that he should go, then go he will, and there is nothing prosaic or limited in his response; and the completeness of his sacrifice is expressed in the prayer he makes and the hope he cultivates—that the Lord will show him the way to the Supreme Sacrifice. He cherishes in his heart the hope of martyrdom. Hence he asks that the hardest mission, the most distant country, the most barbarous and benighted people be made the objects of his zeal. In God's name he goes to conquer and to die.

And so it was that in early years the call came to

Philippine Duchesne to leave her native land, her beloved Dauphiny, to go to some far-off country to be a light-bearer to savage races who dwelt in darkness and in the shadow of Death. She had much to bind her to France and Dauphiny—devoted parents of high culture and splendid traditions. The land of Dauphiny had for its neighbor on the north the home of St. Francis de Sales; while the Alpine range formed its eastern horizon. So its people, as with the dwellers in the higher altitudes, blended the living faith with the love of liberty and lofty thought.

Here among her people she grew up, nursing in her soul her dream and hope that somehow God would bring her the opportunity of going out to serve Him somewhere—anywhere—that demanded all her courage, all His grace. Long years were to pass, and many trials were before her. She enters as a student the Visitation Convent which the gentle Francis had caused to be set up there on the heights above the city— devoted pupil; she joins the Visitation Community to become therein a devoted novice. Parental objections there were, but her goodness and constancy overcame them. Then came the French Revolution. The soldiers of liberty and fraternity closed the convent, and confiscated the property; drove the religious out into the streets, murdering all they could conveniently.

Cast in such a maelstrom one will emerge either an angel or a devil, and out of it came this Servant of God, purified as metal is by fire, her spirit still grandly heroic though all around her was ashes. She essays the task of restoring the convent on the hill, but her sisters are gone—some to God, others in their old age to find some asylum where they may rest. She struggles, she prays, but all in vain. Like one who walks through halls deserted she sees all around ruins and emptiness.

It was then that she felt, as she was often to feel in the future, that notwithstanding all her efforts, all her prayers, all her sacrifices, she had utterly failed. Soon, however, came the benefit of her failure. At that very time there was being established up in the north of France a community that appealed to her in her desolation, because of its warmth, its high purpose, its spirit of sacrifice. The Sacred Heart of Jesus brought it into being, and to the Sacred Heart it promises love and eternal fidelity. Her Visitandine house while it flourished had a like spirit. It too learned "of Him Who was meek and humble of heart." Hence it was for her an easy transition to go over to the Society wherein she saw flourishing all her dead hopes—all her early fervor.

And now as a member of this new Community her hopes of distant service, of complete immolation, returned. Years must pass—years, let us say, of preparation—until at length the Bishop of the Louisiana Territory in Western America comes to the new Community begging for Sisters. Out in that far-off land are colonists a few, and Indians many; but no one to tell them of God or duty. The great Foundress released to this distant mission her best beloved and most trusted daughter, who, with her few companions, starts on a long weary journey with supreme trust in the Sacred Heart of Jesus.

A voyage of months over stormy seas—New Orleans at last. Then the great river to St. Louis; then Florissant and St. Charles—now here—now there, seeking in the midst of many trials and privations to set up the reign of the Sacred Heart—to bring the children whom she gathered to learn the love and mercy and goodness of God.

Then, after years of struggle she sees her life dream come true. Out to Sugar Creek in Kansas, where dwelt the Potawatomi, the voice of the missionary calls her, and though broken in health she responds with alacrity. Among the savages she makes her last stand—teaching, praying, struggling on until the voice again bids her return to St. Charles to die.

There are those who delight in picturing the bigness and beauty that distinguished our colonial life a hundred years ago. They like to tell of its broad freedoms, its generous people, its flowering savannahs, rich vegetation, its glorious sunsets. All of which has literary value. It gives one side of the picture; but nearer to the truth and much more relevant is the story so admirably told in the following pages of the heroic Philippine struggling with the crude world around her—the log cabin, the wooden shack with an improvised door of some scanty sheeting to break the wintry winds; the frozen water, the frozen fingers, the hunger and pain, No—for them in exile, there was only One who could make it bearable, and it is He whom Philippine ever served and loved.

Wherever duty called her, her first care was to see erected the Altar, and with her Saviour present the crude and wind-swept cabin became a palace. Her own cot was always next the little chapel, and at its threshold day and night she kept vigil. There on retiring her Sisters left her and there they found her when morning came. She thought that her life was fruitless and a failure. (It is a way the Saints have of regarding their life work.) Yet, if we look at the rich harvests that have been gathered from the seed that she has sown, the many souls won to God by her zeal, the children instructed, the many religious houses that have been founded by her and by those whom she formed in religion, the marked devotion to the Sacred Heart of Whose Kingdom in this western land she was the John the Baptist, we must conclude that her was under heaven a life most fruitful and blessed.

Her ashes rest in its little shrine out at St. Charles under the maples and the stars. Her strong influence is felt and her blessed memory revered all through this western country. The children's children rise up to call her blessed. Her cause is before the Holy See, and urgent prayers go up to the Sacred Heart that her cause before God and His Vicar may prosper. Mayest thou, St. Madeleine Sophie, who loved our Philippine as in Christ the one nearest and dearest to thee on earth—whom thou scarcely couldst part with even for the while that she might come to establish with us the reign of the Sacred Heart—mayest thou, Oh, blessed Saint, now that we celebrate the day of thy crowning—not forget thy best beloved nor let her linger in the grand processional of heaven. Intercede, we beseech thee, that God's holy will be manifested in her regard and that with thee Holy Church soon may crown another Servant of the Sacred Heart!

JOHN J. GLENNON,
Archbishop of St. Louis.

ST. LOUIS, MISSOURI,
March 19, 1926,
Feast of St. Joseph.

CONTENTS

PART I. THE TRAINING OF AN APOSTLE

PART II. THE APOSTOLATE

ILLUSTRATIONS

xiii

PART FIRST

THE TRAINING OF AN APOSTLE

CHAPTER I

In the School of Generosity

CHAPTER I

In the School of Generosity—1769-1788

"Throughout their history the people of Dauphiny have not ceased to show themselves in love with independence and high spirit; they have been enterprising, energetic and persevering. . . . Their flight has passed beyond the nest. *Pennae nido majores.*"

PAUL BERRET.

Dauphiny, though French in language, customs, nationality and spirit, is in many ways a province apart. It can boast a varied landscape, yet its own peculiar character is typified by its snowcapped peaks, its crystal lakes, its pine forests, rather than by the smiling valley and the flowery mead. Although it was more than once a buffer state, its very history stands apart from that of France. In almost prehistoric times its border line enclosed the thatched huts of the Allobroges, the *"feroces spiritus,"* bold enough in a later day to defy and even to stay the onrush of the conquering arms of Caesar. Their capital, Culario, became Gratianopolis under the Roman, and Grenoble under the Gaul. War followed war; the proud high-spirited people of Dauphiny knew no compromise and would make no truce. The defeated Lombards retraced their steps across the Alps. The Saracens who entered Dauphiny came not as conquering heroes, but to lend their knowledge and their aid in

5

exploiting mines and in the construction of canals. The Princes of Dauphiny led their armies to the Holy Land while their cities struggled for new enfranchisement.

One would expect that with the death of the last prince the history of the province would be merged in that of France. It was not so. Dauphiny was too high-strung to brook control. She took no small part in the great wars with England. To France she gave some of her noblest men, among them Bayard, the blameless, fearless knight. The Kings of France, with the one exception of Louis XI, were not a little afraid of Dauphiny. Charles VIII, Louis XIII and Francis I thought it well to employ the noblest captains of this turbulent province in the foreign wars of France. The Governor de Gordes dared to defy Charles IX, who had ordered him to bring about in Dauphiny a massacre like that of St. Bartholomew. Of de Gordes' successor, Henry IV remarked: "Lesdiguières has made himself a Dauphin"; yet the King did not dare to profit by this insight and to remove the governor who might in some way prove a rival. Thus it came about that through the sixteenth, seventeenth and eighteenth centuries the spirit of independence waxed strong.

In the heart of Dauphiny lies the lovely valley of the Isère, a vale rich in vineyards, wheat and corn, yet flanked by mountains on which the white-starred edelweiss, the Alpine tulip and the blue gentian replace the snow which there comes early and stays far into what in a less high altitude would be spring. Down this peaceful valley Hannibal marked in blood his way to Rome. Later a Roman road showed how wise had been his choice. The Valley of the Isère can boast of one of the most interesting and most picturesque cities of all France—Grenoble, which bears even today the traces of

several successive civilizing forces; for, though flame
and flood have threatened to wipe out what was oldest
in the city, much remains. There are relics of the
Roman, the Gaul, the Mohammedan, the mediæval
Dauphin, the scholar of the Renaissance, the saint who
"is not of an age, but for all time."

Grenoble had no small part in the history of Dauphiny; it was in turn the Allobrogian capital, a Roman
fortress, a mediæval stronghold. It still prides itself
on the Chevalier Bayard. Dauphiny knew only his
youthful promise, and his triumphs in the joust and
tourney, for France claimed him as her son. One day,
however—it was on the morrow of a great Italian victory—he suddenly appeared in Grenoble, which he had
learned was suffering from a cruel plague. There he
spent himself in the service of the sick and dying, he
drove away bands of marauders, and only when his
native city seemed to need him no longer did he return
to the Italian front.

The spirit of independence which was Dauphiny's
had its well-springs in Grenoble. There the French
Revolution took its rise in the rebellion of the local Parliament which, from 1760 on, refused to sanction the
new financial measures of the Government. Among the
leaders in this strife for liberty were the Périers and
their cousins, the Duchesnes.

The character of the Duchesnes was strongly
marked. One who knew them wrote, "They were souls
of strong temperament whom the education of the
ancien régime had made still stronger. The '*caractère
Duchesne*' is a proverbial phrase to express the energy
for good existing in this family." This energy had
brought them a success that by the middle of the eighteenth century made them known the world over as

prosperous manufacturers and exporters of textiles. In France they were famed not only in the world of merchandise, but at the bar and wherever else they strove. At the very time that Dauphiny, at the dictate of Grenoble, was daring to set aside the precepts of Paris, a Duchesne, Pierre François, held a distinguished position in the high-spirited, fiery Parliament of his native province. He was a man of intellect, of energy and of will, possessing an unusual gift of oratory. His was a Christian family of the good old type, and members of each generation for a century at least, had offered themselves to God in the Visitandine Convent at their native town, Romans, or at Grenoble. Yet Pierre François was for many years far less in sympathy with the spirit of his cloistered relatives than with the philosophic and over-liberal views of his political party.

To that liberal party belonged the Périers, Claude, Casimir and Camille. Claude was a successful banker, and a founder of industrial establishments in Dauphiny. He bought Vizille, the ancient château of the Dauphins, and put it at the disposal of the Parliament of Grenoble, to the cause of which he dedicated his five sons. His sister, Rose Euphrosyne, married Pierre François Duchesne, thus linking the families whose traditions, inclinations and characters were remarkably alike.

The Duchesnes and Périers lived next door to each other in the Place St. André, Grenoble. There was something monastic and severe about the very street. These were the characteristics not only of the Church of St. André, and of the Hall of Justice which once had been the palace of the counts of Dauphiny, but also of the houses with grated windows, cloistered courtyards and grand stairways. From the street the Duchesne house looked uninviting, forbidding even, but the door between it and the Périer home was often open, and merry laughter must have echoed in the grim old court-yard where the little girls and their boy cousins played together.

Rose Philippine Duchesne was born on August 29, 1769. She was baptized a week later, on our Lady's Birthday, in the Church of St. Louis, France's crusader king, and the patron of the far-distant mission to which she was to devote herself one day. She was a child of Dauphiny, a true Duchesne. Strength and imperious-ness were visible even in her earliest years. Her good mother saw the dangers and the possibilities for good in such a nature, and the training in the school of unselfish-ness and generosity began before it was time for lessons to be learned from books. The tendencies to wilfulness, to stiffness, to a childish severity were worked upon, her character of iron was tempered by piety and devotion to the poor. Philanthropic giving may be unselfish, but charity based on true, virile piety alone is selfless, and selfless Philippine was to be. That blessed day, how-ever, was still far off, for the sanctifying of this charac-ter took years.

The first incident recorded of her early life is that, when she was three years old, small-pox disfigured her little face that had given promise of real beauty. Philip-pine often heard her sisters admired, and she noticed that her name was passed by in silence, yet no word of bitterness or even of regret escaped her. This unselfish spirit was shown not only toward those nearest and dear-est to her, but also to chance acquaintances, for from her earliest years her greatest pleasure was to give. To the beggars at the door and to the sick poor whom her mother took her to visit she gave all the coins that she had received for herself.

"We give you this money for your own little pleasures," her parents would sometimes remonstrate.

"And if my pleasure is to give it to others, what then?" she would reply.

She was old for her age; her early taste for history proved this. Perhaps she showed one of the shadows in a character that was far from perfect when she read Roman History to an elder sister who was ill, and in need of cheerful entertainment. It takes time and suffering for an autocratic nature such as Philippine's to learn the sympathy and tact that enable one to read at sight another's tastes.

Grenoble had much to offer the lover of history. The Church of St. André just across the street from the house of the Duchesnes was only three centuries old, but a long walk would take the children to the Monastery of the Minims, where was the tomb of Bayard, and to the Church of St. Lawrence which could boast a Merovingian crypt with eight and twenty columns of rare pink and white marble. There were probably summer expeditions to the Grande Chartreuse, perched like an eagle's nest on the heights, some twelve miles beyond Grenoble.

History was in the making, and changes were taking place that were to influence Philippine's life. When she was seven years old, the thirteen English colonies on the Atlantic Coast of North America rebelled against taxation without representation, threw off their allegiance to the Mother Country and declared themselves free and independent. Slowly the news of this revolt reached Dauphiny, whose heart, Grenoble, was quick to throb with kindred feelings. The inhabitants of the province must have taken a lively interest in the American Revolution which followed the Declaration of Independence and which ended in victory for the newly federated states. Beyond the vaguely outlined western border of the United States lay the French colony then known as Louisiana. Missionaries from France and Spain had gone to these far-distant lands to evangelize the Indians. Some of these zealous priests returned to their native land to plead the cause they loved and to beg alms for the cultivation of fields white for the harvest. One such missionary thrilled Grenoble with the tales he had to tell, and the heart of the little Philippine Duchesne throbbed high with longing to share one day the toils and labors, the suffering, even the martyr's death. For there were many who had shed their blood for Christ in far America. One of these missionaries, the Jesuit, Father Eusebio Francesco Kino, wrote in the picturesque style which also characterized Philippine's letters even from her childhood: "And although we had gone to their shores solely to seek the precious pearls of their souls, to nurture them with the heavenly dew of the Divine Word, and to give them their lustre in Christ, showing them the celestial shell, Mary, who for their good conceived with the gentle dew of Heaven, the perfect pearl of first lustre, Christ, yet they (the Indians) thought we came like others . . . in search of the many and rich pearls which were produced in the countless fisheries of their coasts."

The illusion that there were material pearls to be found on the American coast was probably dispelled before the end of the eighteenth century, but, as Philippine listened to the words of the missionary who had visited Grenoble, she made up her mind to go and sell all that she had and to buy the field which held a treasure, the souls of the Indians of North America.

The little girl was no dreamer, however. Madame

Duchesne saw to it that her children were well occupied, and she brought them up in an almost Spartan simplicity. The Alpine cold of a winter in Grenoble did not prevent early rising, even though ice had to be broken in their pitchers. Frost-bitten and chilblained fingers were not taken as an excuse for poor writing or careless sewing. When lessons were over for the day, there were younger sisters to be amused.

Events were few, so whatever chanced to break the blessed monotony of a homelife such as this must have made a lasting impression on the mind of Philippine. She was nine when her city was threatened by the "Deluge de la St. Crespin." The River Isère unites with the Duc a few miles below Grenoble, and when both streams have overflowed their banks the valley is under water, and the lower parts of the city are endangered, but the suburbs, being on the heights, are in safety.

On the Hill of Chalmont stood the Visitandine Convent of Ste. Marie d'en Haut. This house had been founded on April 8, 1618, by St. Francis de Sales, who at the request of the citizens of Grenoble had sent for Mother de Chantal to help him to choose a suitable place for a foundation. Together they selected a rocky site, a considerable height above the city, remote from the traffic and feverish industry of commerce and looking down upon the valley of Grésivaudan with its smiling fields and gardens. The two saints built the monastery of Ste. Marie as an aerie upon a crag above the valley. The eaglets they would there train were now to look upon the sun in contemplation, now to descend to the sick poor in the city of Grenoble. Such was St. Francis' first plan, this the reason why he called the new order "The Visitation." It seemed best, however, to modify this design, and grilles and turns soon proved that Ste.

Marie d'en Haut was destined for an order of contemplatives. Several years after the foundation, as St. Jane Frances de Chantal knelt in the chapel of Ste. Marie praying for him whom she called the Founder of the Visitation, she distinctly heard a voice say, "He is dead." Thinking only of the spiritual transformation she had seen in him at their last visit, she exclaimed: "My God, he is no more, he lives no more. It is Thou Who dost exist and live in him." Then she wondered if the words she had heard might mean that he was dead. Several days later she learned that her saint and protector had indeed gone to his heavenly reward.

It was to this Convent of Ste. Marie d'en Haut that Philippine Duchesne was sent to school. Of a serious turn of mind and caring little for games, she must often have spent her hours of recreation looking out upon the valley where the Isère marks its way in silver, where the only sounds are those of sweet-tongued bells, of rapturous birds, and crystal waterfalls. Above and far beyond are Mont Blanc and St. Nizier, chaste Alpine peaks.

At Ste. Marie, Philippine went on with the lessons learned at her mother's knee. There was more reading, more history, more geography. The child, with her ever-growing hopes for the missions, must have paused over the story of the Discovery of America and of the conquest of the Indians whom she longed to win for God. She must have studied with interest the maps of North America and of still more remote China, wondering on which coast her lot was to be cast. There were lessons too in sewing, an art and science in which she was most skilled. Still more important was the training of character Philippine received, for at the Visitation, "in a constantly serene and maternal atmosphere, the child learns at an early age self-denial, a sense of duty, and of responsibility to God for every action." Thanks to her mother's training, these precious virtues were not unknown to Philippine; in fact, they sum up the characteristics of her early childhood, the good Sisters had but to deepen and to strengthen these traits in the little girl confided to their care.

Once the long days of homesickness were over, Philippine found that at Ste. Marie she had a second home; she felt in her element in those cloistered halls. There, grew her devotion to the Blessed Virgin, there, she saw in chapel, court and cloister symbols of the Sacred Heart, Which, through the humble Visitandine, Saint Margaret Mary, had shown anew to a forgetful world Its Divine and human love.

It was to prepare for her First Holy Communion that Philippine had been sent to the convent. Of that blessed day no details have come down to us. We know only that she was twelve years of age, and that the ceremony must have taken place in the convent chapel, or rather church, which the munificence of the Duc de Lesdiguières had long before enriched. We may be sure that the earnest, loving child did not see the frescoed ceiling or reredos, but that her look was fixed upon the Tabernacle of the fine old marble altar. Napoleon Bonaparte, born the same year as Philippine Duchesne, and probably making his First Communion at the same age as she, looked back from Saint Helena to that day as the happiest of his life. Other Bonapartes have thought the same, but it is often otherwise with those who give their lives to God and to His service, for still happier days are in store for them. Besides, it seems likely that François Duchesne did not follow his little daughter to the altar-rail, even on that great day of her life, and her heart must have throbbed with the pain that children's hearts know well, and must have quickened with high resolve to win her father back to God, cost what it might. This much we know: before her First Communion Philippine had longed for martyrdom upon some distant shore; from this day on she planned another form of self-immolation. She had come to know that the grace to shed one's blood is given to few, and she was now determined to give her life, her all, to God in the daily long-drawn-out radiant martyrdom of religious life—a life which she had seen nobly led at Ste. Marie.

When might she enter? The Superior of Ste. Marie had given up the world at seventeen. Philippine could hardly hope to enter any younger, and she was still only twelve. Young as she was, she knew that natural strength of character, high spirit, independence, would not suffice her in her hour of need. She daily sought for light to know God's Will more clearly and for strength to do that Will. It was not only at the hours prescribed by the school rule and the odd moments she might spend before the Blessed Sacrament that she prayed, but she obtained leave to rise with the nuns and to make a meditation at the same hour that they made theirs. And this was not merely during Lent, which was for her a time of real penance, nor during the month of May, always so dear to her, but day after day during all her school life. She needed light, her desire to work among the savages grew stronger. Was she to save souls as St. Theresa did, by prayer alone, and never to see those for whom she prayed? Or would Christ choose her as an apostle to go before His Face? Was she to combine apostleship and cloister in the "martyrdom of the classroom"? But when she dreamed of saving souls, they always shone out from the almond-shaped eyes of Chinese, the deep-set eyes of Indians or the dancing eyes, set in strange whiteness, of the colored race. However, Philippine was only thirteen, and God knows how to wait—a lesson which she had yet to learn.

Her confessor at that time was the missionary who first had fired her soul with stories of Louisiana. To him she probably confided her distress when her father decided to take her away from Ste. Marie. She had said nothing of her hopes for the far future, but he had doubtless read her secret in

"The deep unwavering eyes
Of 'her' eternity made wise."

François Duchesne's false philosophical principles were responsible for his fear that his daughter might enter religion. Neither he nor his wife could have thought that she would be unhappy in religious life which had been so bright for many of their dear ones. No doubt the affectionate mother dreaded to lose the child who had grown dearer during the year or more that she had spent away from home. She probably thought it wisest to humor her husband, whose prejudices against religion would only grow if his will were opposed. He was becoming daily more powerful in the Parliament of Grenoble.

So Philippine generously and cheerfully gave up the life at the convent school. It was at her own suggestion that she now joined her Périer cousins in their studies. There were eight boys in that family, and their father superintended their education with the thoroughness which he brought to everything he undertook. Time was to be well spent in that novel school conducted by M. l'Abbé Raillane in the square tower of the Périer house in the Rue St. André. The boys were learning Latin, and their cousin, even though she was "only a girl," was allowed to her great delight to study it with them. Arithmetic was certainly a necessity for the four boys who were to be bankers, and to Philippine too this study would not be useless. She made less of a success at music than her cousins did, but with drawing it was far otherwise. The only pity was that the drawing teacher was not a master in his art, for Philippine, with a native gift for sketching, soon outstripped him. M. l'Abbé Raillane, a learned and holy man, must have rejoiced in the promise of learning and of virtue which he saw in the young girl. He found her faith unspoiled by principles such as those her father held, her hope unshaken in the midst of obstacles, her love uncooled in its devotion, in spite of the Jansenism that still chilled France, her humility in her willingness to study with her cousins, the eldest of whom was four years her junior.

Monsieur and Madame Duchesne had allowed Philippine to have her way in the choice of a type of study which only accentuated the virile features of her mind and heart. She in turn acquiesced in all that they planned for her diversion. Though not able to play the piano, or any other instrument, with ease, she delighted in music and loved to go to concerts. Her earnestness prevented her from making light even of a dancing lesson, so that she seemed quite at ease at the gatherings that were probably frequent in that gay double household of Périers and Duchesnes. These gaieties were reminders, by contrast, of a life she longed to lead. However, she said nothing of her plans which had been gradually changing since her return from Ste. Marie.

Philippine's remarkable love of prayer had at first drawn her towards Carmel. True, the cloister door

would close out her savages, but not their souls. St.
Theresa, we are told, won as many conversions as did
St. Francis Xavier. Looking about with maturing
eyes, Philippine saw how necessary was Christian education to the rising generation of a France that was
threatening to become infidel! The Visitation had for
her a strong appeal because she thought its rule resembled that of the Society of Jesus, which she loved as
uniting perfectly the contemplative and active lives.
The Jesuit saints were among her chosen friends in
Heaven, especially Xavier and John Francis Regis.
As a Visitandine, she could work, suffer, pray, in turn,
and all at once.

Still she waited. She was only seventeen. Perhaps
God did not want her yet. Some wise counsellor must
have directed this delay, it was so unlike precipitous
Philippine to bide even God's good time, but wait she
did. The sign came and from those who little dreamed
that thus they were the means of an earlier entrance into
religion than might otherwise have been.

Her parents urged her to marry—even her younger
sister was about to be married. Why not she? Philippine repeated that she had determined to give herself to
God. They were silent. Opposition, it was evident,
had not altered her—perhaps time would.

She was now the eldest girl at home. There were
many ways in which she could help her mother and she
was unstinting in her generous service of each and all.
So things went on until one day she learned that her
parents had a definite marriage in view for her. They
were trying to press her gently but no less surely into a
life she did not care to lead. She now changed her
course. Waiting had not won her parents to her side,
she would not wait longer. Her warning was merely a

CLOISTER AND GARDEN OF THE CONVENT OF SAINTE-MARIE-D'EN-HAUT, GRENOBLE

refusal of invitations to entertainments and balls, a choice of simple, plain dresses, a more noticeable religious regularity in devotional practices which she had marked out for herself. In this warning, which was characteristically rigid, she persevered all that long year.

Philippine's aunt, Madame Périer, a woman full of faith and piety, would probably have been glad to see signs of a religious vocation in her own daughter, Philippine's favorite cousin, whose great charity made her a power in Grenoble. She married, however, and, as Madame de Savoie-Rollin, did untold good in her native city. In this cousin and in her good aunt, Philippine placed all her earthly hope. One day she asked Madame Périer to go with her to visit Ste. Marie to consult the Superior, Mother de Murinais, about her entrance, still in the unknown future. At the end of the visit, Philippine felt that her hour to act had come. She said good-bye to her aunt, informing her that she would enter the noviceship that evening.

All was desolation that night in the home of the Duchesnes. They felt that joy had left their house. They could not know what they would later learn that "when God takes loved ones away, He gives them back with increased power of sympathy" and love.

CHAPTER II

LESSONS OF DETACHMENT

CHAPTER II

"I know that when the stress has grown too strong,
*   Thou wilt be there;*
I know that though the waiting seems so long,
*   Thou hearest prayer.*
I know that through the crash of falling worlds
*   Thou holdest me;*
I know that life and death and all are Thine
*   Eternally."*

JANET ERSKINE STUART.

Philippine Duchesne had been a postulant at Sainte Marie d'en Haut for only a few days when her mother and sisters followed her up the steep, winding street, and past gloomy-looking houses. A sudden turn brought them to an archway surmounted by an inscription which they had often read but which now had a new meaning for each of them. It ran: "St. Francis de Sales chose this place for the foundation of the Fourth Monastery of the Order of the Visitation of St. Mary. The first stone was laid in his presence, October 16, 1619." They raised the ponderous knocker, the door opened of itself and a portress met them at the far end of a dark passageway and led them to the parlor. The monastery grill seemed to the heart-broken mother a true symbol of the barrier which she thought had come between herself and her daughter. To Philippine this visit was not less painful; her mother spoke of how they

23

missed her at home, of how she had counted upon her to help in training the baby sister Mélanie and of her father's displeasure. The young girl was no less loving than beloved, her heart was wrung with pain as she listened to her mother's pleading words. Yet love it was that had brought her to Ste. Marie—again this higher love prevailed and her family returned home as they had come.

They left Philippine, not a they had found her, but strengthened by conflict and by victory though sad at heart. As the door closed upon her mother and sisters, she turned towards the chapel. Ste. Marie d'en Haut had been built in the old monastic style. Its buildings, flanked on the inner side by cloisters, surrounded a court which was open to the sky. In the centre of the grassy quadrangle stood a cross of stone near which were two wells. As Philippine passed around the cloister garth she must have been reminded of One Who, sitting by the well of Jacob, said: "If thou didst know the gift of God." Perhaps the bare stone cross seemed to the postulant the fitting symbol of God's gift to her. She went down the steps, entered the nuns' choir, and as she renewed her consecration before a statue of the Sacred Heart, she prayed for strength.

A few months later in that same chapel she received the longed-for habit of the Visitation which she loved daily more and more. Enthusiasm never fails to interest. It was probably Philippine's glowing, fervent appreciation of the Lives of the Saints which she read with true delight that caused her to be chosen to repeat for the community what had pleased her most in reading. Like St. John Berchmans, she could say, when she had spent more than a year in religion, that she did not remember having broken a single rule of her Order.

With St. Francis Regis, she felt her love for the poor ever on the increase. Another St. Francis Xavier, she hungered and thirsted for souls; to this great Apostle she would sometimes say, "Why do you not call me to follow you? I would do so at once."

St. Francis de Sales and St. Jane de Chantal had founded their Congregation for those whom delicate health, age or infirmity debarred from the older Monastic Orders. "The Rules of this Order," says Mgr. Bougaud, "made for persons of delicate health and generosity of soul, present nothing that can weaken the body, they omit nothing that can crucify the soul." Yet St. Chantal herself had characteristics that would seem to have disposed her for a more rigorous kind of life. "She was very ardent and naturally impulsive. Her strong nature had need of action, her robust health, her warm and sanguine temperament called for penance," and the Rules leave vast scope for generosity guided by prudence and obedience. Philippine Duchesne was also impulsive, strong, active. In those early days she was blessed with robust health. Ardent too she was and sanguine. When there "was a lion in the way," she never hid nor fled, she either refused to see the lion, or, seeing it, she fought it. Her superiors, knowing her constitution, her temperament and her grace, allowed her more activity, more penance, more fasts and vigils than the Visitandine Rule prescribed.

Sometimes as they left the chapel at ten o'clock at night, the Sisters would meet her smiling and radiant making her way down the long passage to the tribune. She had obtained leave for some hours of prayer. Often she lost count of time, and morning would surprise her still on her knees. Then she would steal gently along the corridor where the picture of the Sacred Heart could just be seen in the light of early morning. She knew by heart the words below that painting and gladly re-echoed their message: "With joy ye shall drink water from the fountains of the Saviour."

From time to time throughout that year of her noviceship, Philippine must have heard through the gratings of the old monastic parlor rumors of civil events of no slight moment to Ste. Marie and to her dear ones in Grenoble who were deeply concerned in what was taking place. In May, 1788, the Parliament of Paris declared all provincial Parliaments prorogued until the formation of the great baillie-courts. This and other summary measures fired the populace of Grenoble. The tocsin sounded, the alarm-bell pealed and boomed; mountaineers rushed down with axes and made short work of the coaches in which the members of the Parliament of Dauphiny were about to leave the city. The troops sent to quell the riot were met by violence. The mob broke into the house of the Governor, the Duke of Clermont-Tonnerre. Brandishing an axe above the Governor's head, the leaders of the people threatened to hang him on the drawing-room chandelier if he refused to convoke its Parliament. Thus, says Carlyle, "axe over head, the poor General has to sign capitulation, to engage that the Lettres de Cachet shall remain unexe-cuted and a beloved Parliament stay where it is." Meanwhile other rioters climbed up on the roofs and hurled down tiles upon the soldiers. Marshal Vaux, sent to replace the yielding Clermont-Tonnerre, could only forbid the Parliament to meet within the city walls. He was obeyed. A week after the "Day of the Tiles," as this the "first battle of the Revolution" has been called, the three orders were assembled in M. Périer's château of Vizille.

This famous castle had been built by the Duc de Lesdiguières upon the ruins of the ancient manor of the Dauphins. So large had Lesdiguières made it that he, "the old fox of Dauphiny," could there lodge a court, and hide implements of war for the equipment of ten thousand men. Satan, a quaint legend says, threatened to burn the line of fortresses in less time than Lesdiguières would take to ride past the beetling turrets. "The old fox" took up the challenge and won the day, but his horse's tail was caught in the fresh cement and there it was still to be seen in 1788. In one of the buildings was the hall of the Jeu de Paume, whose walls told in bright frescoes the long story of Lesdiguières' victories. There Louis XIII had visited "the old fox" in his lair. There feudalism had reigned supreme and there it met its deathblow, for from those walls went forth a demand that Louis XVI convoke the States General without delay. There, too, at three o'clock in the morning of July 22, 1788, the Provincial Assembly signed a petition of thanks to Claude Périer for his loyalty to the new cause in opposition to which many royal hearts of France were soon to bleed.

To Philippine Duchesne, the outbreak of the Revolution meant more than danger to her family, more than peril for her loved Dauphiny and France. It meant the indefinite postponement of her religious profession in preparation for which she had now completed the time of noviceship required by the Church. Her father, seeing the danger to religion in the political cause he had at heart, would not consent to his daughter's making her vows until she should be twenty-five years of age. That would mean waiting six more years. Philippine could console herself only with the thought that, if not admitted to the inner sanctuary of religious life, she yet might dwell in the outer courts, for M. Duchesne made no objection to her remaining at Ste. Marie as a novice. Of that time she wrote later: "I saw no light in the future, the trial of the moment seemed to me the hardest God could have sent." Again wise counsel came to her assistance: "Let us adore the Will of God, my child; He knows what He is doing and the result of what He permits, you will understand this later," and the little novice went back to her place in the novitiate. Her hours of prayer lengthened and grew more intense. Her willingness to help others became more evident, all felt that they could count on her in an hour of need.

So things went on for a while. Then France broke with Rome. The law of February, 1790, deprived monastic vows of all legal force, suppressed existing religious orders and forbade the introduction or foundation of any not then in France. All monastic property was thus available for secular purposes. Early in 1791 the Visitandines of Grenoble were ordered either to give up religious life or to abandon Ste. Marie. On January 14, the Superior, Mother d'Auberjon Murinais, drew up a protest which each of her community signed, declaring that they were religious until death. The result of this holy boldness was their expulsion.

M. Duchesne had known only too well the course which events would take. Before the closing of Ste. Marie d'en Haut was effected, he insisted that his daughter return home at once. She obeyed, but in tears. "O Sion," she exclaimed, for to her Ste. Marie was the city set upon a mountain, the city of peace, "O Sion, shall I never see thee again! O Lord, wilt Thou not break the bonds that detain me among the children of Kedar!"

To break these bonds, Philippine now planned to go

to Italy. Her old class-mistress and friend, Mother
Eugénie de Bayanne, was superior of a monastery of the
Visitation in which the banished novice felt sure she
would be received. This her father denied her. Sadly
she put off the dear habit of a Visitandine and took her
old place in the home in the Rue St. André. Grenoble
soon proved unsafe even for a family whose head was
in sympathy with the Third Estate, and M. Duchesne
removed his household to Grannes in the Department
of le Drôme, not far from Crest and from Romans.

The country home of the Duchesnes was on the side
of a hill at the top of which were ruins of an old feudal
castle. The remnants of feudalism were being laid
waste by the Revolution. Even in that remote country
place, the storm seemed to be breaking about their
doors. Archange de Valence, a Carthusian, spoke
against the States General and was promptly sent into
exile while his monastery at Crest was suppressed. The
Convent of the Visitation there and another at Romans
had already been closed. It was a comfort to Philippine
to find at Grannes two members of the Society of Jesus,
which had been suppressed before the French Revolution and by him whom they most revered on earth, the
Vicar of Christ. Some of them had gone to Russia,
where there had been no Bourbon sovereign to wring
their suppression from the Holy See. Others remained
in France, giving individual instead of corporate service
to the Church, with only loyalty in their hearts, and with
but one word on their lips, "*Exspecto resurrectionem.*"

The two Jesuits in exile at Grannes encouraged
Philippine in the life she was trying to lead. She and
her cousin, Julie Lambert, a Visitandine expelled from
Romans, followed the Rule of their Order as well as
they might. In the summer they rose at five, and but

half an hour later in the winter. They made daily meditations and frequent visits to the Blessed Sacrament in the little underground church. There Philippine delighted to find a picture of her dear St. Francis Xavier and one of St. John Francis Regis, whose tomb not far away at La Louvesc she was planning to visit. Her devotion inspired the whole family, even her father, who shared with her a page in his prayer book—the prayer of Xavier for the conversion of infidels which she learned by heart and said almost daily during the rest of her life.

This exile at Grannes was not a spiritual retreat. Philippine was always one to put her hand to whatever work came nearest; she taught her little sister, Mélanie; she helped her mother in the house, learning many a precious lesson in the kitchen, scullery and dining room. The Office of the Blessed Virgin which she said daily as it had been a rule at Ste. Marie, and her fast every Wednesday, also prescribed, were not allowed to interfere in any way with her service to others or to isolate her from those whom she loved more than ever. Kindness and affability are the spirit of St. Francis of Sales and his heritage to his Order.

The terror of the Revolution was daily increasing. The two Jesuits were obliged to leave Grannes. The church was closed. There was no hope for Mass except when a priest in disguise was able to hide for a time in some hospitable home. Among those who thus ministered to Romans and its environs was M. Ravenas, formerly curé of Tolissieux. He was arrested at St. Marcellin, and was sent to Grenoble to be incarcerated in the old monastery of Ste. Marie d'en Haut, then being used as a prison.

One day a stranger called on M. Duchesne at Grannes. He had heard that some mills were to be built and he asked to superintend their construction. So intelligent and reliable did he prove to be that M. Duchesne engaged him as steward of his estate. Meanwhile, the stranger did far more than attend to the material welfare of the Duchesnes for he was none other than the Abbé Pordebard in hiding from those who were hounding him. He directed Philippine and her sisters, giving them solid instruction.

In the early morning hours he said Mass in a secluded part of the house and there, like the early Christians, they received Holy Communion. This good priest may have been at Grannes when, after a long illness, Madame Duchesne died in the arms of her most loving daughter, Philippine.

In a letter written in 1793 to her sister whom she addressed as "Citoyenne Mauduit," Philippine made known her intention of giving this sister the share of the fortune left to herself; among her other sisters and her brother she divided the land apportioned to her by her mother. Her action was explained some years later when she wrote, "After a great sorrow had placed me in possession of a fortune, I thought that the best way to enjoy it was to give it up. Heavenly hopes I kept as my portion."

It was probably at the request of her grandmother, and not on her own initiative, that Philippine now went to Romans to care for this captious old lady. Of this visit she wrote to Madame de Mauduit, "In observing the change which advancing years have made in our grandmother, I cannot refrain, dear sister, from some melancholy thoughts. The same blood flows in our veins and already we often feel in ourselves symptoms of her impetuous disposition. How much I fear that the resemblance may increase in time and that it may make

us one day the bane and torment of our families. Let
us try to overcome this tendency and to resist the first
temptation to a fault which grows with age and becomes
at last incorrigible. Let us try not to expect too much
from our neighbors, for in this life perfection can not be
found and we shall always have to put up with the
defects of others." This picture of her grandmother's
disposition shows how great was Philippine's knowledge
of human nature. She exaggerated neither her own
tendencies nor the effects of yielding to them, as seen in
the old lady who was tyranny and wilfulness personified
and who was a tyrant to her servants, especially to one
whom Philippine describes as a "perfect lamb of a
woman, a model of patience and peacefulness." Rose,
the maid thus described, was encouraged to remain at
her post, for the granddaughter knew that no one else
would endure it. She could not do so herself, for she was
not as yet either a perfect lamb or a model of patience
and peace. Dismissed by her grandmother, she beat a
hasty retreat from Romans, recording one of few lost
opportunities.

Philippine had read her sister's character aright.
Madame de Mauduit, for all her charity to the poor, was
somewhat of a dragon at home and her husband, it is
said, quailed before her.

To help in the study and in the correction of her own
character and to plan for the future, Philippine now
stopped at St. Marcellin to follow a spiritual retreat.
This little city boasts of Roman relics, a belfry and an
arched doorway. To the one now in solitude the sojourning there became a gateway to a new phase in her
life. She made up her mind not to return to Grannes
but to go on to Grenoble to ask the hospitality of her
aunt. She thought that in that city which held captive

so many innocent prisoners, victims of the Reign of Terror, she could be of some use and that there she might better watch for an opportunity to re-enter the Visitation.

Diffident of her own decision, Philippine wrote to one of the Jesuits whom she had known at Grannes to ask counsel in her new plan. He answered that God would surely bless her undertaking and he told her that great things had been foretold for religion in Dauphiny. The holy beggar of Christ, Benedict Labre, had passed as a pilgrim through Vivarais on his way to the tomb of St. Regis. His had been a strange life. After many vain attempts to join one religious community after another, he had come to understand that his mission was to give up his country, his all, and to lead a new sort of life, one most painful, most penitential, not in the desert or the cloister, but in the midst of the world, devoutly visiting the shrines of Christian devotion. Here not far from La Louvesc, he had foreseen a revival of fervor.

It was to hasten this religious renaissance that Philippine made her way back to Grenoble. In answer to the opposition of her family she wrote: "I can do more for my father by devoting myself entirely to God who overrules every event and sways the hearts of men than I could do by my presence and by my loving attentions. I have often prayed that the suffering of this separation may fall on me alone, that I may feel it in all its bitter extent and that the merit of this sacrifice may obtain for my family, union, happiness and peace."

CHAPTER III

THE SCHOOL OF SYMPATHY

CHAPTER III

THE SCHOOL OF SYMPATHY—1794-1801

"He teaches best
Who feels the hearts of all men in his breast,
And knows their strength or weakness in his own."

BAYARD TAYLOR

Philippine availed herself of her aunt's hospitality only while she looked about for a way of life more suited to the task to which she had now set herself. In Grenoble she found a friend, one who had been a nun until the Revolution closed the convent and expelled the Sisters. The two shared the wish to devote themselves entirely to the poor, the sick, the imprisoned. They rented rooms and lived a hidden life in their own city, making their presence known only to those who might buy the embroidery and plain sewing which became their means of livelihood.

The first prison which Philippine visited was that of Ste. Marie, for her loved Sion had now become a Babylon, a place of captivity. Its walls no longer reëchoed the laughter of merry children, but the moans of prisoners. Yet it was still the home of prayer, for many of those imprisoned were captives to the love of Christ. Philippine found there M. de Ravenas, who had ministered to Grannes and who had been taken prisoner at St. Marcellin. The companion of his labors, Father Joseph Martin Guillabert, was his fellow-prisoner and before long would share his martyrdom. There too was

Madame Peret, the foundress of the house of the Ursulines at Grenoble.   Philippine's ministrations to her were to be returned a hundredfold when she should receive abundantly of the kind hospitality of the Daughters of St. Angela in the far-away "Dream town of France"—New Orleans.

Priests, monks and nuns had been imprisoned on the charge that they were dangerous to the Republic.   They had refused to swear to support the Civil Constitution of the Clergy, decreed by the Assembly but condemned by Pius VII in March, 1793, as heretical and opposed to the discipline of the Church.

There were lay prisoners too, whose only offence was nobility of birth or an indiscreet adherence to a lost cause.   Philippine became the comfort and consolation of these victims of a Revolution which her family, however unwittingly, had certainly helped to bring to a head.   She and her zealous friend were joined by others and thus was formed an association dedicated to the services of Confessors of the Faith and other suffering captives. *"Les Dames de la Miséricorde,"* as the members of the little congregation called themselves, fearless in their heroic work of charity, drew new inspiration and fervor from the sight of the priests awaiting their martyrdom.

One of the "Ladies of Mercy," perhaps Philippine herself, for the incident is typical of her spirit, went one day to visit M. de Ravenas at Ste. Marie d'en Haut. It was some little time since he had seen her and he asked what had passed since her last visit.   Tears prevented her from answering.   She had apparently heard that he had been condemned to death.   Gently he reproached her, bidding her rejoice that he was accounted worthy to suffer for Christ.   Then to his joy he learned that her tears were not for pity but for holy envy—her only wish was to share his martyrdom. Soon after this he was removed to the cellars of the Conciergerie which he described as "the vestibule of Heaven." His death came by the cruel knife of the guillotine, June 25, 1794, and his last prayer was "Blessed be Jesus, for Thee I die, I give Thee back life for Life and love for Love."

Relatively few of the non-juring priests were privileged to shed their blood and thus to win the martyr's crown. Far more were banished from France. The Assembly ordered a wholesale deportation; about eight thousand took refuge in Great Britain alone, and Spain, Italy and Switzerland opened their doors to the refugees. Not all those deported attained a foreign strand. More than one ship was deliberately sent to the bottom of the sea. Imprisonment in France was the punishment of priests over sixty years of age unless some excuse could be found for putting them to death. Massacres of prisoners took place in several cities. At Bordeaux, for example, Robespierre had ordered the construction of a huge guillotine having four blades, thus to make short work of the execution of the twelve hundred priests imprisoned there. Four days before that fearful decree was to be carried into effect, Robespierre met his own death by the knife of another guillotine.

Some few of the faithful priests escaped deportation and wandered through France, giving the Last Sacraments to the sick and dying, saying Mass in hiding wherever they might and encouraging the faithful to persevere. So Philippine became a "priest-hunter." She seemed to have an intuition for recognizing those who could give her sick poor what would be their only comfort in their last hours. When she had failed to find one of these outlawed priests, she would pray beside the

dying, exhorting them to contrition and to confidence.
One day she carried a woman to her own lodging, placed
her in the bed which she shared with another *Dame de la
Miséricorde,* and prayed beside her all the night until
she died. Fear seemed unknown to Philippine. Danger was evident, even to her, but she scorned the thought
of it if there were hope of saving souls. In those years
of terror, she would go at any hour of the night to visit
the sick in the hovels they called home and, if she left
them before dawn, it was to find her way to some secluded spot where Mass was to be said.

At last there came a respite when with the death of
Robespierre in 1794 the application of the laws against
the loyal clergy was relaxed. Some of the clerical prisoners were set free and so many exiled priests returned,
that the Convention in alarm gave them a month in
which to quit France once more. Vacillation was, in
most cases, the characteristic of the Convention, which
revoked, renewed, and withdrew the renewal of the decrees which it had made.

The Directory, however, organized hunting for non-
juring priests and hundreds were cast upon unhealthful
tropical shores where they languished and died. It was
the Directory, too, that ordered Napoleon Bonaparte to
attack the Papal States. In 1798 the Roman Republic
was proclaimed and, in March of the following year,
Pope Pius VI was made a prisoner of France. Ill as he
was, he was hurried to Parma, to Turin, then over the
Alps to Grenoble, where he arrived on the 6th of July.
The fidelity of the good people of the Alps and of the
Valley of the Isère was shown in a courageous and spon-
taneous outburst. The homage, expressing their loyalty
and filial piety, is a radiant gleam of light in the darkest
night. Spain sent an envoy to the Pope, and it was at

Grenoble that they met. There the Holy Father blessed the kneeling throng, among whom undoubtedly was Philippine Duchesne. The Pope was then hurried on again, on through St. Marcellin and Romans to Valence on the Rhone. "My bodily sufferings are nothing," the dying Pontiff said, "in comparison with the anguish of my heart." On August 27, 1799, his martyrdom came to an end and he died repeating verses of the Psalms so loved by him.

At the close of the Reign of Terror, Philippine Duchesne's uncle, Claude Périer, had been named to represent Dauphiny in the legislative body at Paris of which he was later appointed a regular member. He did not confine his activity to politics, but by fortunate investments and an economy that made him all but a miser, he amassed a huge fortune that was to pave his way to political success in the new Republic. To him were referred the great financial questions of the day; he laid the foundations of the Bank of France, drew up its statutes, and became one of its regents. His brother-in-law, Pierre François Duchesne, had also been sent by Dauphiny as a deputy to the legislature of France under the Directory, but with an independence of character superior to that of Claude Périer he ardently, though vainly, opposed the policy of Napoleon which brought about the coup-d'état of the 18th Brumaire abolishing the Directory and establishing the Consulate. Napoleon thus scored a greater victory than that of the Pyramids or Aboukir. The French Revolution was virtually at an end. "Yet," says an historian, "though much was to be gained by the concentration of the executive authority and much also by the suppression of extravagant political debate, the price was destined to be such as no one in France imagined on that

November evening while the deputies were rushing wildly through the park and the fog was falling upon the last fevers of the French Revolution." In the ten and a half years since the Three Orders first assembled in Claude Périer's château of Vizille, popular as well as Parliamentary government had fallen. If order had replaced anarchy, so too had militarism supplanted democracy.

Peace fell upon Grenoble. The clerical prisoners were released. Philippine Duchesne's chief work being at an end, she took advantage of this respite to visit her relatives in Romans. This gave her the longed-for opportunity to go on to La Louvesc to pray at the tomb of her dear St. Francis Regis. During the sojourning at Grannes she had hoped to make this pilgrimage, but then her mother and sisters had opposed her plan, and, since her devotion and pleasure alone were at stake, she had yielded to their wishes. Now, however, that her mother was in Heaven, her father in Paris, her unmarried sister at Grannes, she felt free to go. On the 3rd of May she and one of her grandmother's maids made this pious expedition.

There were many disappointments in store for Philippine, even in the fulfilling of her own desire. She failed to see the Jesuit who had advised her to make the pilgrimage, and she afterwards learned that he had died on the very day she had spent at La Louvesc. She missed seeing Mgr. d'Alvan, the holy Archbishop of Vienne, who had been in hiding at La Louvesc and whom she had hoped to find still there. The church which had been built over the tomb of St. Francis Regis was closed and—greatest disappointment of all —the body of the Saint, which had been taken away and hidden during the Terror, had not yet been brought back. She prayed like another Magdalen beside an empty tomb, then went to Mass in a barn near by and returned to Romans, not consoled, but comforted, strengthened in her resolve to dedicate herself anew to the service of the poor. Her loved St. Francis Regis had devoted himself to the unromantic labor of the home missions. His intrepidity and zeal were rewarded with striking conversions, his patience and humility won over even his enemies, while his mortification and prayer told the secret of his success. As he returned to the house one evening after a day of weary labor one of his confrères said:

"Well, Father Regis, speaking candidly, are you not very tired?"

"No," replied the Saint with a laugh, "I am as fresh as a rose."

It was this characteristic of amiable evenness that made him so loved in the cottages and hamlets which he visited. He was undaunted by snow and ice and by mountain and torrent. He had begged to be sent to the Missions of the Hurons and the Iroquois in Canada, and hope had been given him that he might go, but his work lay at home. So, too, did Philippine Duchesne's in 1800.

"As soon as I arrived at Grenoble," she writes, "where good schools were not wanting for little girls, I took charge of a few little boys who had been totally neglected and who were living in the streets like animals. I found it difficult to get hold of even three or four, but food and promises of clothing at last induced them to come for one hour a day. These first scholars brought some of their playfellows, and I had in my class between fifteen and twenty children rather well disposed, but so intolerably wild and noisy that all those who lived in the house where I was lodging were angry with me. It was a trial also to be pursued in the streets by the greetings of these disreputable-looking creatures. They pointed me out to their parents, who were vexed because I had told the boys not to work on Sundays. If it had not been for the thought of St. Francis I should have given up my apostolate."

Philippine Duchesne was for some time the sole member of her family in this city of her birth. Her unmarried sister had not returned to Grenoble. Her father was still in Paris, where he had become a member of the Tribunate whose president he was more than once. In 1802, however, he sided with Carnot in opposing the Life Consulate. They both saw through Napoleon's eloquent thanks to the Senate which had re-elected him for ten years. The crafty Bonaparte had said, "You deem, then, that I owe a fresh sacrifice to the nation. I am ready to make it if the command of the people ratifies what your vote allows." Thus the First Consul slyly called for a plebiscite, feeling sure that the people would vote him the consulship for life. M. Duchesne, convinced that the death blow to liberty had been struck, resigned his position in the Tribunate and returned to Grenoble, not changed, but despairing of the cause of what he considered freedom.

While he craved political and civil liberty, his daughter was yearning to be bound to God by the vows of religion. Ste. Marie was no longer a prison, its inmates having been either guillotined or given their liberty. The Government still claimed the house as the property of the State and put it in charge of a caretaker, who kept it closed except on Sundays, when it was used as a shelter by those who cared to take a long walk up the Hill of Chalmont.

On the Feast of Pentecost, 1801, Philippine went to visit some former Carmelites living at Grenoble. Her longing to return to Ste. Marie became the chief subject of conversation—for she thought she saw the Visitation rising from its ruins. The daughters of St. Theresa, too, had a place in her plans, for she hoped they would establish a Carmel in what had been the chaplain's house on the Hill of Chalmont. Her hopes were never confined to the well-being of her own religious order—every interest of the Church was hers. For years the restoration of the Carthusians to the Grande Chartreuse was one of her dearest intentions; and only when their return seemed impossible did she consider acquiring their old monastery for the Visitandines she might gather together. On the afternoon of that same Whit Sunday she asked her sister, Madame de Mauduit, to go for a walk with her. Philippine's little niece, Amélie, then three years old, went with them. They walked up the steep road leading to ruined Ste. Marie and along the terrace overlooking the Vale of Grésivaudan, of which Gray wrote, "Not a precipice, not a torrent, not a cliff, but is pregnant with religion and poetry." They stood there, these two, Madame de Mauduit, an imperious Duchesne, kind at heart and tender to the poor, but the terror of her husband, a corporal of dragoons, and Philippine, a Visitandine novice now these fourteen years and not yet professed. They were silent as they gazed upon the mountains, of which another author says, "The great Alps, seen thus, link one in some way to one's immortality."

Thus Philippine may have mused, when suddenly her reverie was broken by a voice, the voice of a little girl. "Oh, yes, I shall come to school here and here I shall make my First Communion." It was only precocious, three-year-old Amélie who spoke as she rolled in the long, sweet grass; but to her aunt, ever on the watch for a sign, her words seemed like the *"Tolle et lege"* vouchsafed to St. Augustine through a whisper, and Philippine said aloud, "My God, may the child's words come true."

This prayer was constantly repeated in the months that followed. Philippine resolved to buy back Ste. Marie d'en Haut from the Government, and to Heaven she first turned for aid. She promised St. Regis that, if she were able to get back her monastery, she would send some one on a pilgrimage to La Louvesc, would procure religious instruction for twelve poor persons and would perform many things in honor of him whose intercession she hoped to gain, and, knowing well the power of children's prayers, she obtained those of her class.

Then, having invoked her friends in Heaven, she sought aid upon earth. She received great encouragement from the Abbé Rey, from the Vicar General, M. Brochier, who had suffered much for the faith, and from the Almoner of the Hospital of Grenoble. Together with Madame de Murinais, her former Superior, she drew up a petition in the name of the surviving nuns of Ste. Marie. This they addressed to the Administrator of the Department, saying that they wished to enter into negotiations for the restoration of the property to its former owners—no answer came.

Meanwhile Philippine was helping her old friend and cousin in nursing back to life and health her husband, M. de Savoie-Rollin, and so skilful did she prove that one day her cousin said:

"Philippine, is there nothing that I can do to repay your kindness?"

"There is only one thing which would give me pleasure," was the prompt answer, "and that would be if your husband would use his influence to obtain for us Ste. Marie d'en Haut."

M. Rollin and his wife's nephews, Casimir and Scipio Périer, then most influential in Paris, exerted themselves on behalf of Philippine, with the result that early in December, 1801, the loved home of Ste. Marie d'en Haut was given back to her. Her prayer to the Sacred Heart had not been in vain. Her high hopes had not failed; "We become spiritually, supernaturally sanguine, we expect everything from God, precisely because we have in our veins the Precious Blood that makes the Heart of the Son of God throb with un-limited confidence in the goodness of the Father."

CHAPTER IV

The School of the Cross

CHAPTER IV

THE SCHOOL OF THE CROSS—1801-1804

"Therefore upgird thyself, and come to stand
Unflinching under th' unfaltering Hand
That waits to prove thee to the uttermost.
It were not hard to suffer by His Hand
If thou could'st see His Face;—but in the dark!
That is thy one last trial,—be it so.
Christ was forsaken, so must thou be too."

HARRIET ELEANOR KING.

December the 10th was a glad day for Philippine Duchesne. The good news spread rapidly and friends were not slow with congratulations; others, less friendly, prognosticated ill, for they had seen Ste. Marie in its ruined state and thought it uninhabitable. Among those who had shown kind interest in the "mad enterprise" was Father Jean Baptiste Rivet, who went that very day to visit Philippine. He had another bit of good news for her, he said. The Concordat between Pius VII and Napoleon was to be carried into effect at once. Thus Catholicity would be re-established in fair France, peace would be restored to many a troubled conscience and the Church would be reorganized throughout the land. Even Napoleon was afterwards to say that by signing this contract he had "raised the fallen altars, put a stop to disorders, obliged the faithful to pray for the Republic, dissipated the scruples of

51

those who had acquired new property and broken the last thread by which the old dynasty maintained communication with the country."

But Father Rivet was too optimistic on that December day. It was only in the following April that the Concordat was to be published, and together with it the Organic Articles which would limit its scope and infringe upon its spirit.

Philippine also had been too sanguine. True, Ste. Marie had been restored to its former owners, but where were they? Some had died, while others had become so aged and infirm that it would be all but impossible for them to take up their life in a house open to every wind that blew. Then there were misunderstandings of which Philippine in her eager zeal never even dreamed. The petition sent to the Government had asked for the restoration of the house to the Order of the Visitation. M. Casimir Périer, in renewing the request on behalf of Philippine, had so worded it that when the favorable document came it was found to have been made out solely in favor of Madame Duchesne, who, in the absence of Mother de Murinais, signed the paper. Thus, Ste. Marie belonged neither to the French Government nor to the Visitandines as a whole, but to the novice. To Philippine this probably seemed of little moment, as her only desire was to give up all by a vow of poverty, but to Madame de Murinais and others it looked as though Madame Duchesne had intended to secure the house in her own name and right and thus to assert her independence of the rest of the former community. Supposing that they were to return—what then? The house was unfit to live in. It had no income and no promise of a school, for the Concordat had not yet made religious education legal.

Penury has its dangers, menacing even Holy Poverty itself. Many voices were raised against Philippine and her rash project, yet the more they spoke the more she longed for the life that she had once led upon the mountain, for, as Ozanam says in speaking of the Franciscans: "This life, the hardest that one can conceive, was also the freest and in consequence the most poetic. In truth, the one thing that enchains human liberty is fear, and all fear may be reduced to that of suffering, so nothing stands in the way of one who has made of suffering his glory and his joy."

Nothing, then, stood in the way of Philippine. In January, 1791, she had taken off her religious habit and returned to the world. Now, after eleven years of dangerous, hardy enterprise for God, she was no less eager to give herself to Him in solitude and hidden apostolic work than she had been on that desolate day in the long ago. She still hoped to go one day to a foreign mission, although the ways and means were not in sight. She was probably in ignorance of the fact that since 1799 a little community of American nuns had been living under the rule, the habit and the name of the Visitation. They had asked to be affiliated with the Order in Europe, but that could only be done after European Visitandines had come to join them at Georgetown and to initiate them in the manners, the customs and the spirit of the Daughters of St. de Chantal.

Philippine went alone to visit the old monastery. She had to shovel a path for herself through the snow that had drifted through crack and crevice into cloisters and corridors. Deftly she removed the broken panes of glass from the windows that were most damaged and replaced them with the oil-paper she had brought. She found to her joy that the chapel had suffered but little damage from the Revolutionists. It would be easier to repair the ravages of time and storm than those of man. Yet what would St. Francis and St. Jane have said if they could have seen their loved monastery then? They must have been praying from the heights of Heaven for its spiritual and temporal restoration. Undaunted by what she had seen, unafraid of suffering, Philippine returned to her lodging in Grenoble, determined to move into Ste. Marie in a day or two at any cost. Not one of the former nuns was ready to return just then, so she induced a poor girl whom she was instructing to accompany her.

The rain fell heavily on that 14th day of December; the wind howled about the turrets of Ste. Marie, rattling the loose tiles upon the roof. As evening came on a strange procession rounded the turn, plodded through the archway and entered the outer door of the dreary, desolate house. One ragged urchin after another set down his burden of a carpetbag, a box or an ungainly bundle, and, with stiffening fingers, tried to squeeze the freezing rain water out of his soaking coat. The porter received these visitors with but little surprise, for he would never be surprised at anything again —Madame Duchesne was coming back to the old house, and these lads, her couriers and escorts—volunteers from her catechism class—were carrying her goods and chattels up the long, steep way from Grenoble. Tired as she was, she had a ready word of thanks for her dear boys and another of sympathy, because they were so cold and so drenched. Then sending them home, for it was getting late and their good mothers might be worried, she and her companion went to prepare a place for the night.

Philippine had planned to spend the first night in the chapel, "where no one had praised God for many a long year" and where she would have much to say of deep gratitude, but, as the poor girl was afraid to sleep alone, the pious project had to be abandoned. The night in the chapel would have been lonely even for Philippine, for the Blessed Sacrament was not there. The work of preparing for the Divine Guest began next morning. There was much to be done, for the convent, as she wrote later, "was open to all the winds, but I felt no fears in that solitude, for I knew that God, Who had guided me to it, would also protect us until we could manage to make it secure. This I tried hard to do, spending my time with the workmen, or else in the kitchen, or sweeping every part of the house, which for ten years had been neglected, and I often had to clear away the ice and snow. These occupations were all pleasures, for I felt the joy that St. Theresa says she experienced when sweeping her convent. Never had worldly pleasures given me half so much delight. We prayed in the chapel, where one door and three windows were missing. It was very cold, but we did not feel it."

Her courage proved inspiring and she was soon joined by an old religious, Madame Foucheraud, while one or two others came a few days later, so that they were able to say office in the chapel with its many vacant stalls. Its outer door, through which visitors used to enter for Mass and Benediction and to assist at Vespers, remained closed, as France was still under her self-imposed interdict.

On Christmas Eve Madame Duchesne and her Sisters walked down the Hill of Chalmont to Grenoble. One of the workmen, a lay-brother still exiled from the Grande Chartreuse, went before them carrying a lantern, whose light cast fitful shadows on the snow, shadows of women carrying bundles under their arms. The blackened houses built during the Wars of the League loomed before them, then flanked the steep and stony path which they descended. They crossed the bridge over the icy Isère and entered the city and soon reached the house where a priest awaited them. Untying the strings that bound the mysterious packages, they pulled off the paper and revealed the religious habit which each had made for herself. There was the sack-like gown, the white guimpe, the veil of black tamany, in just the shape in which their Father St. Francis had cut the first veil in 1610. The priest blessed their habits, and in the joy of their hearts they put them on while the Father was vesting for the Midnight Mass. Twelve o'clock struck—the Holy Sacrifice began and they united their consecration to Our Divine Redeemer, Who on the first Christmas night appeared clothed in our mortality. Hidden under the white veil of the host, He came to each one on that blessed, blessed night.

Early in the morning they returned to Ste. Marie, clothed in the religious dress which was still outlawed from France. This was but one of many daring deeds done by Philippine under the habit that she so loved.

A few days later the nuns paused in their arduous labor to welcome to their mountain home Mgr. Spina, the titular Archbishop of Corinth, a consummate theologian, and Father Castella, General of the Servites. These two prelates, who were later made Cardinals, had been in France for more than a year on an embassy from the Holy See, and their signatures may be seen today together with those of Consalvi, Bernier and Joseph Bonaparte at the end of the Concordat of 1801.

The Abbé Rivet and M. de Savoie-Rollin had asked them to visit Ste. Marie and to encourage the nuns in their hazardous enterprise for God. This they did willingly; it was the first sign of religious life that they had seen in France and gladly they gave it their blessing.

That blessing was Philippine's only consolation just then. The nun who had first joined her proved too old and infirm to stand such a life of utter privation. Suffering affected her mind, and in one of her moments of unbalance she deserted Ste. Marie d'en Haut. Grenoble lifted its eyebrows and sneered, "Another proof that no one can live in the same house with Madame Duchesne." Yet the object of their sneers showed no discouragement. She prepared to celebrate the feast of St. Francis de Sales on the 29th of January, and, though the outer door of the church was still closed, priests and friends of the house were admitted through the convent entrance, and many were the Masses said that day in the old chapel, where still stood the humble confessional of the sainted Bishop of Geneva.

The consolation brought by the thought that the convent church at Grenoble was the first in which Catholic worship appeared in all its splendor after the Revolution prepared Philippine for further trials. In vain did she try to induce the nuns to hasten their return to their monastery. They were living good lives in the world, many of them keeping their rule almost intact, just as Philippine and her friend had done in their exile at Grannes, but they naturally feared to embrace religious life publicly before the issuing of the Concordat. Human prudence was certainly on their side, for the house was still dilapidated and its treasury empty. Madame Duchesne, for all the experience gained in practical affairs, was merely a novice, and, though she was in her thirty-third year, several of the former community were more than twice her age. In silence the novice endured from those whom she loved censure and blame, which when taken up, misconstrued and exaggerated by a world eager to criticize, became calumny.

Still she hoped on. She thought that if only the former Superior of the house, Madame de Murinais, could be induced to return, all would go well. This aged nun was well known in Dauphiny for her virtue and prudence and was venerated no less by persons of the world than by her former daughters. Her influence, Philippine thought, would set all to rights. February and March passed by and still she had not come to Grenoble. The novice redoubled her supplications and prayers. At last, in Passion Week, 1802, Madame de Murinais arrived at Ste. Marie, bringing two coadjutrix sisters, one of whom was nearly eighty years of age. With her, too, came a young nun whose sole employment was to be the care of the aged Superior.

Madame Duchesne rejoiced to enter the choir for office with this venerable Mother leaning on her arm, for her optimism, which pain had supernaturalized, made her foresee brighter days for Ste. Marie. The news of Mother de Murinais' installation brought some of her religious daughters back to their monastery. Works of zeal were now planned and some were carried into effect. When, during Holy Week, Father Rivet gave a retreat for ladies of the world in the chapel of Ste. Marie, Philippine's zeal outran her prudence. She had a belfry erected over the church and the cross that surmounted it seemed to be raised aloft by the Alpine spur of Chalmont so that Dauphiny might see the sign in which victory lies, the sign that was still hidden in Grenoble. On Holy Thursday the outer door of the chapel was thrown open and the public were free to enter for Mass or to be present at Tenebrae, and this rashness met with no evil results. On Easter Sunday, April 18, the Concordat was read aloud in Notre Dame, Paris, and was promulgated throughout France. The chapel door which Philippine had opened would not be closed from without. Then, to her surprise and distress, she saw that there was danger of its being closed from within, for the union and fervor she had expected to see were certainly wanting.

In Paris, in Alençon, in Romans, convents of the Visitation had been reopened and were flourishing in a second spring of renewed fervor. Elsewhere the nuns, not allowed to return to their monasteries, were living under their rule. The houses of Meaux and of Amiens were preparing to open their doors to those whose only desire was to live out the plan of St. Francis de Sales in all its perfection—Ste. Marie d'en Haut was the startling exception. There Divine Office replaced the Little Office of Our Lady which had been the rule. There was proof, too, that the work of the education of youth would not long be continued, even if young aspirants should join the aged community. The cloisters and corridors lacked the silence which has been said to be "the element in which great things fashion themselves together." The habit was worn by one only, Madame Duchesne. To understand her anguish we must be able to fathom a heart grown deep by suffering and love. She had not come to Ste. Marie merely to seek shelter from a tumultuous world, and had expected the community to look upon themselves as victims of adoration, reparation and expiation. To appreciate her disappointment, one must be capable of reading her character: "I felt so triumphant," she said when describing her joy at Mother de Murinais' longed-for return. That feeling of triumph, which was of short duration, would have been no training for one who, in spite of her virtue, was still impetuous, stern, imperious, uncompromising even about trifles; the discipline of detachment, generosity, sympathy had raised her love to heroism, but it had failed to touch the faults inherent in the Duchesne temperament—such a character of iron is tempered to steel only through fire and tears. She had been independent—a host in herself. She had been either loved or calumniated, but never ignored. Now her views were made light of, her opinions counted for nought. She, a Duchesne, born to succeed, had utterly failed. She had brought to Ste. Marie d'en Haut those whose chief thought was to live out their lives in peaceful enclosure. Their enforced sojourning out of the cloister had made them unfit both physically and spiritually to take up their religious life in all its primitive fervor. It seemed now that there would never be further foundations made from that house. The voices of children would no longer be heard in the building set apart for the school.

On the patronal feast of the Convent, July 2, of that year, which had seemed filled with promise, Philippine knelt alone in the chapel and put into agonized words the terrible thought that had come to her. As she wept she saw that her handkerchief was covered with blood— her anguish of soul had broken a blood vessel. When she sought advice her confessor said: "You have not yet wept enough, my child; this is only the beginning of sorrow—you must arm yourself with courage." She needed in truth a valiant heart for what lay before her.

She took upon herself all the employments that were irksome and difficult. The sacristy was her joy, but her work there was often interrupted to take up her post at the door, to teach the younger children or to weep over the accounts of an empty treasury.

On the 26th of August Philippine stood alone at the door of Ste. Marie d'en Haut. Through her tears she saw descending the hill of Chalmont the Mother Superior and all those who had joined her at Ste. Marie, all save one coadjutrix sister; and as they were lost to view she turned and made her way to the chapel. This was the anniversary of the consecration of that church, and those for whom it had been built and dedicated had abandoned it. She had offered to go away if she were the obstacle to good in that house; she had remonstrated, entreated, implored, but in vain! Then she wrote to her old friend and teacher, Madame de Bayanne, to ask that reinforcements be sent from Naples, and the kind religious would have come to the rescue herself had not her Cardinal brother intervened, thinking such action imprudent. Was all at an end for Ste. Marie? Before the crucifix Philippine renewed her oblation, which was now self-immolation. Having tasted failure, she could pray:

> *"Yet what can I undo,*
> *I the undone, the undone,*
> *To comfort Thee, God's Son?*
> *Oh, draw me near and, for some lowest use,*
> *That I may be*
> *Lost and undone in Thee,*
> *Me from mine own self loose."*

CHAPTER V

THE TRAINING THAT JOY GIVES

CHAPTER V

The Training that Joy Gives—1804-1806

"Yet many a one a tryst has kept
With the immortal while he slept,
Woke unremembering, went his way;
Life seemed the same from day to day,
Till the predestined hour came,
A hidden will leapt up in flame.
And through its deed the risen soul
Strode on self-conquering towards the goal."

A. E.

Father Rivet was as prompt in offering consolation as he had been in hastening to congratulate Philippine when, eighteen months previously, she had received the monastery of Ste. Marie d'en Haut into her possession. Now it was deserted and Philippine, "alone within those sacred walls as Ezra in the desolate Temple of Jerusalem . . . knelt at the foot of the altar and bathed the holy spot with tears, tears which the Angels of the Sanctuary must have gathered up in pity to unite with the Blood of Christ and to offer them before the throne of mercy and of love." The good Father reminded her—for she was in a certain sense a foundress—of the trials of St. Theresa in her foundations. Then he told her of a new St. Theresa, a Mother Foundress in deed, though she would not brook the name. She had brought into being a little congregation of which he had more than once before spoken to

Philippine Duchesne. It was then some years since the death of Father Léonor de Tournély, one of the four founders of the Fathers of the Sacred Heart, under which title some fervent young men had bound themselves to follow as far as they might the rules of the Society of Jesus, then suppressed in France, Spain, Italy and all the colonies of these nations. The saintly Père de Tournély wished to establish an institute of religious women consecrated to the Sacred Heart and devoted to the education of girls. The attempts he himself made failed, but, when in his thirty-first year he lay on his death-bed, he confided his hopes to Father Joseph Varin. His last words were for the institute that he felt sure would be founded, and, crying out suddenly in accents that thrilled those who stood by, "Yes, it will be! It will be!" he gently expired. The Fathers of the Sacred Heart united with another congregation whose aim it was to live as much like Jesuits as they were allowed. They gave up the name "Sacred Heart," taking that of the "Fathers of the Faith." About a year later they received as a novice a young priest, Louis Barat. During the time in which he had acted as Professor in the seminary of his native town of Joigny, Louis Barat had passed many an hour in his home, a vine-dresser's cottage, where he instructed a little sister, Madeleine Sophie, in the branches which he taught the seminarists. To him this child owed her knowledge of Latin, Greek, Spanish, Italian, history, literature and natural science; to him she was indebted for the strengthening of her will and the training in concentration and constancy; to him she owed the gentler, wiser direction of Father Varin, his own Superior. In Madeleine Sophie, Father Varin found one ready to his hand for the carrying out of Father de Tournély's most ardent desire. Though she had hoped to enter Carmel, the word of her new director became the expression of the Will of God, and the little Society, founded in Paris, November 21, 1800, was to be entirely devoted to the worship of the Sacred Heart and to the propagation of this devotion, chiefly by the education of girls. As they were still in the aftermath of the Revolution, the dear name, "Sacred Heart," was kept secret, and the nuns were known as the *"Les Dames de la Foi"* or the *"Les Dames de l'Instruction Chrétienne."*

Philippine was charmed as she listened to what Father Rivet had to tell her of the new congregation— a society devoted to the Sacred Heart, which had revealed its love to one of her own Visitandines of the Seventeenth Century, an order consecrated especially to Our Lady whom she so loved, an institute founded on prayer, the life of her life, dedicated to sacrifice, her daily bread, and given over to the education of children, whom she cherished—every note found an echo in her heart.

The new Society of the Sacred Heart was still very small; it had but one house, that of Amiens, and but two of its little community had made their vows. The thought came to Philippine Duchesne to throw in her lot with theirs, and then another thought—to ask Mother Barat to take possession of Ste. Marie and of herself. For this Father Rivet had probably been hoping, and so, before he descended the mountain, he had promised to write to Father Roger, a friend of his and one of the Fathers of the Faith, to ask him to interest Father Varin in Philippine and her house.

That promise was made in August, 1802. Time passed and the smile of the Sacred Heart seemed like the first touch of warmth, bringing forth flowers, pale blossoms they were and frail, like the crocuses and snowdrops that herald spring. In Emilie Giraud, a young girl much older than the seven others, who with her made up the school of Ste. Marie, Madame Duchesne saw the hall-mark of a religious vocation, and she found to her joy that Emilie's one hope was to enter Ste. Marie.

In November Father Rivet's sister, who had been a Carmelite until the Revolution had driven her from her convent, and whose one desire now was to join the Society of the Sacred Heart, came to the house on the hill. She asked admittance there as a favor to herself, and she also wished to prove to Grenoble that Madame Duchesne did not make all who lived with her unhappy. In all probability, kind Father Rivet had inspired this action, as Philippine had been alone for two months, except for her little school and for those ladies who spent a day or two of retreat at the convent. Madame Rivet was delighted with Philippine, and she declared that, even at the risk of dying of hardship and fatigue, she would stand by her new friend and remain at Ste. Marie. The admiration was mutual, and Madame Duchesne found in Father Rivet's sister not only a generous support, but a mother and a Superior. They adopted the name of Daughters of the Propagation of the Faith, a title similar to that of the Order they hoped to join. In the meanwhile they asked Father Bouchier, the Vicar General, to give them a temporary rule. During the Christmas holidays a postulant joined them, and then Emilie Giraud was allowed to pass from the boarding school to the community. On the 3rd of March the four made simple vows of poverty, chastity and obedience, and Madame Rivet was confirmed in the

office of Superior, while to Philippine fell the task of
instructing the two younger nuns in religious life and
its duties.   Together the little community prayed and
did penance, longing for the time when they might consecrate themselves to God more completely; and their
work was blessed by an increase in the school, which
soon counted eighteen.

Father Rivet had not forgotten Ste. Marie in his
mission at Bellay.   One day Father Roger called on
him there and told him more of the community at
Amiens and lent him their rules, which Father Rivet
sat up all night to copy and which he then carried in
triumph to Mother Duchesne and his sister, who, reading them, yearned all the more for amalgamation with
"Les Dames de la Foi." A new postulant joined them
in the early summer.   Now there were five to receive
Father Roger when he paid his first visit to Ste. Marie
d'en Haut.   To bring about the desired meeting with
Mother Barat he promised to consult Father Varin,
who was then traversing Dauphiny like a second St.
Francis Regis, visiting the hamlets and villages, praying as if all depended on God and working as if the
conversion of sinners depended altogether on himself.

On the Feast of St. Ignatius, July 31, 1804, Father
Roger returned to Ste. Marie, bringing with him good
Father Varin, whom he had found not over-anxious to
add a new foundation to the Society of the Sacred
Heart, which as yet counted very few members and
which was still in its infancy.   Having said Mass, they
went through the house.   Father Varin amused himself
as he saw turn, cloister and grille, by saying to Mother
Duchesne:

"Yes, that will just do for the Visitation."

She loved her old Order and her heart thrilled at its

name, but now she felt that God intended her for the Sacred Heart. During Benediction Father Varin came to the same conclusion in her regard, but he gave her no sign of encouragement.

The next day the Fathers again said Mass at Ste. Marie and afterwards Mothers Rivet and Duchesne went to see them, hoping for some token of approval. Again Father Varin spoke to Philippine of the virtue of holy indifference and of the time that God allows for the accomplishment of His designs.

"But, Father," she answered with her old impetuosity, "if St. Francis Xavier had so deliberated before doing God's work, he would not have accomplished so much in ten years."

Father Roger and Father Varin smiled, and the latter replied, "Well, I promise you that Mother Barat will come."

Thus the visit ended in joy for the two nuns, who hastened to write to tell the Holy Foundress of their gratitude and their hopes. Father Varin went to Amiens to arrange with Mother Barat for the visit to Grenoble.

"You will find there," he said, "companions who will be a help to you, especially one; and, if there were only that one, she would be worth seeking at the other end of the world!" In Philippine he had found the courage and confidence to which he had been exhorting Mother Barat and her religious family at Amiens.

Mother Barat's answer to the letters received from Grenoble was characterized by the charity and humility for which the Church has exalted her. She wrote: "Your letter has filled me with joy, for from it I see that your souls, inspired by grace, are fitted to carry out the designs of Providence. Such precious dispositions make me tremble at the thought that God should have chosen me to cultivate them, but plants that grow in fertile soil require little care and skill on the part of the gardener; that is why Our Lord has picked out such a poor and wretched creature as I for this work. . . . I long to show each of you my love and my solicitude. Soon our two religious communities will form but one heart and one soul in Jesus Christ, and meanwhile we must realize that we are united in Our Lord."

In the meantime preparations were being set on foot at Ste. Marie d'en Haut. Mother Duchesne solicited and obtained legal recognition for the school. She fired the little community with her enthusiasm for what she and Madame Rivet wished to consider less of a reunion than a merging of the spirit of Ste. Marie in that of the Sacred Heart. In her joy Philippine wrote: "May Providence be blessed a thousand times for having assigned me the task of preparing the abode of those who will come here to receive the Word of God and carry it to distant lands. Still greater will be my happiness if, though all unworthy to enter that holy Society, I am through pure mercy admitted into it, and I can thus strive to rescue souls from our common enemy to give them to our great Master." While awaiting Mother Barat's arrival Philippine began the correspondence which was to last through years and prove to be her greatest earthly joy. In December letters stopped coming from Amiens.

Mother Barat left Amiens on November 22, the day following the fourth birthday of the Society of the Sacred Heart, and reached her destination on December 13. She brought with her Madame Debrosse, who had just made her vows, and a coadjutrix sister. In

her delicate thought for others she had asked Father
Roger to meet her at Grenoble and to bring with him
another confessor, thinking that the custom of Ste.
Marie might have been for each nun to have her own.

It was three years since Philippine had returned to
Ste. Marie, but she was too happy now to be recalling
memories of those dismal years. How different this
home-coming would prove! Suddenly she heard the
knocker sound and hastened down the damp, gloomy
passage to the front door. Almost before she knew it
she was on her knees kissing the feet of her whom she
singled out as her new Superior, and exclaiming: "How
beautiful upon the mountains are the feet of him who
bringeth good tidings and who preacheth peace." On
that glad day Philippine took the last place at Ste.
Marie, for, though not the Superior, she had been
Mother Rivet's right hand and counsellor, and her
knowledge of the house and her training in practical
affairs had given her a prominent place out of which
she slipped in silent joy. "The time has come for me
to keep silence," she wrote. "My part now is to obey
and to exclaim in deep humility, 'Forever shall I sing
the mercies of the Lord!' "

Mother Barat brought joy to the grim old monastery of Ste. Marie, grown grimmer through the years.
Philippine was radiant, while Emilie Giraud and her
young companions were like happy children, loving
their dear Mother Barat, but fearing her a little and
laughingly hiding from her as she passed them in the
dim corridors. She was amused at their behavior, and
said they were so wild that she would not open the
noviceship just yet. There were other reasons for the
delay, as there must have been need of reform in a house
which had been a refuge for those who had belonged

to different religious orders, each with its own peculiar spirit, that intangible something so hard to define, yet so all-important.

Father Varin had given Mother Barat this advice, which she determined to carry out to the letter: "In the work of reform, patience is more necessary than ardor, prudence is better than zeal. We must first win hearts, then all the rest will follow quietly without shock or commotion. . . . Be firm sometimes, never harsh, and everywhere and at all times let gentleness reign."

To her surprise and her joy, Mother Barat found her task not so difficult. Philippine's influence on the community had made them eager for any change that would prove that they had been thrown into the melting-pot and that they were to be moulded to the form of the Sacred Heart. Madame Duchesne showed herself the most docile of all. She had forgotten her added years, her experience, her sufferings during the Revolution and all that in spite of failure she had really accomplished. All was lost sight of as she looked at her young Superior, whose face after Holy Communion and whose action all day long radiated Christ.

At Ste. Marie Mother Barat had free scope for her love of mortification and suffering. The damage brought about by ten years of neglect is slowly repaired. The chapel windows and doors were not securely fastened, and a wintry blast was often felt within. Snow drifted into several parts of the house, and the nuns had scant covering. Only an iron constitution, such as Philippine's must have been, could have endured all this without detriment to health.

Christmas was always one of Mother Barat's favorite feasts, and her influence aroused and increased this love in all whom she met. The devotion to

the Infant Jesus was with her eminently practical.
From Him were to be learned the same lessons of self-
sacrifice, of obedience and submission that He taught
on Calvary. A crib was put in the community room,
and the nuns would sometimes turn their gaze away
from it to look at the saintly Mother whose ecstatic love
of God Incarnate could be read upon her radiant
countenance. The sacrifices she suggested were the
little things which sometimes seem and even become an
obstacle when in reality they are an opportunity. As
one of Mother Barat's daughters imbued with her spirit
wrote just a century after the Blessed Foundress's first
visit to Grenoble: "If you can get to realize Our Lord's
intense interest in you and His delight in all you can
offer Him of obedience, charity, confidence, gentleness
in your every-day life—even giving a nice smile or shut-
ting a door gently for love of Him—you will have the
key to a happy life; and if you keep that sacred happiness like a sanctuary lamp alight in your heart, you
will be a joy to God and His creatures; and this last is
an apostleship."

On the last day of the year 1804 Mother Barat announced that the community of Ste. Marie might now
begin their noviceship. Though united in desire and
love, they had had very different modes of preparation
for their new life. The grille and gratings were removed; a habit uniform as to make and material was
adopted. The unwritten rule of the Society of the
Sacred Heart was made known to the novices and commented upon by Mother Barat. Then she asked Father
Roger to give them a retreat.

This retreat is certainly unique in the annals of the
Society. The zealous director had one only purpose—
to inculcate self-sacrifice, the spirit in which he had long

schooled himself. If he saw, or thought he saw, any special attraction or desire or attachment on the part of the retreatants, he promptly asked that it be given up. They might easily be too much attached to the chapel of Ste. Marie, with its saintly associations, so he announced that the nuns would not enter the church during the retreat. Instructions would be given several times a day in the little oratory above the sacristy, and there they would say office. It was objected that strangers occasionally entered the church through the outer door to attend Vespers and they would be disappointed to have come for nothing. The Father at once arranged that the children would replace the nuns in choir and that Mother Debrosse would train and lead them. He forestalled any further objection by obtaining the permission of the Bishop to say his Mass and to reserve the Blessed Sacrament upstairs.

The retreat began. Father Roger wished to see the faces of the retreatants. Perhaps he was near-sighted; at any rate, he declared the tiny chapel too large and he divided it by a white linen drop-curtain, in front of which he placed a bench for his congregation of five. From the first instruction to the last his teaching was rigorous and austere, his words throbbed with life and went home to the hearts of those who knew well that he had striven to put in practice every ideal which he set before them. So strong were his words that Mother Duchesne took alarm for fear that her young companions would look back after having so generously put their hands to the plough. So, as each succeeding trial was unfolded before them, she would whisper to those nearest her on the bench, *"C'est une épreuve."* "This is a test." Her solicitude amused the others. In vain they endeavored to conceal the emotion which the Reverend Father attributed to worn-out or over-wrought nerves. He sent for Mother Barat and told her that he would preside at a daily recreation which he saw to be needed.

Somehow Father Roger then learned that Mother Duchesne was continuing her old practice of fasting, and he thought this austerity might have its roots in self-will. Before the evening instruction he announced, "Tomorrow all except Madame Duchesne will fast and will have for supper only dry bread." When Philippine went to her cell after Mass the next morning she found there a plate with an assortment of fruit, a large piece of bread, a refreshing drink and a note which ran, "Take all of this; it won't hurt you." She did as she was told, but when time came for supper she went to the Father and, on her knees, begged him to let her share the dry bread with the others, who had had no breakfast at all. This time he yielded.

He next learned that Mother Philippine had held, with Duchesne rigor, to the saying of office, even when the restricted number of the community might have justified or even demanded a dispensation from the rule on this point. So he announced that they were to say Office no more. He meant not during the rest of the retreat. Mother Duchesne, who thought that this service of praise so dear to her was to be given up altogether, had the full merit of her generous sacrifice. Again an announcement: "Tomorrow you will take to Mother Barat the thing to which you cling most." Nothing appeared at the Superior's door. The Father ordered an extra recreation. He had begun to think that they really clung to nothing here below and that he had been too severe.

"Father," said Mother Duchesne humbly, "when

orders are given they should be made possible. I can't take to Reverend Mother's room this house and everything in it, and I care for nothing else on this earth."

Still, the son of St. Ignatius was not satisfied. Detached as they were from all that was material, they might yet cling with self-will as a basis to even the holiest practices. Early on Saturday morning he announced:

"Today, Saturday, is set apart for special devotion to the Blessed Virgin. Not one of you is to say her beads today." In turn the Reverend Director had been ascetic, rigorous and stern. "One does not give two such retreats in a lifetime," he said. "Nor make them," the retreatants might have answered with truth.

This year at Grenoble offers a picture of Mother Barat as Mistress of Novices. She trained her daughters for God, so that He would find each ready for His work when the time should come. Emilie Giraud at first held aloof, fearing that her filial confidence towards Mother Duchesne, who had been her first Mistress of Novices, might be censured. The little novice, who had the virtues as well as the faults of a child, soon saw the mistake and gave herself into her new Superior's hands to be trained.

Mother Duchesne "needed no spur, but a check." Mortification was the means by which she praised, thanked and implored grace of God. Their frugal repasts seemed too good for her and she seasoned her portion with bitter herbs. Mother Barat objected to this, fearing that her health might be injured. Philippine obeyed, but later on begged that the prohibition be removed. The saintly Mother Mistress said:

"Well, I consent, on condition that I do not see you do it."

Philippine thought her case lost, as she was next to Mother Barat at table and the young Superior was noted for her power of observation—nothing escaped her. However, Philippine determined to try, and that very day she powdered her food with wormwood. Nothing was said to her. Mother Barat had not seen her, for she was lost in profound recollection. The novice was too prudent to boast of her discovery, and thus nearly a year passed. On one of the last days of Mother Barat's visit to Grenoble Philippine hung on the wall just above her Superior's chair these words from the Canticle of Canticles written in large script: *"Ne suscitetis neque evigilare faciatis dilectam, quoadusque ipsa velit."* "Stir not up, nor awake my beloved until she pleases."

There was general laughter in the refectory that day. Philippine had expanded and softened under Mother Barat's gentle touch. She had grown so gay and light-hearted that she found herself laughing with the other novices when her conscience, "stern daughter of the Voice of God," told her she should be serious.

Mother Barat trained her novices also in the work of education. There were twenty children in the boarding school that year; the little ones were confided to Sister Emilie. Mother Geneviève Deshayes was sent for from Amiens to take charge of a small school founded for the poor children of the neighborhood who attended Mass at 7:15 and remained until evening. Mother Duchesne taught the older girls in the boarding-school. It was a great joy to her when, in 1805, her little niece, Euphrosyne Jouve, came to Ste. Marie. In her grandmother Philippine had seen the Duchesne temperament at its worst; in this golden-haired, blue-eyed little girl she saw its possibilities at its best.

Euphrosyne in turn saw in her "Tante Philippine" the Duchesne character as trained by Mother Madeleine Sophie, and she sat herself to imitate her. She soon showed herself an angel at prayer, an athlete at games, and at study a true "knight of learning." Mother Barat often took the children, sometimes together and sometimes individually, thus sharing in the great work of education, the principles of which she was laying deep in the hearts of her novices.

The year was not without its trials. Calumnious reports were circulated in Grenoble with regard to the old house, and those who did not calumniate criticized. The gratings and grilles had disappeared. There was a young, inexperienced girl at the head of the convent. Only young subjects were received. What did it mean? It was indeed novel to hear of religious who were only semi-cloistered, who went from one house to another of their own order, whose only grille was their rule. St. Francis de Sales had been ahead of his time when he had established his first three foundations for nuns who would go to visit the sick poor in their homes. He had found it necessary to modify his plan, and Ste. Marie, the fourth house of the Visitation, had been, in fact, the first to be founded for the work of contemplation alone. Why, then, had this change taken place on the mountain? At Lyons, as well as at Grenoble, obstacles were placed in the way of those who had intended to enter the Sacred Heart at Ste. Marie. In prayer and in silence Mother Barat found the peace with which she smilingly endured all these evil reports. There at prayer she and Philippine met. These two souls, "one of marble, the other of bronze," were united in their love of this holy exercise in which they took their delight. Thus, Mother Barat wrote to her dear Philip-

pine from Lyons, where she went for a flying visit in
Lent, 1805: "I am not blaming you for what you
sought so eagerly last Sunday, provided that you have
the courage to sacrifice it should your Mother have sent
you to bed." She alluded to the Holy Hour that Philippine had not the permission to make at night as often
as she would have liked. In the same letter she says:
"Happy the soul which sees only the cross, a large
share of which is reserved for you, but have courage
and, without asking for sufferings, be ready to accept
them with all your heart."

The cross was more than ever the portion of the
holy Foundress just then. It was said by outsiders
that her prolonged stay at Lyons meant that she had
deserted Ste. Marie. Her meekness under reproach
was doing much in a quiet, hidden way for Philippine,
who had once complained of having been deserted by
those whom she had gathered together at such great
price. She was silently learning by the most forceful
of lessons—example—the love of the cross. While she
was living in the city of her childhood God was taking
away all her dear ones in turn. Nearly all her own
sisters had married and gone to live in other cities of
France. Mélanie had entered the Visitation at Romans,
and, though this brought great joy to Philippine, she
acknowledged that she missed sorely the frequent visits
that had meant so much to both.

Meanwhile the political affairs of France had not
come to a standstill. In March, 1804, the last of the
Condés perished at the order of Napoleon, to whom the
Senate soon voted the coveted title of Emperor. His
shabby invitation to crown him in Paris met with a
gracious acceptance from Pope Pius VII, who, thinking that his action was for the good of the Church, left

Rome for the French capital in November, 1804. On the 2nd of December the Holy Father blessed and consecrated the diadem in the Church of Notre Dame, but Napoleon crowned himself and his Empress. "It was on a stern and gloomy brow," says Lockhart, "that he with his own hands planted the symbol of successful ambition and uneasy power, and the shouts of the deputies present, carefully selected for the occasion, sounded faint and hollow amidst the silence of the people." On his return journey to Rome the Pope was ordered to follow in the wake of the Emperor's triumphal march, awaiting at each relay the horses which Napoleon had tired out. At Lyons the humble suite of Pius VII had to wait for some time, and there Mother Barat had the privilege of kneeling at the feet of the Pontiff, and, strengthened with the blessing which he willingly extended to each of her little congregation, she returned to Grenoble, bringing with her Henriette Girard. This postulant, "a person of experience," Mother Barat called her, thought that there must be at Ste. Marie some mystery that was being deliberately withheld from her, for she frequently heard the novices speak of the cross of religious life, and she saw only faces beaming with joy. Mother Deshayes, who possessed in no small degree the spirit of the Society, enlightened her by saying that for a religious of the Sacred Heart the great hidden cross is to see God so loving and so little loved in return.

This was the Holy Year, and Fathers Lambert, Gloriot and Varin, who preached the Jubilee at Grenoble, befriended Ste. Marie and did much to dispel the cloud of ill-repute that still hung over the house and to win for the new Order the good-will and patronage of the Bishop, Mgr. Claude Simon. To him they sent

an epitome of the Rules of the Society of the Sacred
Heart, a summary which had just been drawn up by
Fathers Varin and Roger in concert with Mothers
Barat and Duchesne. This document served as the
basis of the Rule when it came later to be written in
full. Thus Ste. Marie, where the first writing was
done, became all the dearer to the Society and to the
first Mothers. The Bishop's approbation was given,
and on November 21, 1805, Mother Barat renewed her
vows together with Mothers Deshayes and Debrosse;
and Mothers Duchesne, Rivet, Emilie Giraud, Henriette Girard and three others pronounced the vows that
bound them to God and to the Society of the Sacred
Heart.

It was about this time that Mother Duchesne made
the acquaintance of Father Louis Barat, who seems to
have inspired her at first with an awe that she seldom
felt for anyone. In him she soon found a kindred
spirit, one stern and ascetic as she was and one who,
like her, pined for the distant field. An event was preparing which was to give Philippine some hope that
such a mission would one day be confided to her.
Mother Barat had longed to devote herself to the
savages in some remote land, but it was from Grenoble
that Father Varin sent her to Amiens for the election
that in January, 1806, made her Superior General, thus
binding her irrevocably to France. If the Sacred Heart
was to have a missionary, it must be someone else.

Three months later the Mother General went again
to Ste. Marie, which she had left in charge of Mother
Deshayes. There she remained several weeks until
Father Varin sent her to arrange for a foundation at
Poitiers. This house was to be the fourth of the Society,
as one had been founded at Bellay since the acquisition

of Grenoble. In bidding good-bye to the little mountain community which Mother Barat had grown to love dearly, she said: "Saint Theresa acknowledged that her greatest suffering in making foundations was that of leaving her religious daughters. I can easily understand that, and I, poor creature that I am, feel the same. God must sustain me in this separation."

Philippine, too, felt this parting. In this mother she had found her ideal.

CHAPTER VI

Transforming Years

CHAPTER VI

Transforming Years—1806-1817

"Lord, Who thy thousand years dost wait
To work the thousandth part
Of Thy vast plan; for us create,
With zeal, a patient heart."

J. H. NEWMAN.

Early in January, 1806, Dom Augustin de Lestrange, the Abbot of La Trappe and its saviour, visited Grenoble and Ste. Marie d'en Haut. When Master of Novices at La Trappe he had been expelled by the National Assembly. In Spain, Belgium, Italy, Switzerland, England and Russia he had successively prepared refuge monasteries for the monks driven from France. In 1803 he had sent a colony of his religious to North America, and his great hope was to follow them. He was fired with zeal for the land which he described to the nuns and the children of Ste. Marie as plunged in the darkness of error. The very name of the Indians sent a thrill through the soul of Philippine. She felt her hopes rise, and wrote to Mother Barat. The saintly Foundress had for Mother Duchesne the same aspirations, and her answer was most encouraging. She had indeed found at Ste. Marie one who was not merely "worth seeking at the other ends of the earth," but also one worth sending so far. With this in mind and heart she answered: "How

87

happy should I be if Our Lord, having so much reason to disdain my service, should receive yours; while we await the moment which we will hasten by the purity of our lives and the fervor of our prayers, we now know that soon perhaps a way will be opened to us." Philippine replied:

So I am allowed to indulge in my longings! You do not deprive me of the hope that my wishes will one day be fulfilled! In my desires and my yearnings I may fly to the countries where I shall be able to render some service to Our Lord and to be rich in Him alone. What a strong goad to self-reform is the fear of being unworthy of my high destiny! With what respect and emotion I should hear from your lips the delightful words, "I send you." With what transports would I take your venerated hand and place it upon my head so that you would bless me, saying: "Mayest thou be blessed by Him in Whose honor thou wilt be consumed." In spirit I am often at the moment of decision, and oftener still in the places where I promise myself one day to be. But would you believe this, knowing that I am still as worthless as when you left, perhaps more so? The more I look forward to my mission, the more I realize my cowardice. It is long since I have passed a Lent in such weariness. I am not only merely natural, but immortified, centered in self. . . . I long to know what you wish to say to me, and in spirit I kneel to listen. It was a sore trial to learn that I must wait until the end of May for your return to Ste. Marie which you so solemnly promised. I fear these multiplied delays far more than sufferings. Reverend Mother will have told you that the building is finished. I am all the more pleased because it will be possible for me to say my "Nunc Dimittis," as I shall be needed no longer.

I hope that you will write to me before Holy Thursday and take back that cruel injunction never to spend a whole night in the chapel. Have pity! I shall need all that time to speak to my Divine Master at leisure.

Your counsels regarding economy have been carried out faithfully. I am inclined to be thrifty, and necessity has always been on my side, but now that obedience makes it a sweet duty, we shall be all the more careful.

Philippine prepared herself for her mission by daily fasts, nightly vigils, constant mortification. Her meals were scraps of bread and cheese—her choice—whatever no one else could eat. Mother Barat restrained these pious excesses and wrote often to her to bid her work upon her character by hidden practices of meekness and humility. Self-conquest was rewarded by the longed-for permission to spend in the chapel the whole night of Holy Thursday, 1806, and Mother Duchesne wrote to thank her loved Superior General:

Your letter gave me great pleasure and did me untold good. I needed that letter badly, for my soul had been as hard as a stone for three weeks. At your words it melted like wax before the fire. My eyes were no longer dry, and joy flooded my heart all that night, for the permission you gave me for the vigil came just in time. O blessed night, when for the second time I thought that my prayer had been granted. Oh, that I may go before the end of the year. I have almost persuaded myself that I shall. All night long I was in the New World, where I journeyed in good company. First, I reverently gathered up all the Precious Blood from the Garden, the Prætorium, Calvary. I took possession of Jesus in the Blessed Sacrament. Closely embracing my treasure, I carried It everywhere to share most lavishly without fear of Its ever being exhausted. St. Francis Xavier interested himself in bringing my precious sowing to harvest, and from his place before the throne of God he prayed that new lands should open their doors to the Gospel. St. Francis Regis himself piloted the missionary nuns; so too did many another saint on fire for the glory of God. And so all went well. My heart seemed incapable of even the holiest sorrow, because I felt that the merits of Jesus are to be applied to souls in the New World.

The twelve hours of the night passed quickly and without weariness, though I remained on my knees; yet in the evening I had feared that I could not hold out an hour. I had many sacrifices to offer—a Mother, and what a Mother! Sisters, relations, a beloved mountain home! And then I seemed to be alone with only my Jesus; alone, except for children, black and uncouth, and I felt happier in their midst than does a king in his court. . . . Dear Mother, when you say, "Lo, I send you," I shall answer at once, "I go."

I tried to be sad all the rest of Good Friday, but I had little inclination to sorrow, my hopes beat so high.

On that Good Friday morning of 1806 Philippine thought her desires all but fulfilled. How often in her life she had set times for God, and He had kept her waiting! She was indeed to sail for America, but not before she had spent twelve years in God's novitiate of suffering. Dryness and combats were now her lot. When we speak of her "gift of prayer" we mean the "gift to pray" rather than that which would have made this holy exercise easy. Often, it is true, she lost the sense of time and of weariness, so that the children, who had quietly slipped small scraps of paper on her habit as she knelt at night prayer, found them still there when they came to the church the next morning. But she received less consolation than comfort in the old-fashioned meaning of the word—strength. Mother Barat's letters bring repeated exhortations to patience, to courage, to confidence. There were indeed some moments of calm, when the clouds rolled back, and she saw the West beckoning her on. Then she would write begging and imploring that the going be no longer delayed, and the prudent Mother Foundress would reply, as she did on May 4, 1808:

"It astonishes me that with your good sense and fair judgment you can conceive such an idea, attach yourself to it and then think that it must be God's Will. There is question of nothing less than preventing a solid and lasting good, in order to go in search of one not only uncertain, but almost impossible, on account of circumstances of which you are ignorant."

Now and again Mother Barat would send a word of encouragement, a hinted hope that the dream would one day be a reality. And always, whether she gently reproached Philippine for her imprudent eagerness or raised her hopes high by a story of missionary activity in some remote land, she held aloft the ideal, the virtues that a missionary should possess. "One preparing himself for the foreign missions," says M. Marinais, "must be constant in his resolve; he must be a man of method, of prayer and of study."

Thus was Philippine being trained. The constancy she needed was not that of desire for the missions, but of calm peace in waiting and of impersonality in her zeal. To her the saintly Foundress spoke severely, knowing the iron of which she was made: "Have you forgotten the words so often heard in your heart, that you must be a victim and one immolated for Christ? Have you forgotten your solemn promise to follow Him whithersoever He goeth? . . . Courage, my daughter. Take as your motto, 'To love and to suffer.' . . . You see that we have been accepted for the colonies. Does not this news give you pleasure?

Have patience, then, and remember that the works of God are done slowly."

Mother Duchesne must surely have had the method required of a missionary. How else can one account for the prodigies of work done by her at the very time when her prayer was prolonged beyond reckoning? She was the "business manager" of Ste. Marie, ordering what was needed, overseeing workmen, trying to keep the old house in repair and paying the bills. As infirmarian, she was unwearying in her care for the sick of the community and of the school. When Madame de Terrail, who had worn herself out in the classroom, went to her eternal reward, Mother Barat wrote to the Mistress of Health:

"And so, my Philippine, our dear sufferer is in Heaven. What an advantage this will be to you, for she will not forget all the tender care which you lavished upon her, and if a glass of water given in God's Name is not left unrewarded, how much more will acts of charity of a higher order be recompensed?"

Of her devotedness to the children when they were ill, one of them wrote: "Our Mothers having arranged to separate from the rest the youngest and most unmanageable children, Mother Duchesne took charge of this wild set and never lost sight of them. If any of us were indisposed she was nurse and infirmarian, and she used to sit up half the night by the sickbed. Especially if there was anything repugnant in our illness, she never gave up what she called her right. With the tenderest care she nursed two who had contagious diseases. Yet it was she who gave most life to our hours of play, joining in our games with charming gaiety."

Office always found Philippine in her stall, for she was Mistress of Choir. She was her Superior's devoted secretary, and she taught religious instruction, at least to the older girls in the boarding school. When she took upon herself the duties of calling the community at five in the morning and of being the last to visit the house at night to see that no unnecessary light had been left burning and that no doors were unlocked, it was probably allowed because in any case she would have been up at those hours. Her short night's rest was taken on a hard board with but a single covering, even when the Alpine spur of Chalmont lay deep in snow. It was not that she did not feel the need of repose, for sometimes she was so weary that she would fall asleep at her work while her pen wandered aimlessly over the pages of the account-book, in which she later found scrawled among the figures the words, "I love God. I hate the world." It was what Christ abhorred in the world that she hated; with Him she loved its inhabitants and sought to do them good. Only at prayer did she never have to contend with sleep.

In 1807 Mother Barat spent a few weeks at Grenoble, and while there wrote to Mother Emilie of her appreciation of the virtue of her dear Philippine:

"Your good Mother Duchesne teaches in the school all day, sits up at night with the sick children, has the whole exterior management of the house, but she never shows distress and scarcely seems to be over-worked. What a valiant woman!" At the same time, however, she sought to restrain Philippine in the course of her utter devotedness and neglect of self.

For the life of study considered essential for the would-be missionary Mother Duchesne had little time left. Her preparation of class was always thorough, but there was so much copying to be done of texts needed by the younger mistresses that she had not the

chance to delve deeply into books. She would have
liked to learn a new language, but the first mission of
the Society might be in China or in America—North or
South; the future was too indefinite for Mother Barat
to encourage her learning Chinese, Spanish, English or
Indian, which she hoped would be useful. The study
of the Heart of Christ, the open book of every successful missionary, was unceasingly carried on by both
Mother Barat and Mother Duchesne.

Prayer was Philippine's life. She had said, "As I
am not allowed to work for my poor savages, the least
I can do is to suffer for them." At night in the silent
chapel of Ste. Marie she wrestled for the souls of the
Indians, where she seemed to be saying like Jacob of
old: "I will not let You go until You bless me."

Her loved Indians were not forgotten during the
day. The most difficult, restless children would put
their mischief aside and listen enrapt while the Mother,
ordinarily so reserved, spoke in burning accents of the
missions and of martyrdom. "Who wants to go with
me?" she would say with shining countenance, and the
children would catch her enthusiasm and express their
longing to go. Some of them said years later that the
ardor which she inspired was so real that had the ship
been there they would actually have embarked. Not
one of them was ever to go to the missions, but several
felt that to these outbursts of childlike, generous
enthusiasm they owed the grace of a religious vocation.

One of these children recorded in writing their love
for Mother Duchesne. She says in part: "In order to
show the impression produced on us by her strong and
pure virtue, her humility, fervor and boundless devotedness, I must needs return to the dearest memories of
my childhood. . . . During two entire years she

was charged with the youngest and most troublesome children, who were separated from the others in order to give peace to the school. She was a real Mother to these mischievous children, whom she would allow to help her in her multifarious occupations. Thus she found an excuse to take them to the garden, where they romped while she interviewed the gardener. Sometimes she led them to the pantry, where she allowed them to core apples, an occupation which they preferred to study. When she had to spend an entire day in the sacristy she found means to employ them even there, some in sewing, others in going through old cupboards in order to make an inventory of all that they should find. These treats were not allowed to take the place of class, at which she insisted on attention, never being known to repeat for the benefit of the dreamers, who were thus made to realize that there was no time to lose; her teaching was both forceful and clear. . . . As a reward for a painstaking writing lesson she would read aloud the Iliad or the Odyssey."

The children of Ste. Marie wanted to show their Mistress General their grateful love on the feast of her patron, St. Philip. One of them says, "But how could we do it? It would be difficult on account of her humility. We thought that we should surely be able to slip in a word of gratitude on her feast day, May 1st. But, alas, on the eve she found on our beds the white dresses which we were to wear in her honor. She collected them all and carried them off. . . . Yet the more she sought to evade honors, the more she revealed to us her virtue and her rare gifts. We knew that under a rather dry and austere exterior were concealed the tenderest affection and the most sympathetic heart, and we could always count on her love."

In glowing colors Mother Duchesne would paint
on canvas and even on the walls of her convent
allegorical scenes of nuns rescuing lost sheep from
brambles and briars. St. Francis Xavier dying on the
island of Sancian in sight of China, to which he had
longed to go, and St. Francis Regis, her special patron
and friend, found prominent places in her gallery.
Though these pictures showed talent, they were far
from being works of art, save inasmuch as they laid
bare the soul of the artist. She contrived to interest
her relatives in the missions and their many needs. The
Périers were most generous, and her sisters proved
willing listeners. She probably did not mention her
hope of leaving France to her father, upon whom old
age was beginning to tell. She realized this and wrote
to one of her sisters:

"I had yesterday the agreeable surprise of a visit
from Father. I found his face still young, but his legs
are stiff and he has difficulty in walking down our hill.
I cannot realize that he is growing old. His kindness
makes one want to see him live to a great age, but, alas,
the joy of every meeting is disturbed by thoughts of
separation and death."

So passed the years of 1807 to 1812, with little
variety as far as exterior things were concerned, but
each succeeding year found Philippine more ready for
what God had in store. The great virtues mentioned
by M. Marioni as essential for a missionary she had
possessed in greater or less degree from her youth.
Little virtues so necessary for an apostle were being
developed in her by the training of Mother Barat, continued in her occasional visits to Grenoble and in her
more frequent letters, as well as by the example of the
gentle, saintly Mother Thérèse Maillucheau. The

"little virtues," says Mgr. Retord, Vicar Apostolic of
Tonkin, "which win success for a missioner are untiring
patience, self-surrender, great prudence, angelic sweetness and an even disposition under the most trying circumstances." On this score Mother Barat wrote to
Mother Duchesne: "Since you so dearly love the good
St. Francis de Sales, why have you not acquired his
spirit while in his school? With what gentleness he
teaches one to act not only towards others, but towards
oneself!" And, again, "Do not behave like a lion which
gets angry and lies down at the bottom of the pit into
which it has fallen. I want you particularly to have
patience with yourself. Never be cast down and
gloomy when you have done something wrong, for our
faults should serve only to increase our humility and
our trust in God. . . . Endeavor to acquire those
virtues which will win children's hearts—sweetness,
serenity and evenness of soul, the fruit of perfect
patience."

A spiritual director has said: "When Our Lord calls
a soul to follow Him closely He begins by sending it
many rough helps from the exterior. Gradually the
soul receives finer helps, but at last the time comes when
Our Lord takes up the chisel Himself." Opposition
at home, the horrors of the Revolution, the trials of the
following years on the mountain had been Philippine's
rougher exterior helps to perfection. The Divine
chisel was reserved for the mission to come. In these
intervening years she was receiving the training, delicate though exacting, of Mother Barat and of her
gentle Mother Thérèse, whom the Foundress had left
at Ste. Marie in 1808.

During that visit the saintly Foundress frequently
saw among the little First Communicants Mother

Duchesne's niece, Euphrosyne Jouve, and she spent many of her precious moments correcting this little girl's Latin exercises. In her frequent visits to the mountain after 1809 it was her joy to see this child of promise growing in wisdom and grace as in age, and emulating her aunt in desire for the foreign missions. Philippine constantly renewed her prayer to be sent, but the more prudent Foundress hesitated, as it was impossible to look far ahead with France still in an unsettled condition. Political affairs had taken great strides during these years. "One of the most marked characteristics of great men of action," says a modern writer, "is their refusal to rest even when they seem to have gained a surfeit of glory and to have climbed to almost incredible heights of power." Napoleon, undaunted by the signal defeat of Trafalgar, overwhelmed the Allies of Austerlitz on December 2, 1805, the anniversary of his coronation, his "lucky day," as he called it. The next three years marked his rise to triumphs of which few but himself would have dreamed. Over Naples, Northern Italy, Holland and Lucca, which he had conquered, he placed one after another of his relatives. He brought Prussia and Austria low while the Holy Roman Empire, ten centuries old, lay in ruins. The Czar Alexander said that he had discovered in Napoleon one only weakness—vanity—and that vanity it was that brought about his egregious mistakes; he desired to end in one year the Russian campaign that required at least two, and, fearful that it might fall into the hands of England, he sold to the United States the vast territory of Louisiana, lately acquired from Spain. His chief mark of vanity, however, was the standing up against God and His Vicar. "It was," he boastfully said, "by turning Catholic that

I finished the War in the Vendée, and by becoming a Mussulman that I established myself in Egypt. If I governed a people of the Jewish religion, I would re-build the Temple of Solomon."

Pius VII had come to realize in sorrow that the Concordat of 1801 had been merely a subterfuge of the Emperor, who now expected the Holy See to side with him in his wars. Having asked this assistance in vain, he ordered his troops to invade Rome. The Pope was arrested and taken a prisoner to Savona, then on to Fontainebleau through Grenoble, where he paused on July 20, 1809. He spent ten days at the Prefecture just across the Isère from Ste. Marie, whence his car-riage, surrounded by *gendarmes,* could be seen. The morning after his arrival the convent had the privilege of lending a Missal and cruets for his Mass. One or two of the nuns went to pay their homage to the im-prisoned Pontiff, who also deigned to receive the sixty children of Ste. Marie d'en Haut, and each evening the little community knelt at the convent window to share in the blessing which the Holy Father gave to the throng kneeling in the street below. On the Feast of St. Peter in Chains he was hurried off towards Fon-tainebleau. Then the tide turned against Napoleon, the victorious Allies demanded the release of the Pope, and the Emperor knew he must yield. Yet, thinking that to let his captive return freely to Rome would be "a dangerous proof of magnanimity," he sent him south under escort before the Allies could have time to act. Napoleon had kept secret his own excommunication, but the bull was published and circulated in France by a pious Congregation, which thus brought down the wrath of the Emperor on all religious orders. To the Minister of Public Worship the Emperor then wrote:

"If on October 1 (1809) there are any missions or congregations still in France, I shall hold you responsible."

This was why Mother Barat feared for the future of her little Society; the Fathers of the Faith had already been suppressed, and its turn might come next. In heroic silence she practised the patience she had taught Philippine Duchesne. She placed little trust in the authorization of her congregation solicited by Mother Baudemont, drawn up by Portalis, the Minister of State, and signed by the Emperor in camp at Osterode. She waited, watching each change taking place in her loved France. Napoleon's disastrous retreat from Moscow in 1812 was the first of a series of defeats. He fought desperately, like a lion at bay, until the surrender of Paris in 1814, when he retired to his miniature island empire of Elba. Meanwhile Pius VII from Rome revoked the suppression of the Society of Jesus, and nearly all the French Fathers of the Faith, with Father Varin at their head, joined the re-established Order, to the great joy of the religious of the Sacred Heart.

Another event gave new happiness to Mother Duchesne. On Christmas Day, 1814, four postulants entered at Ste. Marie. One of them, Octavie Berthold, was to play a prominent part in the life of Philippine. Another was Euphrosyne Jouve, who shared Octavie's intense love of suffering. Their time of first probation was stormy; the old monastery walls re-echoed the boom of the Austrian guns, while cannon balls whistled through the terraced garden. Aloysia, as Euphrosyne was henceforth to be called, loved the sound of arms, for it reminded her that she was a soldier, a cadet of Christ. On the 29th of March Grenoble offered an heroic resistance to twenty thousand Austrians. That very day witnessed the burial of Aloysia's grandfather, Mother Duchesne's own beloved father. As the rules regarding enclosure were not formulated then as they are today, Philippine had been sent to attend him in his last illness, and hers had been the incomparable joy of bringing back to God the one who was nearest to her on this earth.

In the early spring of 1816 France vibrated with the news that Napoleon had slipped away from Elba. Dauphiny opened her gates to him and a regiment met him. He unbuttoned his coat, and, facing the armed men, said:

"Soldiers, which one of you wishes to fire on his General?"

A shout of welcome greeted this theatrical deed. At Vizille, as he gazed at the old château which had belonged to Lesdiguières, and in a later day to Casimir Périer, he remarked:

"Liberty was born at Vizille in 1788. It is born anew at Vizille to-day."

The peasants and mountaineers took up the soldiers' shouts of welcome when on March 7 the Emperor entered Grenoble, for "with their chief city the people of Dauphiny had given him an immense arsenal, an army, the keys of Lyons and the way to Paris." Then came Waterloo and St. Helena. "Napoleon was," says de Tocqueville significantly, "as great as a man can be without virtue."

Between the years 1809 and 1814 there was not a single apostolic decree concerning sacred rites, and the first proclamation following upon this unusual interruption was that which established a commemoration of Our Lady of Sorrows to be made on the third Sunday of September. In alluding to this fact the author of "The Liturgical Year" says: "1809 to 1814 were five sorrowful years during which the government of Christendom was suspended—years of blood which beheld the Man-God agonizing once more in the person of His captive Vicar. But the Mother of Sorrows was still standing beneath the cross offering to God the Church's sufferings, and when the trial was over Pius VII, knowing well whence the mercy had come, dedicated this day to Mary as a fresh memorial of the day of Calvary." That third Sunday of September was the first commemoration of Our Lady of Sorrows, and a year later within its octave Philippine Duchesne made her perpetual vows.

As France grew calm in the wake of the banished Napoleon it seemed to Father Varin time to draw up the Constitutions which he and the Foundress had prayerfully worked upon in the Château of Chevroz in Franche-Comté, where he had taken refuge in 1813. Therefore, in October, 1815, Mother Barat summoned to Paris the Superiors of the houses of Poitiers, Grenoble, Cuignières and Niort. Mother Duchesne was also invited as the travelling companion of her Superior, Reverend Mother Bigeu. As the two travellers looked back at "the snowy summits of the Alps that surrounded Grenoble like a coronet" Philippine probably thought that she was leaving her mountain home forever and that Paris would be but a stepping-stone to the missions. God's thoughts are so often not ours! She was in truth never to see Ste. Marie again, but the day of her departure from France was still far away. The journey to Paris was through Lyons, where, since the rules of enclosure had yet to be established by the Council, Mother Duchesne stayed with her sister,

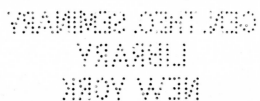

Madame Jouve, to whom she had much to tell of Aloysia, now a happy, fervent novice.

The Council was held in the Convent of St. Thomas of Villanova in the Rue de Sèvres, Paris, where the nuns found an altar dedicated to the Sacred Heart and the famous statue of Notre Dame de Gras, before which St. Francis de Sales had prayed for and gained peace of soul. The results of this Council must have reached all the houses of the Sacred Heart in time to add to the joys of Christmas, and soon after that came a pontifical rescript approving the Constitutions and Rules of the Society.

Philippine had thought that, now that the Society of the Sacred Heart was firmly rooted in France, it would speedily branch forth in other directions. Her dismay then was great when the Council, instead of confirming her hope for the missions, named her Secretary General. She wrote to the Community of Ste. Marie d'en Haut:

S.C.J.M.   PARIS, JANUARY 8, 1816.

To the Mothers of the Society of the Sacred Heart of Jesus at Ste. Marie of Grenoble.

My very dear Sisters:

Since I am not to see you again, I am pondering deeply the initials S.C.J.M. with which we are henceforth to begin our letters.

I was grateful for your New Year's greeting, and, though I put off writing until our Mothers should be ready to leave for Grenoble, I have remembered you before God, telling Him of my desires for you. I have rejoiced in the hope that He will be glorified in your house which is so dear to me, and whose interests I have often taken too much to heart. God watches over it even more lovingly than I did, and in His Divine Providence we can be at peace. Of His Goodness you now have a proof in the return of your Reverend Mother. Her two companions will be of great assistance to you.

I am not to blame for our prolonged stay here; indeed, I grow weary of life outside of our own cloister, for which all the beauties of St. Sulpice cannot make up. . . . It is good to hear that you are all well. As to colds, it seems that the way to avoid them is to go out of doors frequently, for, since we have been out in all weather, we have had none.

Reverend Mother will have much of interest to tell you. Your curiosity is laudable in what concerns our holy rules. We are indeed happy to know our duty more clearly so as to be ever more faithful. Let us beg pardon of God for the past and begin all over again.

Pray much for me, dear Sisters, and believe me
Ever yours in the Sacred Heart of Jesus,

PHILIPPINE.

Reverend Mother Bigeu returned to Grenoble, but she was not to remain at Ste. Marie, for she had been named Assistant General. She was replaced by Mother Thérèse Maillucheau, to whom Philippine wrote the following words of sympathy from Paris on February 26, 1816:

Your letter has reached me, and I have taken a real share in your present sufferings and in those that will come to you with the burden of being Superior. But at the same time God has consoled you by the courage and virtue shown by your good daughters in a circumstance painful to their grateful hearts. . . . Euphrosyne's letter has given pleasure to all to whom I have read it. We are still at St. Thomas and we do not know how long we shall have to remain. . . . I beg you, dear Mother, either to have the prayer to St. Regis said faithfully in fulfilment of my promise or to have the vow commuted if the prayer is not being said.

The new Assistants General, Mothers Bigeu, de Charbonnel and Grosier, stayed in the Convent of St. Thomas in the apartment which had been occupied by Madame de Gramont d'Aster before her entrance into the noviceship. Mother Duchesne accompanied them in their daily visits to the prospective Mother House in the Rue des Postes and soon found ample scope for her devotedness. Not satisfied with urging on the workmen, she helped them as painter, mason and as glass-fitter, or in outlining on the walls the stone-like impressions that would make them look monastic.

During the seven months spent at the Convent of St. Thomas the nuns who were to form the community of the new Mother House went out daily to Mass, now in one church, now in another, and Philippine prayed long in the chapel of the Foreign Missions and in the most celebrated shrines of Paris for her cherished desire.

On the 15th of April, 1816, the house was ready for the Superior General, her Assistants and her Secretary. In choosing Philippine for this office Mother Barat saw in her the qualifications which the Council had laid down as essential for the office. In looking through the letters and the journals so faithfully kept by this able scribe we can read between their lines the rule of the Secretary General. In these letters Mother Duchesne shows herself "the hand and the memory" of her Superior. Varied and numerous as her duties were, hers was ever "the spirit of recollection and prayer;" she had been trained, "yet so as by fire," to the prudence and discretion required, and of this the journals kept by her are proof. Her letters were clear, precise, observant of all due courtesy, and they bore the impress of that piety and unction which the sainted Foundress hoped would characterize her little Society. The new Secretary so identified herself with the mind of her in whose name she was writing that to each expression she gave the color of Mother Barat's thought and the seal of her authority. The impersonality of letters written in the name of the Superior General is quite different from the simplicity with which she speaks of herself when the letter is her own. For example, she wrote on August 18, 1816, again to Mother Thérèse:

Your illness has given me great pain, for I could not be indifferent to the loss which your absence causes in a community of which I once formed a part. I have prayed for you, as well as for the First Communicants.

I am indebted to you for your kind attention in sending my notebooks. A large exercise book containing notes of History is missing. If it can easily be found I should be grateful to have it. In what has already been sent I recognize the kindness of the good Mother and Sister in charge of the linen room, and I thank them, but, as they should love my soul more than my body, I beg them to forget the one and to care for the other by leaving me some privations and by praying for me.

Again she wrote to the community of Ste. Marie d'en Haut:

I expected no sign of your remembrance, being well aware that I deserve only to be forgotten. It would be well to forget me, for the thought of me must recall the many faults by which I have done harm to a house dearer to me than life—faults which are the object of my keenest regret. But, knowing by experience that

charity is the bond of our holy Society, I am not astonished at your thinking of me, and I beg you to pardon
my past faults and to pray that I may improve. You
must be merciful to me even as God has been. He
generally gives to each soul but one grace that is the
first link in a chain of many others. This signal grace
was in my case my return to Ste. Marie and my
entrance into the beloved Society of the Sacred Heart,
a blessing far beyond what I could ever have hoped.
Nevertheless, although I have profited so little by
teaching and example, God in His Goodness now points
out to me a new Mission which calls forth all my
gratitude.

I have shed many tears over America before the
statue of Our Lady, at whose feet St. Francis de Sales
received peace. This statue is now at St. Thomas,
where we have spent these last months. I owe much to
the prayers said both there and at Montmartre. Pray
for me, especially as one's heart should be on fire with
zeal. . . . We cannot have a foundation in Poland,
but we are asked for in Spain, Normandy, Lorraine
and Languedoc.

The installation at the Mother House in the Rue
des Postes was blessed by the cross. Several of the
community and of the school fell ill, and Mother
Duchesne spent days and nights going from one infirmary to the other and replacing her Sisters in the
school, ever thoughtless of self if she might lighten the
burden of others. So indispensable did she become that
even Mother Barat began to fear that Philippine also
would have to sacrifice her dear hope for the missions.
She was thinking such thoughts as these one day when
Mother Duchesne broke in upon them asking when she
might go. Mother Barat told her once more that there
was no opening then and asked her not to allude to this
subject again.

"What!" Philippine answered. "How can this be? You want me to think no more on this subject? But, Mother, don't you remember that it was you who inspired it by reawakening in me that desire? Could I give it up now?"

"Well, dear Philippine," was the reply, "let us talk sensibly. Should I tell you to go and convert the savages, what would you do without companions, money or help, and with not even the wherewithal to set out? Do you expect Providence to work a miracle and grant you the privilege of walking on water? . . . But wait; go on praying. Perhaps later we shall think about it; for the present it is out of the question."

"I'm not asking for anything," Mother Duchesne sadly answered. "Say only, 'Go,' and I shall leave at once with nothing but the grace of obedience."

So things stood when on January 14, 1817, a visitor called at the Rue des Postes.

CHAPTER VII

THE TRAINING CONSUMMATED

CHAPTER VII

THE TRAINING CONSUMMATED—1817-1818

"That which I chose, I choose;
That which I willed, I will;
That which I once refused, I still refuse.
O hope deferred, be still.

That which I chose and choose,
And will is Jesus' Will,
He hath not lost his life who seems to lose,
O hope deferred, hope still.

CHRISTINA ROSSETTI.

Catholicity came to North America with Columbus in 1492, when its sacred symbol, the cross, was planted on our soil. Her priests were pioneers—the first to thread the great arteries of the vast continent, to plod over many an Indian trail, to discover, study and exploit the vegetable and mineral wealth of the land; to learn and to perpetuate in scientific form the unwritten languages of the native tribes, to discharge unflinchingly the duties of a sacred office and for this to die, as full one hundred did, by savage hands. This was the story of the Church in the colonies. Some missionaries followed the Indians westward as they were driven back from the Atlantic seacoast; others remained in the East, and because of the work which they accomplished the Church grew with the growth of the new Republic. The year 1789, made famous by the inauguration of

111

George Washington, the first President of the United States, was likewise the date of the consecration of John Carroll as first Bishop of the country. The French Canadians, scattered through Kentucky, the North-western Territory, the Illinois country and Michigan, as well as the few Catholics in Tennessee, were under the jurisdiction of Monseigneur Flaget, the saintly Bishop of Bardstown, Kentucky. In all these districts there were still Indians, some of them the Catholic descendants of converts of the first French missionaries who came to America in the seventeenth and early eighteenth centuries.

Louisiana was the name originally given to the territory lying on either side of the Mississippi, a river two thousand odd miles in length. It was a colony of France, having been founded by French Canadians, and its people, nearly all Catholics, were at first under the rule of the Bishop of the distant city, Quebec. In 1762 France gave up Western Louisiana to Spain, and in the following year by the Treaty of Paris she lost in favor of England both Canada and that part of Louisiana which lay east of the Mississippi. After that date Louisiana was placed under the ecclesiastical government of the Bishop of Santiago, Cuba, but was soon transferred to the jurisdiction of Havana, under which see it remained until the erection of the diocese of Louisiana and the Floridas to be governed by a Bishop resident at New Orleans.

In the meantime France had got back the secular government of Louisiana and had lost it again because of Napoleon's jealousy of England and President Jefferson's daring seizure of a golden opportunity. After this exchange, made in 1803 and known to history as the Louisiana Purchase, the Holy See entrusted the administration of the new territory of the United States to Bishop Carroll, the Metropolitan of Baltimore. The impossibility of governing properly a land which was then as far removed from the thirteen original states in tradition, spirit and customs as it was remote in geographical miles led Bishop Carroll to suggest to Rome that Mgr. Du Bourg be named for the administration of the Louisiana Territory.

It was no easy task that confronted the new administrator when he went south in 1812. Spiritual life in New Orleans was at a low ebb, for the repeated change of power, ecclesiastical no less than civil, had given a rare opportunity for cockle to grow apace. Moreover, a British army was encamped at the gates ready to attack the city. General Andrew Jackson, the leader of the opposing American forces, showed real appreciation of the patriotic stand taken by Mgr. Du Bourg at this critical moment.

In 1815 the Bishop-elect of Louisiana went to Rome, where he was consecrated. While in Europe he sought to enlist for his mission priests, seminarians and religious. In Italy he obtained the services of several saintly Lazarists, among them the Venerable Felix De Andreis and Fathers Rosati and Aquaroni. Belgium also furnished many zealous volunteers.

The Bishop saw clearly the need of nuns to serve as auxiliaries to the priests in their labors in America. There had been a convent of Ursulines in New Orleans since 1727, when Governor Bienville, the Canadian founder of that city, realizing the necessity of an educational institution for the daughters of the colonists, had applied to the nuns of St. Angela at their convent in Rouen, France. After a perilous voyage of six months a band of heroic women arrived in Louisiana. Bienville's country home, the best house in the colony, was put at their disposal, while their monastery in New Orleans was building. The Ursulines were the first nuns to enter the vast region bounded by Canada, the Gulf of Mexico, the Atlantic and the Pacific. In their good works they knew no distinction either of race or of color, for, besides a prosperous academy for young Creoles, they had classes for little negroes and Indians. They adapted themselves loyally to each successive régime and their prayers helped to win for Jackson a victory almost miraculous when, on January 8, 1812, they watched from the convent the smoke rising from the battlefield of Chalmette as the fighting went on in woful ignorance that peace had already been signed in far-away Ghent.

Fully appreciative of the good done in his vast diocese by the Ursulines, Bishop Du Bourg did not fail to visit their convents in Europe to solicit and obtain new recruits for Louisiana. Then he turned to the Society of the Sacred Heart and called at the Mother House in January, 1817.

The knocker sounded, the door opened and the Bishop gave his name to the portress, who was none other than Philippine Duchesne. Quickly she went in search of Mother Barat.

"Reverend Mother," she exclaimed, "this is the hour intended by Providence. Do not lose this opportunity. You have but one word to say. I beg you to say it."

"My child," the Superior calmly answered, "only if His Lordship takes the first step shall I speak to him of our hopes. That will be the sign by which I shall know that God wills it."

No doubt the portress prayed that the Bishop would ask for aid in his mission, but his only request was that

he might say his Mass at the Rue des Postes the
next day.

He did so, and Mother Barat saw him afterward.
He spoke of the United States, of his vast diocese and
its needs spiritual and temporal, and then added that
he would like to have some religious of the Sacred
Heart for his mission just as soon as they could be
spared from France.

"As soon as that can be, Monseigneur," said Mother
Barat, "I shall have someone quite ready to go."

Then she told him of Mother Duchesne, of her longing to be sent, of her eleven years of preparation. The
Bishop asked to see Philippine. She was called. She
felt that her one desire had been granted, and in the
joy of her heart she could only find words in which to
beg the Bishop's blessing. With that benediction on
the work that she now knew would be hers there disappeared a malady from which she had suffered for nine
years; she was to need all her old physical strength in
the far-away field of her future labor.

Even now that she had leave to go, she could not
depart at once. Bishop Du Bourg continued his tour
through France and Belgium, recruiting missionaries,
begging money, sacred vessels, even farm implements
for his vineyard. Winter passed, spring came and
when the chestnut trees in the Champs Elysées were
snow-white and rose-red, the American prelate returned
to the Mother House to arrange definitely with Mother
Barat for the sailing of her little colony.

To his great disappointment the Foundress gently
told him that, having consulted those whose judgment
she preferred to her own, she had decided that it was
still too soon to launch out into this new enterprise,
that the time was not opportune to send her nuns to

America. The Bishop was not pleased, and the saintly Mother showed her anxiety as she accompanied him to the door. But before they reached it they heard a step behind them, and there stood Mother Duchesne, who had read the truth on her Superior's face and in the fact that she had not been sent for. She fell on her knees, and with clasped hands entreated:

"Your consent, Reverend Mother, do give your consent."

Touched by this perseverance and feeling now that God's hour had struck, Mother Barat said:

"I do give it, dear Philippine, and I shall try to find companions for you."

Then and there Mother Barat promised Mgr. Du Bourg that, in spite of many obstacles—a new foundation at Quimper, the serious illness of several at the Mother House, the lack of funds everywhere—she would send a few nuns to America in the spring of the following year. After expressing his satisfaction he said that St. Louis in Upper Louisiana, or Missouri, was to be his episcopal city and that he was going there by way of Annapolis, but that it would be better for the nuns to go via New Orleans, where at his request the good Ursulines would give them hospitality for a few days.

This fulfilment of her highest hopes seemed to increase Mother Duchesne's almost superhuman power of work and endurance. She returned to the sick in the infirmary, went on with her work as Secretary and with her class in the school and at the same time prepared, as she had been bidden, for the temporal needs of her mission.

Mother Barat now rejoiced more than ever that she had persisted in refusing to accept for the Society the

The little colony was not to leave Paris until May, 1818, but at the end of January a letter from M. Martial, Bishop Du Bourg's Vicar General, announced that he was sailing for New Orleans in February and that he counted on meeting the five nuns in Bordeaux. Preparations continued and Mother Duchesne took no end of trouble to see that the trunks contained suitable clothing for each of her sisters, but when she was asked to see if what had been made ready for her own use would be satisfactory she refused to look, saying, "Oh, give me whatever you like." This was not her sentiment with regard to the things being selected for the sacristy —these she both saw to and packed.

Mother Audé was hastily summoned from Quimper. Sister Lamarre had already arrived at the Mother House. On February 7 Mother Barat assembled the whole community and named the privileged ones, exhorting them to fidelity to the Constitutions and to an intimate and inviolable union with the Society in France. Her burning words influenced all those present with holy envy for the "missionaries."

"If your going to Louisiana were to be the cause of but one more Tabernacle being erected, would you not be too happy?" she said, and, calling the favored ones to her, she gave them the objects which she had for her own use and showed that she would gladly have despoiled herself and her house for the mission she loved.

Mother Duchesne had often shown a more than ordinary repulsion for the office of Superior. So well did all know her feeling on this point that in speaking of her longing for the missions she could say nothing stronger than, "If I could only go, I should be content even to be Superior."

To her dismay she now learned that this was the post she was to fill towards the other four nuns; on her would fall the final responsibility of all that would be said or done, undertaken or carried through, of all success as well as of all failure. Mother Berthold, almost devoid of experience; Mother Audé, who was to make her profession the next morning, and who was Mother Duchesne's junior by many years, seemed to the humble Mother more fit than herself for the dreaded office. Instead of heeding her expostulations the Superior General gave her exceptional powers which the distance of the mission from the centre of the Society and the months that must intervene between a letter and its answer would make essential.

After the ceremony of Mother Audé's profession on the morning of February 8, the travellers received the congratulations of friends of the Society, among them the good Abbé Perreau, who brought gifts for the first chapel of the Sacred Heart in America. Mother Duchesne steeled her tender heart for the parting, but when the moment came to leave, Octavie Berthold was in tears. Philippine took her hand and led her down to the *diligence*. She herself had shown not a whit of the sorrow she felt in leaving the loved Mother General, who returned to the chapel to lay her own grief at the feet of Him Who alone is able to

> "*Express the words that die in utter helplessness*
> *Unsaid through tears.*"

The holy Foundress then read the letter that Mother Duchesne had left for her. In it Philippine asked forgiveness for all the suffering she thought that she might have caused, and she added: "God is putting me in the way of expiation by imposing upon me the charge of Superior. My greatest happiness will be to form for you religious worthy of the Society and of you. Otherwise I should prefer to die."

The travellers found the stagecoach surrounded by curious groups of those who had heard of the impending departure for America. The journey was a noisy one, for a young ecclesiastic, afterwards a Jesuit, did his best to drown with hymns and canticles the loud voice of an officer who distracted the nuns with drinking songs with which he whiled away the hours. There were pauses at Orléans and at Tours, where they went to Church, and they had a "day at home" in the convent at Poitiers, where Sister Manteau joined the little band of missionaries. Another stop at Angoulême, and finally they arrived at Bordeaux. There the Vicar General met them with his carriage in order to drive them to the house of Madame Vincent, who was offering them generous hospitality. Dreading the ovation which she feared would greet their arrival, Mother Duchesne sent Mother Audé with the sisters in the prelate's carriage, while she and Mother Berthold started off on foot to get another conveyance which would take them near to the home of Madame Vincent. To her consternation she found the omnibus surrounded by a crowd and she heard voices saying in triumph: "Here is the Superior of Louisiana." She climbed hastily into the shelter of the *diligence,* wishing that she had accompanied the Vicar General in his carriage.

Madame Vincent gave them the kindest of welcomes, saying that she counted on their remaining with her and her little teaching community until they should embark. They hoped the embarking would not be long delayed, but contrary winds were an insuperable obstacle at that time and the sailing was indefinitely postponed.

Philippine wrote to Mother Barat:

My very dear Mother:

I have been touched by the kindness of your last letters and by the mercy of God to me. I am impatient to be on the boat that will carry me to the goal of my desires. We shall sail only when the weather is favorable, so the delay may continue. I leave in France much that I love, and I shall always be bound to my native land by the strongest ties. These bonds seem to be drawn all the closer when I think of the benefits I owe to the Society which I am now allowed to carry to new lands. What a joy it will be to see devotion to the Sacred Heart flourish there!

You desired this privilege for yourself. God makes use of you where you are, but, since I could do nothing, He will try me out elsewhere, like those nuns who are changed from house to house so that different trials may bring to light the good that is in them. Pray that I may not be unfaithful always. My companions keep up their courage and inspire others with envy. . . . I am deeply grateful for all the prayers said for me. The whole merit of our mission will be yours; the peril both to body and to soul will be ours.

At about the same date Mother Duchesne wrote to the children of Grenoble:

BORDEAUX, FEBRUARY 15, 1818.

My very dear Children:

I am leaving things as completely as though I were about to die, since it is almost certain that I shall not return to France nor see you, dear children, and my many loved ones again in this life. This is why I feel justified in confidently repeating St. Peter's question:

"Lord, we have left all things. What, then, shall we have?" Ah, the reward I ask is the great and ineffable consolation of learning that you are all fervent in the love of God and that with His grace you are doing good and acquiring the solid piety which will win for you happiness both in this world and in the next.

Across the vast ocean that will soon separate us my heart will seek you again and will devise plans for your happiness. I shall ask the interesting children whom we shall bring into the flock of Christ to remember you in their prayers. When surrounded by innocent and simple souls I shall say: "Let us pray for the French children, the memory of whom adds so much to my sacrifice. Let us pray for your benefactresses, who are praying for your conversion and who have sent you these gifts without dreaming that you were to receive them from nuns whom they knew and loved. Their generous deed was done only for God and for you." In this way I shall get the Indian children to pray for you.

I hope to send you details of our foundation in the New World if God puts no obstacle in the way. I was to have left to-day with my four companions, but we are to be delayed for several days longer, so I have this opportunity to write and ask you to put by small things that might serve as rewards and as baits to draw the little savages whom we shall teach. I hope to see them in two or three months. Our voyage will end at New Orleans and will be much longer than if we were to land at Baltimore, but this route is less dangerous. We shall ascend the Mississippi in boats made like little ocean steamers, with rooms having beds, and shall be twenty or twenty-five days on the river.

On account of the uncertainty in which we are as to the success of our voyage and as to what will follow, pray much for us.

I am, in the Sacred Heart,

Your entirely devoted Mother,

PHILIPPINE DUCHESNE.

At Bordeaux the five missionaries found Father
Barat, whose encouragement was needed just then, for
there in sight of the sea they felt the first temptation
to look back. Of this Philippine wrote to Mother Barat
on the 18th of February:

It would be impossible to receive more attention and
kindness than is shown us by Madame Vincent and her
Sisters, who have given us great edification. But all
their solicitude does not make up for your absence and
that of my Sisters. Although God upholds my strength
and even the ardor of my longings, nevertheless, since
coming here I have been in a state of such anguish and
hardness of heart that on entering the Church of St.
Andrew his very own words came spontaneously to my
lips: "O good Cross, so much desired, and now prepared for the one who longed for it." My Sisters also
have their little moments of weakness, which I foresaw
and share fully. We see in ourselves new miseries that
make God's gracious choice of us all the more astonish-
ing. Your brother is famous for pushing on towards
perfection souls that hang back.

It was also of Mother Barat's brother that Mother
Audé wrote: "If the only grace I had obtained on this
journey had been that of seeing a saint, I should not
regret having taken it." He was then prolonging his
stay in Bordeaux in the hope of being sent to Louisiana,
for he knew that Bishop Du Bourg had asked for him
for his diocese.

Before sailing Philippine learned of the serious illness of her loved niece, Aloysia Jouve, and wrote to
her: "I sometimes think that God will raise you up from
this state of infirmity and then make use of you to the
uttermost. Set no limits to your self-sacrifice, even if
it should send you to America without any hope of our
ever meeting, but with the great consolation of being

all the more generously devoted to God. Good-bye, dear Sister. Think of my happiness; envy it if you like, but do not wish to take it from me. We are expecting every moment to sail. Once more, good-bye."

And to Aloysia's Superior, Mother Thérèse Maillucheau, she wrote on March 2:

This is my last day in France, for the boat has come in at last. M. Martial will be the only priest on board, and if he is ill—and he is not very well now—we shall be deprived of Mass. How can I be disconsolate when you lavish on me so many good wishes and such help which stirs up all our gratitude? I shall never be able to repay you for what you have done for us.

As to the hope of seeing you again, I count little upon it. You are doing much good in France, and if Aloysia is to accomplish it elsewhere she will have to be parted from you. Perhaps God is only waiting for this sacrifice to cure her and then to use her for His Glory. How I thank you for your goodness to her!

On February 20 Mother Duchesne had written to Mother Barat:

We have seen here Madame Fournier, a lady who has crossed the ocean six times and knows just what is needed. I find her even too ready to suggest precautions. I should have liked to have only what St. Francis Xavier had. However, as you do not want us to neglect human means, reasonable precautions will be taken and I shall be sure of doing God's Will in obeying you and in following the advice of your brother, our good Father Barat, whose counsels I carry out faithfully. He enters into every detail, even with regard to sugar, of which I have none except a box of sweets from Madame Fournier. I have much greater reason to be solicitous about you, my dear Mother, but you tell me nothing in particular about your health.

Your letters, which are always a joy, will begin a second volume of my collection and will be even more needed now that a greater distance will separate us. We are all valiant, but God has begun to try us. The retreat was difficult—I am as hard as iron and my head is full of troublesome details. You have no idea of the difficulties of the journey, and they are not over. Our boxes, sent on Saturday of Quinquagesima, have not yet arrived.

Madame Vincent continues her kind attentions. Nevertheless, we cannot help feeling that we must be a burden, and this increases our longing to sail.

There was still further delay and it was only on the 13th day of March that Father Barat addressed a last exhortation to the travellers whom he envied. After receiving repeated blessings they left Bordeaux, going down the Garonne to Royan, where they went aboard the *Rebecca* on Holy Thursday, 1818. On Holy Saturday the boat left the harbor and on Easter Sunday they lost sight of France, which only one of the five would ever see again.

For a week the *Rebecca* was tossed on the Bay of Biscay. As it neared the Azores another storm rose. The Captain suggested casting lots in order to discover the Jonas. He had been assured before sailing that if he took aboard these nuns, a priest, Abbé Martial, and a student for the priesthood, M. Evremont Hulissard, his ship would most certainly be wrecked.

On April 21, when the storm had subsided, they found themselves alongside an American corsair, armed with eleven cannon and manned by one hundred and twenty sailors. It was on the lookout for Spanish vessels, probably on account of suspicion that American seamen had been impressed into the service of Spain.

Towards the end of April the heat became intense; capricious winds drove the boat five times across the Tropic of Cancer. Barrels of wine in the hold burst. The stench so produced spread through the vessel; the drinking water became stagnant; the plate and the copper corroded. Even the woodwork showed signs of decay.

A violent wind and rain made it necessary to lower the sails, and the ship drifted aimlessly. At other times it was becalmed. The nuns were rarely able to make use of the privilege of having a priest on board, for storms and seasickness made it impossible for them to have Mass. So small was the *Rebecca* that there was little privacy. The daily instruction given by the Father, no less than frequent Confession, provoked such irreverent criticism on the part of the crew that these consolations had to be abandoned.

In spite of their sufferings, the religious were not indifferent to the natural beauty before them; even storms aroused their admiration. As they neared the West Indies schools of porpoises and of flying fish surrounded the vessel and myriads of polyps colored the waves. The sun rose and set in glory such as had never been dreamed, and when its light had dimmed, the waters sparkled with the splendor of phosphorescence. Two months of patient endurance won for the nuns the sympathy of the other passengers. The captain and the crew grew to consider the little community no longer as Jonas, but as a pledge that the *Rebecca* would at last reach port in safety. Sister Manteau had a fine voice, and when the captain would say, "Come, ladies, sing your beautiful evening song which always brings a favorable wind," she would intone the Ave Maris Stella, and the others would sing with her, while the sailors paused in their work or their games to listen as the *Rebecca* ploughed her way through the waters.

One night as they neared the West Indies a little rowboat hailed their boat, for an officer who had been put off an eastbound ship because of some defect in his passport wanted to be taken aboard. He was able to give the nuns some news of what had happened in France since their departure. Rumor had somewhat exaggerated conditions at Paris and Bordeaux, and Mother Duchesne took alarm for the dear Society in France, fearing more, as she wrote to the Mother General, for the "trunk of the tree than for their little branch, which so far was useless."

After nearly two months on the open sea the *Rebecca* sighted Cuba, and in the halcyon weather was able to glide along the whole length of this large and beautiful island. Among the passengers who boarded the boat was one from Havana, who invited the nuns to make a foundation in Cuba, and gave them forty piastres. They received with humble gratitude this increase of the small bourse which Mother Barat had been able to spare. Saint Theresa once said that for a foundation Theresa and three ducats would avail nothing, but that, with God on her side, Theresa and three ducats sufficed. The seraphic Carmelite had too much saintly common sense to despise the three ducats, even when she had God on her side, and Philippine Duchesne, who had declared herself ready to set out without companions, destination or money, was beginning to realize that even Divine Providence generally makes use of natural means to attain Its high ends. It was in sight of the West Indies that Mother Duchesne wrote her first letter from the New World:

S.C.J.M.   MAY 16, 1818.

Dear Reverend Mother:

A year ago today at this very hour (9 A. M.) we were receiving at Paris the last visit of the Bishop of Louisiana, and you then gave your consent to a foundation in the New World. Happy as I was, I did not dream then that the anniversary would find us so near the goal of our journey, for what are a few hundred miles as compared to the thousands which we have already traversed?

We impatiently long for a letter from you and hope to find one awaiting us at New Orleans, for the vessel that was to sail soon after we did may have made a speedier voyage, and it is sure to have on board letters from you.

We are nearing the end of our journey in fairly good health. As it is summer, we are able to sail the whole length of the coast of Cuba, a way not always passable because of the currents. The other route, which is longer than this by four hundred leagues, lies between Martinique and Guadalupe. After avoiding this detour we were so becalmed that there was question of passing between San Domingo and Porto Rico, or of first taking a northerly course and then coming south through the Bahama Channel, which separates Florida from the great bank of C——. For fifty-two days we saw only the sea and the sky. Only on the 11th of May did we sight land; it was Caicos, one of the Antilles belonging to England. For some time we were on a sandbank, lying between it and Marignano until at last we got off into deep water enough to keep us afloat. All rejoiced at the sight of these islands, as land is more attractive than water. The sea holds such terrors that more than once I was on the verge of writing to tell you to send no more missionaries until you received assurance that all is well with us and that their coming would make such a voyage worth while. You can scarcely hope to hear before October that we have ar-

rived in St. Louis and to know what help we shall need.
So I shall not count on receiving before next spring
any assistance that you may be able to send. I shall be
the first to entreat that you send only those of whose
solid virtue you are sure, those who are not presump-
tuous, but who have received from God a well-tried
vocation.

I have been told that those who have been in Louisiana have generally spoken only of what might attract,
lest they might discourage others from going there. I
shall tell you the whole truth, however, and shall hide
from you neither the perils of the deep nor the
cowardice of my heart. A stormy sea is a most terrifying sight, and its roar, mingled with the crash of the
tempest, is ear-splitting and would drown thunder or
the boom of a cannon. Above the din of the storm-bat-
tered boat rise the shouts of the sailors at their work.
Even more dismal is their silence and that of the captain as he walks the deck deep in thought. A ship in
distress gives one some idea of what the end of the world
will be. The star-studded sky disappears behind mountains of water. The sea, nearly black during the storm,
seems to gape, revealing a bottomless abyss. Rolling
waves sweep over the deck, then the billows recede.
Twice during the night the high sea forced open our
portholes and flooded our berths. The bending mast,
the sails furled or torn, the steering wheel abandoned
lest the boat be too strained—all this is not reassuring
if one fails to see God in a storm. If I have thought
that many would not have the courage to undertake
such a voyage, I have also sorrowed to think that others
could not survive the close air of the cabins, the hard
and small beds and the noise which is constant. In addition to the manipulation of rigging and cordage which
often takes place at night, there is as loud talking as
though it were day. Eating and drinking go on in the
saloon in which two of us are trying to snatch a little
repose and which adjoins the cabin occupied by the
other three. Seasickness is demoralizing in the extreme;

one becomes fit for nothing, not even for prolonged
thought. One's suffering is such that one can hardly
drag from one's heart the shortest aspirations of love.
I could say nothing but, "Yea, Father," and, "I have
left all things for You, O my God!" And if in this
state one asks for water it arrives only five or six hours
later. If one can take only soup, that which they bring
is made from cabbage and bad meat and is covered with
grease. It is a mistake to think that one should make
oneself eat when one is seasick. For several days I took
nothing but soup, and that only once or twice in
twenty-four hours, during which time I remained on
my back, and so I recovered. Eugénie and Marguerite
were either more courageous or more fit for the voyage,
for they were less ill.

After having traversed the Atlantic the expanse of
water between Cuba and Louisiana might well have
seemed small to the nuns as they looked forward to
landing. They did not know that while they had awaited
the sailing of the *Rebecca* from Bordeaux a political
issue had been raised in the corner of the vineyard to
which the Bishop had summoned them, and an issue
which Mr. Jefferson, the President, said, startled him
"like a fire bell in the night." It arose out of the application on March 6, 1818, of the Territory of Missouri
to be admitted into the Union. From the settlement
of this question was to develop a situation which would
have no slight influence on those who would succeed
Mother Duchesne in the work in Missouri. The mere
fact that such a question could be raised in 1818 shows
us the spirit of the people among whom her lot was now
to be cast, the timbre of the souls which she had come
to save. "The boatman's song on the long Western
rivers, the crack of the teamster's whip in the mountain
passes, the stroke of the woodman's axe ringing out in

the stillness of the forest, the sharp report of the rifle of huntsman, pioneer and scout on the fast-advancing frontier filled the air as if with the very voices of change and were answered by events quick with the fulfilment of prophecy. The tidelike movement of population into the Western country, the setting up of new States, the quick transfigurements of economic conditions, the incalculable shiftings and variations of a society always making and to be made"—each of these changes was to have its influence on the pioneer work that awaited Philippine Duchesne in Missouri.

On May 25, a date which was one day to be endeared to the Society of the Sacred Heart for other reasons as well as for this, the *Rebecca* entered the Mississippi, or Father of Waters, which unites the North and the South and which has not been allowed to be a barrier between East and West. The boat sailed past a vast mud-bank, the Balize, dotted with rude huts of settlers who lived on the game that abounded or on what they could earn as pilots or wreckers, and entered one of the passes or arms by which the river reaches the ocean. Coarse grass covered the island and swamps, while water-soaked shrubs appeared at the edge of the bronze flood, which at this place is a mile and a half wide. Farther up low banks were seen covered with ferns with here and there an ill-shapen tree, and in the distance a dark line indicating a well-developed forest. The scream of the bittern, the whoop of the crane, the moan of an alligator alone broke the stillness, unless now and again a whirl of wings followed the flight of wild duck or a pelican splashed at the brink. Through the poplars which fringed the bank the travellers glimpsed a prairie, the long grass of which

rose and fell like the swell of a high sea on the greenest
of oceans.

On Friday, May 29, the boat stopped, though it
was still some distance from New Orleans. Carriages
were sometimes sent from that city to meet travellers
who wished to disembark at this point, and the nuns
prayed that such might be their good fortune. It was
the Feast of the Sacred Heart. The Abbé Martial said
Mass and preached to the happy religious, who followed Mother Duchesne's example when she knelt and
kissed the ground, and for the first time watered with
her tears the soil which she hoped would bring forth a
hundredfold.

They renewed their vows in union with the Society
in France, and in her heart Mother Duchesne made the
renovation as she habitually did in these words: "I consecrate myself to Poverty, but how rich I am in Thee.
I pledge myself to Chastity, Thou art my soul's delight. I vow myself to Obedience—to serve Thee is to
reign. I dedicate myself anew to the education of youth
—Thou art the Shepherd of their souls."

The religious were not disappointed in their hopes
that their voyage was over. Night was well advanced
when they climbed into the carriages that were to take
them to New Orleans, some fifteen miles from the spot
where they had been allowed to land. The road lay
along the Mississippi; there was then no levee there to
block the view of the river. It was a glorious night and
the tawny stream scintillated with the silvery reflection
of a thousand stars, which in a southern sky hang low
like lamps, for there are no mountain peaks to mark
their distance, only the marsh and the swamp and the
prairie stretching on and on until the weary eye can

see no further. Fireflies sparkled in the long grass and
flitted in and out of the giant trees whose draperies of
dark gray Spanish moss curtained the starlit sky. The
air was filled with the overpowering sweetness of magnolia and orange blossom. All was still, save for the
vibrating undertones of insects, with now and again
the rapturous melody of the mockingbird or the eerie
scream of an owl or the roar of an alligator in a neighboring bayou. Once they turned off the road and drove
into a plantation to buy the bread they had not tasted
for two long months. They could hear in the distance
the sound of a banjo accompaniment to a sweet, sad
song, strange to them, for it came from the negro quarters, the tiny cabins of the slaves who worked all day
long in cane-brake or rice-swamp or in the fields of
indigo or cotton or Indian corn. The heat of the day
had gone and the night air that rose from the river
chilled, though it did not cool.

It was half-past two in the morning when they
reached New Orleans. The narrow streets were dark
and still, except in the neighborhood of an old café,
where candles gleamed and whence loud laughter rang,
or when a banjo was played in one of the many balconies, or when a lantern-bearing slave hurried past,
heralding home a lady whose dancing slippers were carried by the maid walking behind her. And Mother
Duchesne knew that not in New Orleans, the Crescent
City, the "Dream City of France," would she find the
savages, the unsophisticated, other-worldly folk that she
had come so far to seek.

Soon the travellers reached the lodge of the Ursuline
Convent on Chartres Street. Having entered the iron
gates, they approached the house, a massive building
with high, latticed belfry, arched dormer windows and

a sloping roof. They were most hospitably welcomed by the Superior, Mother St. Michel Gensoul, and her good religious, whose kindness then and in the weeks and months and years that were to follow was one of Mother Duchesne's strongest motives for thanks to God. This hospitality made them feel at home at once, so when a little colored girl came running by, Mother Duchesne called her and petted her. Won by the notice, the child ran off to catch a hen. When asked what she wanted it for, she answered, in a patois spoken by the slaves of Creole households: *"Mi veux tuer li pour Dame nouvelle manger."*

The "new nuns" were delighted with all that they saw and heard. There were then three hundred children profiting by the education and instruction given them by the Daughters of St. Angela. In a large and prosperous Academy they carried on the work for which Bienville had invited them to Louisiana in 1727. There were Catechism classes for the Indians and negroes, which the nuns just over from France delighted to visit. Mother Duchesne did not delay writing to France:

S.C.J.M.   NEW ORLEANS, JUNE 3, 1818.

My very dear Mother Thérèse:

I carry with me the affectionate remembrance of a Mother and friend whom I can never forget, one all the more loved at the moment of our separation when you despoiled yourself of all that might be of use to our mission. We are still a thousand miles from our destination, where, we are told, a house is being got ready and where the Bishop is building a new church.

While we wait we are fortunate in the good example and perfect charity of the Ursulines, who care for us like tender Mothers. Far from finding us a burden, as we really are, they speak only of their sorrow that we are not to remain in New Orleans.

I shall not give you any details of our voyage, as I feel sure that our Very Reverend Mother will have shared with you the two letters and the journal we sent her. If they never reach you, we shall send you copies brought up to date. I am writing to the children and am sending you a small Indian basket. Please give my love to each one of my Sisters, to whom I should like to write a word individually. The lack of time and postage does not allow this, but before God I forget not one of my Mothers, my companions in my employment, the pupils and the poor. Tell these last that on Sunday I assisted at the instruction given here to three hundred persons of all colors and countenances. I noted especially some old negresses who would much like us to stay here with their Mothers in Christ. That same day forty creoles, negroes and mulattoes, etc., received their First Communion in the chapel of this house. When would *we* ever see so large a ceremony?

This convent, as old as the city, was founded at the expense of Louis XV. The first nuns almost died of want, living as they did more in the marshes than on dry land, but now the house is well established. These religious are almost alone in upholding religion in this city. We cannot tell you what they have been to us.

To Father Varin she wrote of her hopes on June 4:

S.C.J.M.

Here we are almost at the end of our journey, for several hundred miles seem little when compared to the thousands which we have travelled, and steaming up a calm and beautiful river is agreeable in comparison with a voyage on a storm-tossed sea. It is only the entrance into the delta that is dangerous—and soon the Mississippi will be as crowded with traffic as our rivers of

France, so progressive is commerce in this country. The physician who attends this convent says—but perhaps he is too optimistic—that New Orleans will soon be as large as Bordeaux. St. Louis he compares to this city, and Upper Louisiana or Missouri when converted will be another France in climate, fertility, commerce and civilization. So great is the progress made by this nation in such a short time that my thoughts keep pace with my hopes. Already I picture myself in the far North, or beyond the South Seas, or in Korea or even Japan—there to win martyrdom. Worldly ambition is boundless; not so mine. Having obtained martyrdom I shall ask nothing more. Since that day may still be far distant, I am making plans for our mission. The most important of these both to you and to us, Reverend Father, will be the coming of some Jesuits to Louisiana. Will you not send some?

I see more and more clearly how difficult our work is to be and how powerless human means are to set it afoot, but God's Will is evident and He will be with us. The dryness of spirit which I suffered both at Bordeaux and while crossing the ocean is far from increasing. On the contrary, I feel my soul once more dilating with hope. Many are the graces lavished upon us. I am the more guilty not to be better. Help me by your prayers and recommend me to those of your sons.

In the course of a few days the *Rebecca* docked at the port of New Orleans, and Mother Duchesne and one or two of her companions went to the steamer to claim the baggage which they had left on board. In that little expedition to the docks and back again to the convent they saw New Orleans by daylight. Huge palmettos rivalled in height the masts of the sailing vessels in port and the white spires of the Cathedral. An esplanade bordered by trees ran along the low levee that kept the "Father of Waters" from invading the city. Even in the French quarter, or *"Vieux carrée"* as it was called even then, the Spaniard had left his mark. The old *cabildo* and *calaboza,* Spanish buildings, had covered carriageways leading to inner courts, with parterres of red and yellow flowers. Adobe houses with curving tiled roofs were to be seen, and stuccoed dwellings with iron lattices, huge locks and hinges and miniature balconies. Moats and palisades, unlovely remnants of warfare with the Indian, lay in ruins. The colonial homes, with white columns and wide galleries on each floor, spoke of the hospitality of the South. In gardens enclosed by white fences bloomed the fragrant jasmine, the fluffy crepe myrtle and the pale bluish wistaria. The Ursuline convent was surrounded by an adobe wall and the garden was sweet with orange blossoms and magnolia. This was especially so in the heat of the noon-day, when the sky seemed like a brazen bell overhead, a saffron heat-haze hung over the city and river. The great batten shutters on all the houses were closed tight and the world went to rest.

In a letter to Mother Barat, Philippine gives the reason for their prolonged stay in New Orleans:

Perhaps before this is sealed I shall have heard from St. Louis—the Bishop's silence has been far from consoling. Two or three days ago we saw someone from the North who told us that both a college for boys and an academy for girls are much in demand. The college is to be in St. Louis; our school is to be seventeen miles from there in Florissant or St. Ferdinand, a village situated in one of the loveliest and most fertile parts of the country. It seems that there is no suitable house in good condition. The inhabitants build quickly, but not solidly. There is no question of stone; brick or wood alone is employed there, as here in New Orleans. In this convent, for instance, the partitions between cells and rooms are wooden. So, too, are the ceilings which are finer than any I have ever seen.

No one could be more hospitable than the good nuns who would want us to stay on with them if they did not fear our getting ill. They have made us buy many things and have insisted on paying for them. The Superior told me today that we must use this house for storage and that our nuns coming from Europe must always stop here, choosing for the voyage a season in which a long stay in New Orleans would be desirable. They have also offered to do commissions for us after we are settled in St. Louis.

I hope that in time we shall have many other convents in this country, but it will be necessary for us to have English-speaking and Spanish religious. St. Louis is now more English than French, both in language and in customs. In New Orleans one language is as common as the other. Nearly all the children speak both and many of the parents only English. I have never met with more manner and charm than these Creoles possess. Education on the plantations may be neglected, but among the Americans in the cities there is a true zeal for it. I have seen a little girl ten years of age who will finish school at twelve. To keep her occupied along the line of her talents they are teaching her Latin. Her brother, who is two years her senior and who speaks and writes French, English and Latin and is studying Greek, is to go with us to St. Louis. Although there are means of secular instruction here, his mother, a true mother of the Machabees, is to send him a distance of one thousand miles to make sure of his being under religious teachers. Father Martial, who already has three scholars, will take him in charge.

Do not forget, dear Reverend Mother, to send us the rule of the School, the plan of studies, an astronomy, an atlas, a geography, the poem *La Religion* by Louis Racine and *Esther,* a breviary, the definite formula of vows and the Summary of the Constitutions of the Society.

If you are able to spare someone to help us with the work in the garden, it would be well that she should have leather stockings and gloves to keep off mosquitoes, a small mosquito net and light garments. For the journey she will need bouillon and mint tablets, a coffee pot with an alcohol lamp, vinegar and lemons. Provisions are a necessity. I brought rice and other things, but nothing proved superfluous.

Some of our belongings are still on board the *Rebecca,* although yesterday three of us went to the boat to get the first load. The kind Ursulines sent with us the convent wagon and three negroes, whose combined labor equals that of one of the workmen. As soon as the nuns appeared at the landing there was general delight on the boat. All the sailors came to bid us welcome. The cook, despite his ribs, three of which have caved in as a result of seventy years of service, rushed forward to make us sit down; each tried to outdo the other in kind attentions. With tears in his eyes, the captain's small boy flung himself upon (Sister) Catherine (Lamarre), who had often dressed his wounds. His little dog, even more amiable than that of Tobias, leapt about barking with delight. The captain was not then on board, but he had declared that he had never been more pleased with any passengers than with us. To be guarded, I did not say that I should never forget him, but rather that I should always remember the *Rebecca,* and this seemed to please him.

The kind Ursulines are most solicitous about our journey. If it depended on them our expenses would be small. I should not be surprised if they offer to give us more help. I am really anxious, not being able to count on the 10,000 francs which you sent for us to Bishop Du Bourg by way of Philadelphia. This sum may already be spent, and then there will be debts if we buy or we build. I feel sure that Providence will come miraculously to our aid! Money collected with

difficulty in France is worth far less here. If ever you
make a foundation you must secure temporal founders,
else you will be ruined.

These good nuns, whose charity overwhelms us, are
expecting three religious and some priests who are to
sail from France in September. Will you please send
by them a beautiful embroidered flounce for an alb? I
should be most grateful, as they have none in this house.
They will have lavished upon us one hundred times its
value, and that with a delicacy that I cannot express.

Two weeks later Mother Duchesne wrote to Father
Barat:

S.C.J.M.   FEAST OF ST. ALOYSIUS.

My very, very dear Father:

My first letter may never have reached you, but how
glad I should be to hear from you. I wrote to you on
sea and sent the letter ashore from the boat as it came
up the river. We have now been three weeks with the
Ursulines in New Orleans and we do not know when
we shall be able to continue our journey. During the
greater part of the voyage I experienced the same dryness of spirit from which I had suffered at Bordeaux,
but as we approached this land, the goal of my hopes,
my heart leapt with joy.

The excellent Father de Moni has left his beloved
parish, some twenty-five miles from here, to lend his
help in this city, but, as his French is not fluent, he is
unable to do all the good he otherwise would accomplish. He spoke to me of you and of the Society, which
he loves. He hoped that you would come to America,
where you would find a fine harvest and very few
reapers. Things are pitiful here, but we are told that
in the North the cause of religion progresses surely if
slowly. The Protestants are leaving their sermons to
go to hear the Catholic pastor who preaches in English

and whom they love as much as the Catholics do. I foresee many difficulties, but I foresee them in peace such as I have never had before, and this although I have no consolation. I have left all things spiritual and temporal without hope of success, so well do I realize my incapability of governing souls. I fear to be an obstacle to good, yet I cannot regret having come, for God's Will in this mission is evident.

As our convent is not to be in St. Louis, many want us to stay here, and these charitable nuns whose goodness overwhelms us urge us to remain. They also want to keep Father Martial, and I only wish that they might, so dear are their interests to me. This does not appeal to him, although he would willingly help the nuns. We do not know where we shall be, but wherever it is God is there. We are all getting along well, especially since a convent wall encloses us once more, but how we long to be where we can follow every detail of our own rule.

I am sending you a package for our Mother General so that you may see the interesting handiwork of the Indians. Will you please send these articles on to her afterwards?

I am with deep respect,

Your grateful child,

PHILLIPINE.

The unaccustomed heat told on the religious recently from France. They suffered, too, from the mosquitoes, which fell upon the newcomers in droves, so that Mother Duchesne could write that she looked like a leper. Their kind religious hostesses were distressed and even offered their guests tobacco to burn in their rooms to ward off these insects that gave them no rest day or night. Then Mother Duchesne became really ill. The want of vegetables on the long voyage had brought on a malady which the doctor declared to be scurvy. The invalid saw in this humiliation what she thought was a warning that her death was near. Her missionary labors were only beginning, however, and the good Ursulines, with untiring kindness and skill, nursed her back to life and to health. Mother St. Michel had noticed the mortification that prompted Mother Duchesne to take for breakfast nothing but a small cup of unsweetened coffee. She obliged her guest to drink daily a large cup of coffee so sweetened that to one unused to sugar "it seemed just like sirup," and she asked the doctor to tell Mother Duchesne that in America a substantial breakfast is not a luxury but a necessity.

When the invalid grew better she wrote to Mother Barat:

S.C.J.M.   NEW ORLEANS, JUNE 22, 1818.

Very Reverend Mother:

The captain of the *Rebecca* reports more promptly than he had given us reason to hope and I am taking advantage of his offer to send by him some handiwork of the Indians which I believe will be as precious to you as it is dear to me. The note attached to the package will give you an explanation about the things enclosed.

I fear that I have often repeated and even contradicted myself in my letters to you, for I told you things as they were taking place and quoted various opinions; besides, one's heart is bruised by a sacrifice whose value is manifest to faith and to hope alone. But even in distress love cries out: "My God, with joy I have offered You all things." I felt this, indeed, when the doctor declared that I had scurvy. He seemed astonished that the physician who had met us on the river had not noticed it. Others asked me why I ever left France. Octavie begged me not to be disturbed. I was not anxious, but only serious at the thought that God wished no more of me; that Eugénie would steer the little boat, which would only gain by the change; that, more happy than Moses, I had entered the Promised Land and had brought there a colony destined to wage war for the glory of the Sacred Heart, and that I had left more than did this great Law-Giver, for he gave up only captivity, and I another Land of Promise. I assure you that death had for me every attraction, for I have every reason to fear that I may spoil the work of our foundation. God has shown me only His charms.

I cannot tell you of the touching kindness of the Superior of this house in this trial; it is quite inexpressible. We are the continual object of kind attentions from her and her nuns. After having cared for me during my distressing illness she now wants to help to defray the expenses of our journey, calling the 500 francs which she offers to give us a "widow's mite," which I scruple to accept. I have spoken to her frankly of the expected 10,000 francs without concealing my fear that it may already be disposed of. She shares our anxiety and she made me write to the Bishop and approved what I had written. Moreover, she asked me to say nothing to her nuns of the possible 10,000 francs, lest hearing this might diminish their sympathy. You see, they make every decision in Chapter. We shall never be the losers in dealing with these religious, so I beg you to pay for the flounce for the alb ordered for them from Lyons. They are delighted with Eugénie and Octavie. They want to keep us here, at least in the city, and promise us every success, assuring us of their help with a disinterestedness that is admirable. However, while they wish to help on our work, they see as we do that it is more for the glory of God that we go on to St. Louis in the Illinois country.

Everything in this convent is in the greatest simplicity. The chapel is a large room with walls bare, as are those of the choir; the parlor is furnished with

wooden benches and the pupils have many inconven-
iences. The vocation of the Superior, which was lacking
in any attraction, was decided by the Holy Father himself. She came here when the United States took over
the government of Louisiana, and sixteen Spanish nuns
left here to go to Havana. Seven religious came with
her. Ten more arrived last year, and they are hoping
for still others and will pay the travelling expenses of
any who come, being especially eager for such as have
been formed by their Order. One sees here saints who
have taught for thirty years and who have won many
souls.

The kind merchant from Havana has been here to
see us. He would like us to go to his country, but makes
no promise of aid. The Ursulines advise us not to go
there, although Cuba is an earthly paradise and the
Spaniards contribute willingly and generously to the
upkeep of religious institutions. The island, though
further south than Louisiana, has a more healthful
climate, is cooler and is free from venomous insects;
and yellow fever, if taken in time, is easily cured. Our
difficulty would be the language and we should need
at least one who knew Spanish perfectly. We find English very difficult. Even Octavie, who is the one to succeed best, is not yet able to converse with the children's
parents, who in St. Louis will be chiefly Americans, and
therefore not to be satisfied with mediocrity. The
Creoles, who are in the majority in New Orleans, are
softer, lighter and more pleasure loving. They marry
at twelve or fifteen and consider sixteen too late. One
of them after one month's music lessons was able to
compose. They are like those trees which grow quickly
and die early. Their appearance is charming.

I beg you not to forget the novena at La Louvesc
which I asked my sister, Madame de Mauduit, to have
made. I should have had this done, in fulfilment of my
vow, before I left France.

Yesterday St. Aloysius Gonzaga was chosen as
patron of the noviceship here; the little seminary is also

to be under his protection. Father Martial, who is much liked here, preached at this ceremony. The Ursulines have invited any of our nuns who come over to stay in this house. They have also offered to store here things sent us from France so as to save us the expense of storage. School furniture, books, apparatus, etc., if addressed to an institution of learning in St. Louis will not incur duty, which is so high here that in one year the government gained 40,000,000 francs from the customs.

We have been told that the journey up the river is not dangerous, but that, as the men's quarters on the river boats are entirely separate from the women's, we shall be able to have neither Mass and Communion nor Confession. Not having heard from the Bishop, we do not know when we shall leave. Travellers tell us that we are much wanted in the North, that we shall lack nothing, but that every success will be ours. We need an English-speaking postulant; the one who has offered herself is too delicate. The priest whom we have seen most often here is a Benedictine from Florence who wanted to be a Jesuit and loves that Society dearly. He looks upon us as sisters and daughters and we are able to appreciate him in spite of his difficulty in speaking our language. He was delighted when Eugénie and Octavie understood what he said in Italian.

Under Louis XV, who built this house, everything needed was sent over from France free of charge. The Jesuits procured the foundation and the Jesuit missionary, who visited Ste. Marie when I was a child, got the Ursuline recruits to keep the work going. I have been much struck by the details of the trials endured by the foundresses of this convent and by the loving intervention of Providence. One of these stories centres about a statue of the Blessed Virgin and is much like that connected with my picture of St. Francis Regis.

You will see from the letters of our other nuns that they are suffering; fortunately they are kept busy. All are longing from a letter from you; the long silence is not to be attributed to you, but to delayed boats. While we offer to God the privation of news, we find some consolation in telling you how we are longing to hear. Please have prayers said for us.

I am in spirit at your feet,

PHILIPPINE.

During her convalescence Philippine's isolation became less complete. She sat out on the broad gallery overlooking the garden, and there her little community gathered around her. They talked of their hopes and plans and of France, and one day she read to them the first lines from their loved Mother General, to whom Mother Duchesne hastened to reply, on June 24, as follows:

I took your letter to the chapel before I read it, so that we might all thank God for this blessing. You can imagine how all were touched by it. The Superior of the Ursulines in bringing it to me asked me most graciously to speak to you of her. This great-souled religious would love to know you.

Forgive me for my letter from Bordeaux even as you have borne patiently with so much from me. I naturally expressed my fear at being named Superior, and I see more and more how unfit I am to guide souls, but God acts without me, and my Sisters are satisfied, as they will tell you. We are told much that is cheering about our foundation in St. Louis and about one that we may some day make here. Mother Rivet will not be too old to come over; some of the Ursulines were fifty-two when they came, but on the sea all will need to be strong and ready to die. Believe, my incomparable Mother, in the profound respect of your daughter, so full of faults, who kneels in spirit before you.

PHILIPPINE.

June had passed and July brought no word from Bishop Du Bourg, so Philippine wondered whether they should remain in New Orleans any longer. This was the first affair of importance in which she, as Superior, would soon have to make the ultimate decision and take upon herself the whole responsibility, and for the first time she knew by experience the utter solitude and loneliness of a Superior's life. Prayer had ever been her support and her comfort, and it was all that was left to her now. She received consolation from the Ursuline nuns, whom she had grown to love dearly. There was Mother St. Michel, who during the French Revolution had had experiences not unlike her own, and, as Mgr. Baunard says, "The French Revolution made saints." Mother St. Michel had had painted in Rome, in memory of a remarkable dream or vision vouchsafed to her, a large picture of the Sacred Heart. This she showed to her guests, and Mother Duchesne confesses that she felt disappointed when she learned from it and from a book of prayers which she found that she was not the first to bring devotion to the Sacred Heart to America.

Her other great devotion, to Our Lady, was fervent in New Orleans at least. Mothers St. Joseph, St. André and St. Scholastique told how in 1812 the city had been partly destroyed by a conflagration which threatened the convent, but at the prayer of the nuns, through the intercession of Our Lady of Prompt Succor, the flames suddenly turned back. On the eve of January 8, 1815, they had kept prayerful vigil before the shrine of Mary Immaculate, and her statue was placed on the main altar during the Mass celebrated that morning by Bishop, then Father, Du Bourg, for General Jackson had sent a messenger to ask their prayers. They saw the smoke rise from the plain of Chalmette, and they afterwards heard that "the squirrel hunters of Barataria" under Andrew Jackson had put to rout General Pakenham with his twelve thousand men, "veterans, for the most part, from the fields of Spain." Jackson sent a courier to the monastery of the Ursulines and went himself to the Cathedral to give thanks for the prayers offered and the victory won.

At the shrine of Our Lady of Prompt Succor Mother Duchesne prayed for counsel as to the step she should take. Thus she came to decide in accordance with the wishes of Mgr. Du Bourg, expressed in a letter which was unaccountably delayed and which was to reach her only after her meeting with the Bishop in St. Louis. "You say you have come to seek the cross," he had written. "You are so well placed to find it that you will not have far to seek. If I were not assured of finding in you these blessed dispositions, I should tremble and not rejoice at your arrival." Mother Duchesne's decision was to go on to St. Louis as soon as they could get a boat. The last letter from New Orleans is dated July 9:

We expect to leave here on Sunday. All our boxes and baggage from France arrived in good condition and we have had to unpack nothing, using only what we had brought in our valises. The good Ursulines have had our clothing laundered every week. The doctor has insisted on our buying dresses of light material; they are of black cotton with a single white thread. We wore our religious habit on the ocean and no one thought it extraordinary. The Ursulines, even those who have come during the last thirty years, wore secular dress, and we may have to make some change in our habits during the journey up the river, when we shall

be deprived also of Mass and Communion. Father
Martial wants to leave for St. Louis at once. I asked
him to write you a line, but he may not do so, as he
did not relish the idea. He said that he had no complaint to make of us, and that if he wrote in our praise
you would easily see that we had asked him to do so.
He reproved me for having told you any unpleasant
impressions, saying that it is a mistake to put on paper
and to send such a distance opinions likely to be changed
by a contrary impression. I am sorry for anything un-
favorable that I may have said and I beg you to subtract
what may be due only to my rigorous temperament.
He has been very kind to us.

Why should I be solicitous for the future, since
when the time comes to act, Providence is always on our
side and on that of the missions? Though there are so
many accidents, for the last one hundred years no boats
carrying missionaries have been wrecked. The *Peter-
son,* which sailed soon after we did, was lost off the
Isles of the Wind. Happily the passengers were saved.
The *Rebecca,* in spite of bad weather, a fire and an en-
counter with a corsair, was safe while we were on board,
but the other day on her return trip, as she sailed down
past the Balize, she was pillaged by pirates.

I do not know what adaptations we may have to
make of the French Plan of Studies. How can we put
in the same class a child of sixteen who has learned
neither to read nor to write and one of eight who knows
both English and French? Reading is difficult to teach
here. More and more want to learn English; some
speak French, with a mixture of Spanish and negro
dialect. In all, five languages are heard in this
Academy. In spite of the difficulties, I am concerned
about a foundation in New Orleans. The Ursulines
with a rare disinterestedness urge it upon us and will
not let us lose by it. To their kind entreaties I have
opposed the following facts:

1. Our mission, which is for St. Louis.
2. The climate.

3. Our vocation, which is for the Indians.

4. We are too few for a foundation in a large city.

To this they replied:

1. That it will be impossible to make a foundation in St. Louis just now, since nothing is ready for us.

2. That the voyage up the river is dangerous in hot weather.

3. That Indians, negroes and mulattoes are not lacking here.

4. That many begin a foundation with less and succeed; that we should not offer ourselves, but should wait to be asked for; that there are not enough churches here and that we should add one to the number existing; that a building would be put up for us in a healthful suburb far from them, it is true, but, as we are both cloistered, the distance would make little difference; that we could easily get enough children for a boarding school, and that, if it should take from their boarding school, they would always be able to fill up with day pupils.

They say that a foundation here is indispensable, as it would be the centre of all the houses we may one day have in America, and that this is the place suitable for our noviceship, since the city is large and cosmopolitan. They think, too, that we should have a house here for those whose delicate health cannot stand the cold of St. Louis. Finally they made us understand how glad they would be to have us and those who will join us.

I saw the wisdom of the inducements which were held out to us, but answered that God's Will is for us to go to St. Louis, and this thought outweighs all other considerations, though I am so deeply touched by their reasons for our having a foundation here that I beg it of you for next spring. I shall consult on this subject both His Lordship and the French consul here, if I can see the latter before we embark. I shall send you their answers and I hope that you will not object that there are too few subjects, for, if we are making no new foundations in France, we should make them here, where they are in demand. I am so glad to have come here that sacrifices made in order to multiply foundations will be sweet. I think I should be ready for anything, even to face again the terrors of the sea or to cross uninhabited forests. One thing excites my jealousy, and that is to see Father Martial already overworked while we remain idle. There is much to do in New Orleans, for the city is growing fast, and we have seen twenty steamers pass in two days. The mulatto, creole, negro and American boys flock after Father Martial, who has three classes in Catechism every day. It would be the same for the girls. Again I beg you for a foundation here. Madame Rivet has great good will and at her age would be more easily acclimated than were she younger. Madame T. also wants to come. This country would just suit her, and her sweetness, her culture and facility for languages would make her most useful. You can count on Eugénie as a future Superior; she has religious maturity and always acts wisely and in the presence of God.

In spite of the distractions of starting out again, our uncertainty for the future and the punishment which I have reason to fear, I cannot forget how much pain I must often have given you, and in spirit I kneel to beg your forgiveness for

Your daughter,

PHILIPPINE.

At last the religious of the Sacred Heart said good-bye to the little colored children whom they had been allowed to help and to instruct; and they took leave of the Abbé Martial, the companion of their voyage across the Atlantic, who was to remain in New Orleans as the third priest in a city of fifteen thousand souls, to help the Ursuline nuns in their hard work with the mulattoes. From the poor Indians Mother Duchesne bought knick-knacks to send to France. Then the time came to say farewell to the loved and hospitable religious. They tried to leave some material token of thanks, but the nuns of St. Angela refused to accept anything, saying in their delicate charity that their visitors had been of invaluable service in the classes among the poor children, and pressing upon them a generous gift for their mission.

It is likely that the five travellers, as they left for the Mississippi landing that July 12, had no idea of the journey that lay before them. The Mississippi, with its tributary, the Missouri, is the longest river in the world —four thousand, three hundred miles. In one part of its course it uses up thirteen hundred miles to go the distance the proverbial crow would fly in six hundred and seventy-five. Its banks are often unstable, and in flood time it brings with it giant trees torn by the Missouri from the great Western forests. At the New Orleans port the nuns saw huge-hulled ships bound for Europe, keel boats, barges and rafts and new steamers to carry passengers and freight up the river as far as St. Louis. It was then just a year since a steamboat had first made that trip, and the Indians in Missouri, dismayed, had fled from the banks, accusing the palefaces of having chained up the Great Spirit and of forcing Him to speed the boat even upstream.

The *Franklin,* the boat on which the nuns took passage, moved slowly away from the landing and on up the river, through groves of orange trees which bear bud, flower and fruit at the same time; past plantations of sugar cane, great bamboo-like stems with bushy tops like palmetto; past fields under water, which the nuns learned were rice swamps. At La Fourche a priest, Father Richard, and two seminarians, Mr. Portier and Mr. Evremont, all bound for St. Louis, embarked, making the number of passengers seventeen. The *Franklin,* a small boat of 125 tons and the eleventh steamer to make the trip up the river, was not one of the comfortable boats which twenty or thirty years later could be seen on the Mississippi. It was primitive and could boast of no staterooms. The passengers were crowded together in a narrow space where the nuns tried to pray and to study in surroundings which were distracting at least. However, the view from the deck was calculated to raise to God hearts less hungry for Him than were theirs. The boat glided between dark forest-walls of angular-limbed, moss-bearded cypresses that seemed centuries old, while in the undergrowth palms grew as weeds. There were weird pictures, too, for, as it was the dry season of the year, the swamps of the springtime were shallow or parched and showed fantastic "cypress knees," strange twisted roots and stunted limbs. The Spanish grey moss swathed many a tree it had killed.

In flood time the southern part of the Mississippi River has no bounds and has been known to be seventy miles wide at such times. In consequence there are all through Louisiana backwaters called bayous, and these the travellers saw from the *Franklin.* Some were covered with huge water lilies, pink, yellow and white; while from others, which were stagnant, rose hordes of mosquitoes, which, says a traveller of that time, "fell on one like burning coals." On July 17 they reached Natchez, a city set upon a hill, or rather a green bluff wooded with pawpaws and orange trees, gently contrasting with the black green of the cypress forests.

Mother Duchesne had described the Mississippi as "a quiet river." It was not long before she saw her mistake. The pilot shouted directions or rang a loud, clanging bell constantly to warn the man at the engine that danger lay ahead. They had to steer clear of snags —huge skeletons of water-logged forest trees torn up by the raging river two thousand miles away and now replanted in the river-bed, some protruding mast-high above the surface of the water, some lying just concealed, while others swayed with the current. To avoid the planters, sawyers, the shallows, the floating islands formed of masses of logs, it was necessary for a boat to shift its course, so that sometimes in one trip from New Orleans to St. Louis it crossed the river at least three hundred times. In all the thousand miles of the Mississippi's course there was not in 1818 one buoy or beacon light or lantern, and flickering, smoky, pitch-dropping torch baskets, noisy shouts and the blast of a bugle or the clanging of a bell were the only warnings at night that they were in danger of collision. Washed up on the banks and shoals were countless skeletons of boats that had met disaster.

The sunrises were beyond description. There was a deep hush, the dark forest softened to gray, a light mist lay upon the water, then the very air seemed to be singing, for there was not a bird in sight. Bluffs were outlined against the blushing eastern sky. The atmosphere grew golden—day had come.

On the 11th of August the *Franklin* reached the place, now the site of Cairo, Illinois, where the silvery Ohio empties into the bronze melting pot, the Mississippi. Semi-tropical trees and flowers and birds had been left far behind and green cottonwood and catalpa were entwined with the leaves and flaming blossoms of

the trumpet-vine. Instead of water pelicans there were
heron and cranes, and green and white paroquets chat-
tered in the branches. The larder of the *Franklin* needed
replenishing, and the wild turkeys that the crew and
passengers shot in the woods were most acceptable. The
boat made many stops, and, as it remained at Kaskaskia
for twenty-four hours, the nuns went to visit the church
and the priest, a venerable missionary seventy years of
age. They were deeply impressed by his utter poverty.
The furniture of the presbytery consisted of two poor
chairs, one tied up with a rope, a worm-eaten table, a
mattress on the floor, a water-pot and a single goblet.
There at Kaskaskia the chief of the Illinois came with
other Indian braves to welcome Father Richard, the
seminarians and the nuns.

At St. Genevieve still more consolation awaited
Mother Duchesne. This little French village had been
built on the bank of the Mississippi, but the river had
changed its course, and when the religious of the Sacred
Heart first saw the town it was about a mile from the
main stream and on a small creek, the Gabourie. The
church at the centre of the village was the heart of all
the interests of the people. Crosses surmounted
the houses and garden gates, and the good inhabitants led a life not unlike that of the early
Christians, raising in common fields their wheat,
corn and pumpkins, so that by working side by side
they would be protected from the Indians. The nuns
were not able to disembark, but the curé, Father Pratte,
went down to the landing to greet them and received
from them a letter of introduction brought from his
aunt in France. Father Henri Pratte was the first
native of Missouri to become a priest, and St. Genevieve was to be the only mission of this young pastor

who was to die after having run a long course in a few short years. He had interesting details to give the travellers about St. Louis, where he had spent part of the preceding winter, as Bishop Flaget, the saintly prelate of Bardstown, Kentucky, had found the presbytery of that city in ruins and had summoned the young pastor of St. Genevieve to make it a little less unworthy of becoming the episcopal palace of Bishop Du Bourg, then on his way to Missouri. During Father Pratte's absence the fervent town of St. Genevieve had not been without a priest, for he had been replaced by Father Félix de Andreis, a young Lazarist and one of the thirty priests whom Bishop Du Bourg had won for the missions during his fruitful visit to Europe. The religious of the Sacred Heart then learned that Father de Andreis had been named Vicar General of the vast diocese stretching from the Great Lakes to the Gulf. With such information Father Henri Pratte entertained and cheered the nuns, pointing out the house of the Commandant Vallé, where in later years Mother Duchesne was to meet with kind hospitality.

St. Genevieve was their last halting-place before their destination, St. Louis. This city of their dreams, then a town not half the size of the New Orleans they had left, had been founded by Pierre Laclede Liguest in 1764. He built the first house, and Indian women and children carried away in blankets the soil from the excavated cellar. The Indian braves scorned such menial labor—theirs it was to hunt and kill; to dig they were ashamed—and they made themselves so troublesome to Liguest, to his step-son, Chouteau, and to the other settlers that the founders threatened to summon the French troops from Fort Chartres down the river if the sullen savages did not retire. The city was called

St. Louis in honor of the patron saint of King Louis XV, in whose domain the settlers thought they were, not knowing that by a secret treaty Louisiana had been ceded to Spain the preceding year. However, St. Louis was not the only name borne by the town. It was called the Mound City because of the grassy tombs of Indian warriors there, and on the hills just across the river it had been "Paincourt," whether because of the sufferings of its founders, or because there was a shortage of grain and the loaves were so small, or merely in memory of another French village of that name, no one knows. Be that as it may, the colony survived its hardships, and in 1818 the town numbered some five thousand souls.

PART SECOND

THE APOSTOLATE

CHAPTER I

LETTING GO

CHAPTER I

Letting Go—1818-1821

"O pretious Prodigall!
Fair spendthrift of thyself! Thy measure
(Merciless Love), is all,
Even to the last Pearle in thy treasure.
All places, times and objects be
Thy teare's sweet opportunity."

CRASHAW.

On August 21 the passengers on the *Franklin* were
told that their voyage was drawing to a close. The
limestone bluffs grew higher and at last were crowned
by a line of shimmering white houses thrown into relief
by the ruins of an old Spanish fort and the ruddy glow
of the setting sun as the boat moored at a spot one
mile from the landing. The nuns decided to spend the
night on board, as they did not like to trespass at that
hour on the hospitality of Mr. Bernard Pratte, to whom
they had letters of introduction from France and messages from his brother, the good pastor of St. Genevieve. The captain, however, insisted on taking the
nuns at once to the Bishop's palace, so Mother Duchesne
and one or two of her little community went ashore.

The city had three streets, the Rue Royale, the Rue
de l'Eglise and the Rue des Granges. Crossing them
were rough ascents from the river. None of the streets
were paved, and the travellers of the time speak of the
"unfathomable mud, fit only for a frog or a tortoise."

163

A few houses were of stone or brick; there were more log cabins with clay-filled chinks; all, of whatever material, were whitewashed. As the religious entered the episcopal palace they must have wondered what it could have looked like before Father Pratte had repaired it. It stood in the northeast corner of the church lot, which was fenced round about. It was of stone, but the mortar was earth; there were no doors and no glass in the holes meant for windows. The furnishings were poorer still. Judge Pratte had sent the Bishop a bed, which was returned with a note saying: "My palace is too small and too shabby to admit so decorative a piece of furniture. You will, my friend, allow me to exchange it for something more useful—bread is what I need." Of his repasts the prelate had written: "I have suppressed coffee at my house at the evening meal. We have potato or cabbage soup, which with a dish of meat or cheese makes a glorious supper. I shall perhaps at last find a substitute for coffee at breakfast also."

This was typical of the spirit of the grand Bishop, who cordially welcomed the religious of the Sacred Heart to his diocese that August day, 1818. He has been described as "a San Domingan by birth, a Frenchman in education, an American in principle, a priest by vocation" and as one "endowed with the elegance and politeness of a courtier, the piety and zeal of the apostle and the learning of a Father of the Church." It was with his characteristic courtesy that he told Mother Duchesne what she had heard rumored in New Orleans and what was a great disappointment to her and her daughters—his regret that there was no suitable house for an Academy for girls in St. Louis as yet, and that he would send the little community elsewhere. He had thought of placing them at Florissant, a village about

The First Convent in St. Charles

seventeen miles from his episcopal city, but another
small town, St. Charles, would probably be their first
home in America.

The captain escorted the nuns back to the boat,
where they spent that night, and early the next morning they left it, never to see it again. A year later the
Franklin sank near St. Genevieve.

The Cathedral of St. Louis, they found, was a poor
wooden structure, some sixty feet long and about one-
half as wide. In this log cabin, falling into ruins,
Bishop Du Bourg had been installed on the Feast of
the Epiphany of that year by Bishop Flaget, who had
come on with him from Bardstown. No sooner was the
installation accomplished than the Prelate began to
plan for the erection of a new cathedral. Like David
who grieved: "Dost thou see that I dwell in a house of
cedar and the Ark of God is lodged within skins?" the
royal-hearted missionary Bishop was sad because the
House of God was even shabbier than his own. The
cornerstone of a brick church was laid on March 29,
1818, but when the nuns saw it nearly six months later
it was still far from complete.

The day after they landed Mother Duchesne wrote
to Mother Barat:

S.C.J.M.   ST. LOUIS, AUGUST 22, 1818.

Reverend and dear Mother:

We are now nearly four thousand miles apart, but
the farther I go the nearer I feel to you in my longing
to carry out your intentions and to accomplish your
desires. Our distance from France is so great that at
times one is downcast by the prospect of being often in
situations requiring our acting without your advice and
direction.

This is our third halt since we left Paris. The other two, Bordeaux and New Orleans, are only to be regretted inasmuch as they delayed the joy that is now ours in St. Louis. We are lodged in a nice home where we are making the acquaintance of some of our future pupils. In about a week we are to leave for St. Charles, where a house is being rented for us. His Lordship is to take us out there and to remain for a day or two to help in our installation. To-day he deigned to hear our Confessions and to say that he regrets not being able to let us make a foundation here, where there is not even a single room to let. He puts before us the great advantages possessed by St. Charles, which he expects will become one of the most important cities of North America, as it is situated on the Missouri River, whose banks become daily more populated and which is about to give its name to a new state of the Union. No day passes without the arrival of four or five families with their belongings who come to settle in a country whose wealth is always increasing. If the plan for constructing a canal to join the Ohio, a tributary of the Mississippi, with an Eastern river is realized, St. Louis will be connected with New York by water and we shall thus hear more promptly from France than now, when letters come by way of New Orleans.

We left that city on the 12th day of July on the steamboat the *Franklin,* which only docked today, but last night, as we had stopped at a place only a mile from the town, the captain brought Octavie and me ashore and conducted us himself to the Bishop. His Lordship was more than kind and brought us himself to the home whose hospitality he had asked for us. He has promised us as our chaplain Father Richard, who knows Father Barat well. Monseigneur says that he will visit us often at St. Charles, which can be reached from here in a morning. Although St. Genevieve is further away from St. Louis, I asked him to send us there instead. When the steamboat stopped there the parish priest, who, though born near here, was educated in Canada by the Sulpicians, came to see us, bringing a conveyance in hope of taking us to his church and presbytery for Mass and for breakfast, but the captain said there was not time. This the Father regretted and added that he had asked the Bishop to send us to his parish. He loves nuns and told us that he had been under their care in Canada. He says that there are over forty young girls in St. Genevieve who would have run to the landing to see us had they known that we were there. This visit consoled us, as we found in him a father and an apostle in his zeal for his widely scattered parish, in which he is the only priest. He told us that the Indians there still remember the first Jesuit missionaries, welcome all visiting priests and have their children baptized.

We stopped at Kaskaskia, a village with a large church, which is visited only every two weeks by the pastor of a distant parish who is too aged to give instruction. The only school is a secular one to which the children go to learn English. That language is being more and more spoken in this part of the country. His Lordship says that we must be in no hurry for a foundation in New Orleans, but that the country along the Missouri is constantly increasing in value. You will see by our journal that between Natchez, which is about three hundred miles above New Orleans, and the Ohio River, which enters the Mississippi not very far south of St. Genevieve, there is on the east bank only a forest inhabited by Indians, and on the west, woods broken here and there by a clearing on which is a miserable hut. There are no stones for building and no men to plane trees. On nearing the Ohio one sees Kentucky on the east and to the west several villages, and the scenery has completely changed from that of the South. Instead of the uniform green curtain formed by impenetrable forests there are more houses, flocks, cultivated fields and a rolling country.

At Kaskaskia the Catholic Indians work in the fields, live in the village and go to the church which we visited. The chief of the Illinois and his daughters came to the river bank to see the steamboat, the first to enter the Kaskaskia River to unload merchandise. They were on horseback and were dressed in beaded garments, while other Indians formed their suite. From a distance they presented a spectacle which, far from being ridiculous, was rather imposing and full of interest. The journal will tell you many things; I have only to beg you not to be anxious about us. You expected us to have something to suffer, and the example of our holy Bishop, whose career at Paris might have been brilliant and who chose instead poverty, labor and suffering, is an inspiration to us.

Before leaving the boat and setting foot on the land of promise I read again the words of Deuteronomy which once made such an impression upon me, and I singled out these: "Hear, O Israel: Thou shalt go over the Jordan this day. . . . Say not in thy heart: 'For my justice hath the Lord brought me in to possess this land.' Therefore love the Lord thy God and observe His precepts and ceremonies, His judgments and the commandments which I command you this day." This, Reverend Mother, is our resolve. May God bless it!

I find Eugénie always more suited because of her virtues to those offices which would put her in touch with people of the world. The Bishop is going to send us a young girl, a convert from Protestantism, who speaks English and has a religious vocation.

Bless your devoted daughter,

PHILIPPINE.

Mr. and Mrs. Pratte were disappointed to learn that the nuns were not to remain in the town. They promised Mother Duchesne that they would send Emilie and perhaps Céleste to the Convent of the Sacred Heart, even though it was to be in the country. Mr. Pratte was of the opinion, however, that a school

in St. Louis would flourish, whereas one on the outskirts would not. But the religious had heard their
Bishop's wishes in the matter, so they went with him
to visit the neighborhood of St. Louis—one of the first
visits was to Florissant.

They drove past the Calvary which had been
erected by the Spanish colonists on the highest point
within the city walls not far from the Cathedral, between Church and Barn Streets, near where to-day
Olive Street crosses Second and Third. There in earlier
days the pious inhabitants had gone each evening to
pray at the high cross of cedar which Mother Duchesne
saw falling into ruins. So, too, was the old Spanish
fort of San Carlos, just beyond the city wall. Between St. Louis and Florissant there was no house nor
inclosure, except a small shanty, three miles out from
the city. Deer and prairie wolves were abundant. Of
the Valley of Florissant, so· called from its fertility, a
traveller of note said: "No description can do justice
to the beauty of this tract." The Florissant common
offered a fine range for horses, cows and hogs belonging
to the inhabitants of the village. It was well wooded,
affording fine shade, and every villager cut from it all
the firewood or house logs he needed. Wild roses and
a variety of other flowers adorned the prairies, and
strawberries, blackberries and May apples were to be
gathered at will.

We have no way of knowing which house it was
that Bishop Du Bourg had thought might do for a convent. The largest one in the village, the country-seat
of the Spanish *Intendant* in days gone by, "a roomy
building facing on St. Charles Street," belonged to Mr.
John Mullanphy, who had rented it to the Trappists
when they had come over from France under Reverend

Father Urbain. The monks lived there for several years and drew the blessing of God on the valley by their prayers and their labor. Before 1818, however, they had gone to Looking Glass Prairie, Illinois, where they supported themselves by making clocks and watches. Finally they all returned to France; all, that is, except one, Father Marie Joseph Dunand, who remained as pastor of Florissant. He was more beloved by his flock there than by that of St. Charles, which he also served, and he was known at both places as "Le Père Prieur." In 1818 he was living, not in the Mullanphy house, but in the pastoral residence, a cottage of two rooms, which Bishop Du Bourg pointed out to the nuns. It "stood next to the nice old wooden church and the graveyard." Mr. John Mullanphy was an Irish gentleman who had seen service in the French army and then had come to America and to St. Louis. He had helped to win the battle of New Orleans in 1812; he was "a true and zealous son of the Church" and he was always ready to rent or sell, at a low price, or to give property for the cause of Christian education and other good works. The Bishop agreed with Mother Duchesne that they had better not make a foundation in Florissant, as there were too few inhabitants and the one house available was quite unfit for a school.

It was a joy for the nuns to hear French spoken in the New World, as it was the language that they heard on the streets of St. Louis, and it was in that tongue that the drivers loudly urged on the oxen drawing the wagons and carts that they passed as they returned to the city.

The Bishop reverted to his previous plan of sending the nuns to St. Charles, and Mother Duchesne wrote to France:

S.C.J.M. ST. LOUIS, AUGUST 29, 1818.

My very dear Mother Thérèse:

I wrote from New Orleans to thank you for the picture, which we have not yet been able to look at, as we cannot unpack before we get to St. Charles, where we are renting a very small house. As the roads are so bad, freightage is probably more costly than the things you could buy us in France, so please send no more for the present. We shall be in the midst of poverty with nothing to spend on transportation, besides one can purchase here many of the necessities of life, and, although shoes are very expensive, we can buy clothing and linen at the same price as in France. Silk, pearls, silk cord, spangles, rings, buckles, etc., in small packages, if addressed to the *Academy* at St. Charles via New Orleans, would come free of duty.

How God tries me in keeping me so long without news of my dear convent at Grenoble and in withdrawing us from the city of our Bishop, the true source of light! There is in St. Louis no house anywhere as fine as our convents in France. It costs thousands to build and everything looks as though we should sow in tears—to our happiness—if thus others will one day gather in joy and see the children of our prayers eagerly thronging about them.

I saw Indians of all kinds along the Mississippi; most of them are clothed and good, some even half civilized. Some speak English or French, are mindful of favors, ask a blessing on the houses they enter and have their children baptized. They say to the Methodists who want to instruct them: "Who are you? You have a wife. The Blackrobes have none. Go away!"

I cannot write to Aloysia, but she does not doubt of my love. My hope is for her to go to China, which is said to be converted, and she is young enough to learn Chinese. How much can be done by a soul truly zealous! The Bishops of Boston and Kentucky achieve wonders

even with the Indians, but in what poverty, journey-
ings and dangers! Here they regard a journey of one
thousand miles as we did one of a hundred in France.

On the same day she wrote to Father Barat:

God deprives us of news from France and the sacrifice is indeed great. I told you, I think, that Father
Martial stayed in New Orleans, where he was badly
needed. We had as a fellow-traveller up the river none
other than your friend, Father Richard, who is to be
pastor of St. Charles, where a small house is being
rented for us. The Bishop who wanted us here in St.
Louis is having all he can do to collect for a new church
to replace the present cathedral, which is of wood and
in ruins. He can do nothing to help us except by his
example which shows us what we shall have to suffer.
In his episcopal palace, which is like the poorest farmhouse in France, he lodged four or five invalid priests
and shared with them one very small room which did
service as dormitory, refectory and study; they are now
only a trifle better off. The Seminary is being built at
a place about one hundred miles from here, inhabited
chiefly by Americans, who live as the primitive Christians. In six weeks they constructed a church under the
direction of a good Lazarist who gave them religious
instruction and who in his success and candid, simple
manner resembles Père Ferdinand. He wanted us at
his parish, St. Ferdinand, but this very beautiful village
is neither sufficiently populous nor otherwise suitable.
The pastor of St. Genevieve, who was born in Missouri but educated for the priesthood in Canada, is admirable for his zeal. He visited us at the landing and
spoke of his wish to have us in his parish, a wish shared
by the young girls of the village. As we are not to be
in St. Louis, I thought it well to suggest to His Lordship that we should go to St. Genevieve, suitable on
account of the spirit of its pastor, its proximity to the
Seminary and the good nature of the people. He op-

posed reasons for this step and then said, "Well, you may *also* go to St. Genevieve."

Kaskaskia, which we were allowed to visit, is in dire need of help, for, although for some months it has been the chief place in the country of Illinois, the children go to schools in which they hear not a word of religion, nor are they taught to read French. As a result they know and understand only the Protestants, and among the Methodists there are many missionaries.

Now that I am on the spot, I see the impossibility of beginning on a large scale with an establishment any larger than those of Cuignières or St. Pezenne. As we increase in numbers our best hope will be to have small houses in several places rather than one large foundation. St. Genevieve might be a good place for a noviceship, for the time being at least. Nothing but the intervention of Providence will bring us back to St. Louis. English is now indispensable and we do not learn it with ease—which offers an insurmountable obstacle to plans for our convents, as all classes must be given in both English and French. Badly housed and few in number, how can we hold to enclosure? I must write to our Mother General to tell her of the difficulty of our position.

The semi-civilized Indians offer a rich harvest to our zeal, but Jesuits are needed to attract them to the missions. All that I saw of them on the journey up the river only increases my interest in their welfare, but I cannot make myself understood. Nothing has been set on foot, nothing can even be planned for our houses. The Bishop shows us his position and tells us of the Ursulines when they first came, and bids us love our abjection, saying that fruit will come later. I go on with eyes closed—Providence will clear the way if It so desires. They say that China is converted. Can this be true?

One must make journeys such as these we have made to learn how to overcome delicacy and how to practise poverty. At New Orleans, here and at St.

Charles they drink river water as dirty as or worse than that of the Seine. My Sisters are more courageous and fervent than I. They see the cross and embrace it.

To her Superior General she wrote as follows:

S.C.J.M.   ST. LOUIS, AUGUST 31, 1818.

Very Reverend Mother:

It is painful to have no word from you and to have correspondence so delayed when one is in such sore need of advice. In spite of having written to you more than five times since we skirted Cuba, I have so much to say that the expression of sentiments gives place to business affairs and details of journeys; thus my letters are dreadfully dry and I must be abrupt in order to give a fuller account. If the last ones have reached you, you will know that we were forty days on the river, nearly all the passengers were ill from the heat and we had nothing but suffering.

The Bishop's palace is like a tiny French barn, and he is trying to replace his old cathedral, of wood and in holes, by a new one for which he is collecting from people already overtaxed, so he could only rent us a house at St. Charles, a village some twenty miles from St. Louis. We had received such a warm welcome from the pastor at St. Genevieve, and so eager are he and the young girls of his parish to have us that I asked His Lordship to let us go there instead. I have told you what reasons the Bishop alleged against this, but he allows us to hope for a second house there, disapproving as he does of our making any plans for New Orleans. I have refused Florissant, for, though the country is beautiful, it is but sparsely inhabited and we should be obliged to build there. St. Louis seemed inaccessible, for it has grown so quickly in these last two years that a piece of land sells now for five times what it did; a rich man refused one hundred and twenty

francs a square foot. We could not get a piece of land
apparently worth less than the property and house in
Paris combined for less than 500,000 francs. The
Bishop paid 2,000 for the rent of four wretched rooms
in which to begin his college. As this apartment is not
yet occupied, he offered it to us, as well as a lot on
which we might build, but a house no better than that
of Cuignières would cost at least 36,000 francs, and in
the meantime we should have to pay rent. The brother
of the curé of St. Genevieve, Mr. Pratte, who lodges
and boards us while we go about house-hunting, is so
anxious to keep us in St. Louis that he has not consented to hire a vehicle to take us to St. Charles. He
wanted to buy here a house such as would cost 36,000
francs to put up, and then to rent it to us. I saw the
house, which is very well situated and quite new, but
would need changes such as we could effect only if we
owned it. On the advice of His Lordship I proposed
to Mr. Pratte that he sell it to us cheap. The lot (which
the Bishop wanted us to buy) is not large enough to
afford us a garden, whereas the land around this house
would suffice. I do not think that my proposal was
rash, for at least 7,000 francs must remain of what you
sent to the Bishop. I count also on being able to borrow
money without interest from the kind Ursulines. They
have given me reason to expect this, and I am
about to write also to the merchant from Havana who
may help us. Mr. Pratte, who is going to confide to us
each of his five daughters in succession, may also offer
to come to our aid. He deserves already the title I give
him of "temporal father." He owns well-equipped
stores where the prices are moderate and he has promised us credit for as long as we like. His wife is the most
esteemed person in the city. She has five little girls,
who, though dreadfully spoiled, have taken such a fancy
to us that they want to come to our school wherever
it may be. When we go out they are distressed lest
it may be not to return. Céleste, in season and out of
season, at least four or five times a day torments her

parents to send her to school before the time that they planned. These interesting children, who have the happiest dispositions and pleasing voices, seem to be related to almost everyone in St. Louis. A great number of their cousins, all with charming manners, came to see us and want to be our pupils. One of them could not sleep for joy the night on which we arrived. Such eagerness is to be attributed only to the inspiration of their angels.

The colored children feel likewise towards us and with mouths agape stare at us. One of them whom Mother Octavie placed beside her at church was the envy of the others, who exclaimed, "You lucky chile!" You see how attractive the children are; so, too, are the Indians whom one often sees here. This fact, the presence here of His Lordship, your hopes for us—all this makes us want to remain in St. Louis. We should prefer to suffer inconvenience here for a time than to be elsewhere. We cannot hope for large institutions in this country; for the first few years we must be satisfied with those on the same footing as Cuignières. The houses here are like the log cabins in the vineyards of France, or our suburban cottages. This is a motive for dividing our number and doing more good carrying on our work in very small groups. If the people of Kaskaskia and St. Genevieve wish to prepare and present us with a small school, we should, I believe, go first to these places. St. Genevieve is near the new Seminary to be built in an American settlement modelled on those of the early Christians. In Kaskaskia, the chief city of the Illinois, there is but one school, and that secular, whereas most of the inhabitants are French Catholics; the church is large and one might build alongside it. I cannot forget New Orleans nor the thought of the good we might do there. See how I stretch forward when my foot is not yet firmly placed, but desires are unruly when one sees so much need.

Mr. Pratte is working hard to get us a house and some pupils with whom to begin. The Bishop is not opposed to the monitorial method of teaching and re-grets that the Jesuits have not taken it up. He will not force it upon us here, even now. His kindness does not prevent him from being very firm. He knows me already and tells me the truth. Eugénie and Octavie please both him and the children's parents. He found fault with me for seeming to prefer Eugénie. Of this I had not been conscious, but I said to him as I have said to you that she has more weight than the others. However, I am not pleased with two things she has done. Without saying one word to me she proposed to the Bishop that she be put by herself in a house where only English is spoken so as to be forced to converse in that tongue; and when I, in accordance with your intentions, clung to St. Louis, she, in the hope that our little sapling should first take root at St. Charles, insisted that all details should be carried out as in France, which is impossible and must be taken into account. Our only hope will be to make our houses as nearly like those in France as we can. We shall not be able to have beds such as you have, as, on account of the lack of space, they will have to be taken down every day. Enclosure will be difficult to arrange, as we shall have very little money, for what resources have we?

On the 7th of September the nuns said *au revoir* to Mr. and Mrs. Pratte and to their two boys and five little girls. They were driven to the new home by Father Richard, while the Bishop rode his horse and led the way. Mother Duchesne had probably been told that at St. Charles they would see more Indians than they would in St. Louis, for the tribes of the Pawnees and of the Illinois at times encamped on the banks of the Missouri not far from where the religious were to live.

There would be spiritual help there, for, though the village had been without a resident pastor for some

time, Father Acquaroni had gone there a few months
before. He had, of course, other missions to serve and
was often away, but, now that Father Richard had come
to Missouri, the Bishop felt sure that he would be able
to arrange so that the convent would have regular
spiritual assistance. St. Charles was then not very much
smaller than St. Louis; it was about the same age, too,
having been founded in 1765, so it has been claimed, by
Chasseur Blanchette, or perhaps even earlier by Bernard
Guillet, a French outlaw and chief of an Indian tribe.
It had first been called *Les Petites Côtes.* The nuns
saw the reason for this when the Bishop pointed out
the slopes that had given the village the name it had
kept until it was Christianized by the friar, de Limpach,
who, aided by Blanchette, built the little log church.
Mother Duchesne looked across the fields, purple and
gold with the flowers of late summer, and saw in the
distance the hills sloping down to the Missouri River.
The travellers were ferried over the chocolate-colored
waters to St. Charles. Their carriage was not the only
vehicle at the ferry, for prairie schooners, as the cara-
vans of the emigrants were called, were waiting their
turn to cross. Each of these wagons was attended by
slaves who cared for the domestic animals that were to
turn some far-western tract into a farm. On the first
bluff rising steeply up from the river was the little
church of St. Charles Borromeo, and on the second terrace a few squares to the north stood a small log cabin,
destined to be the first convent of the Sacred Heart
in America. The house belonged to the widow of
Francis Duquette and the ground was part of a grant
made to him by the Spanish government. Two years
before she had rented half her house to a Protestant
clergyman, Timothy Flint, and his small family. He

described the cabin as "sheltered by fruit trees and shrubbery," and says, "It is remote from the noise of the town and commands a fine view of the river, which spreads below in a wide and beautiful bay, in which there is a tiny island. In summer the trees around the house bend under loads of apples, pears and yellow Osage plums. Above the house on the bluff is a fine tract of high and level plain covered with hazel bushes and wild hops, grapes and red prairie plums." This clergyman, who seems to have been an excellent farmer, had been gone for some time, and the nuns soon noted the tangle of underbrush and the weeds in the garden. The house, they found, had five small rooms and one larger one in the centre that would serve as a chapel. Madame Duquette would continue to occupy one room in the house, and she was to prove a kind and "neighborly" lady.

On the next day, the Feast of the Nativity of Our Lady, the first Mass was said in the house. Then the Bishop left with Father Richard to visit Portage, where there was a mission, chiefly for Indians. The religious were glad to have a few pictures to send to replace those of Bacchus and Venus, which ignorance had placed on the walls of the little church there.

Two days later the Bishop returned. He gave permission for the Blessed Sacrament to be reserved in the tiny chapel, and approved of Mother Duchesne's desire to consecrate their first house to St. Francis Regis, as she had so long ago promised to do. It was in allusion to this promise that she wrote at this time: "My promise to take to America a picture of St. Regis gave me such confidence that I have had an abiding sense of his continued assistance, except in certain times of suffering necessary in the designs of God to make me tremble lest my many infidelities should annul the effects of the saint's blessed protection."

A few days after the installation at St. Charles Mother Duchesne wrote to Mother Barat:

S.C.J.M.   ST. CHARLES ON THE MISSOURI, SEPT. 12, 1818.

Very Reverend Mother:

Having been in thought and in person at St. Louis, St. Genevieve, Florissant and St. Charles, we are settling down in the last named village, the furthest of all from you, since it requires so many detours and halts to get here. The Bishop, whose gaze is ever on the distant future, considers this place as important, since it is the largest village on the Missouri and only some miles from the junction of this river with the Mississippi. The Americans, who flock here from the East and are a restless people, hope that St. Charles will be a great link of commerce between the United States and China, because the Upper Missouri is near another river which flows into the Pacific Ocean at a place whence the crossing to Asia by sea takes only two weeks. While we await this event we find everything here is both rare and expensive; one cannot get a workman to accept even ten francs a day; the rent of our tiny house seems exorbitant. The village is willing to give the Bishop a lot one hundred and eighty feet wide and three hundred feet deep for us, but two Presbyterians withhold their signatures and thus prevent the donation from being effected. The parish would build for us near the centre of this lot and next to the church, whose pastor also will be our chaplain and will say two Masses on Sundays. Even if we do not succeed in St. Charles, we shall be able to count on a large lot offered us at Florissant. As for St. Louis, there is little hope! Monseigneur has enough trouble there! He was more than attentive during our journey out to St. Charles, riding close to our carriage, seeing us safely in and out of the river boat and bringing us finally to this house, which he has since visited frequently. He leaves us to-day and I do not know when we shall see him again. He spoke of writing to you. Though he had not the time to read our Constitutions, he bade us be faithful to them. We have no difficulty about wearing our religious habit, but cloister is less marked than at Cuignières and St. Pezenne. We hope to open our school for the children of the poor the day after to-morrow. For the academy we have only two or three pupils promised. No Indians have come to seek instruction; those here are less well disposed than those in Canada, who are good Catholics. However, we can hope for a harvest one day.

The Bishop destines for the Missions some priests who are to come here from Rome. The Holy Father is most interested in this part of the country, which is no longer called Upper Louisiana, but the Territory of Missouri, and it will soon be a state. In St. Louis a trading company has been established to regulate commerce between Missouri and the Indians beyond this territory. As a result, the savages are more friendly with the white men and come down the river. We met quite a number who had come to confer with the representatives of the government of the United States. They followed us to the river, touched the hands of the Sisters and gazed after us until we had attained this bank. Those who ferried us across the Missouri and then put our baggage on a cart and brought it up to the house refused to accept a penny, saying that we represent Our Lord, Jesus Christ. The Protestants, whose children the Bishop wishes us to receive in our schools, say that those educated with nuns are never willing to leave. Monseigneur inspires us by his example and encourages us by saying that we are the grain of mustard seed and that great good will come of it all. He was very pleased with our sacristy and still more so with Eugénie and Octavie. When they laughed at the sight of our poor little house he said to me, "See these young people who might have shone elsewhere and who are so gay. Oh, it is splendid, splendid! As for you and me, we are only old sinners." On another occasion he told me that the nuns are all well disposed and that more than one is making strides in perfection. He was afraid we might waste the priest's time, but was himself the first to speak of Confession. They say that we must allow six months for a letter to come from France, and three or four for one to reach you. It is hard not to hear from you. Please send some English books; the prospectus, newspapers, bills and addresses must be written in English. It is only at this distance that I realize how strong are the bonds of respect, thanksgiving and love that attach us to the best of mothers.

In spirit at your feet,

PHILIPPINE.

Emélie and Céleste Pratte soon arrived; they were joined by their cousin, Pélagie Chouteau, and class began in earnest. There was so little room that the children's beds had all to be taken away during the day. The poor, who came from the village for religious instruction and to learn to read and to write, had already filled the tiny house to overflowing. These children of the poor of St. Charles formed the nucleus of the very first free school to be founded west of the Mississippi River.

Mother Duchesne's letters and her fidelity in noting down in the journal of the house the events that might serve for the history of the Society allow us to follow the little community through the first winter. She characteristically made light of the privations and sufferings and dilated on the good being done by the zealous Bishop and his clergy, especially Father Acquaroni, curé of St. Charles, until he was succeeded by

Father Richard. He found in her an eager and interested listener when he spoke of his experiences with the Indians. He was most kind to the little community and urged the people of the town to build a suitable home for the nuns.

In October Mrs. Pratte drove out to see her little girls; she brought letters from Father Barat, who was at Bordeaux, still hoping to come to Louisiana. There were letters, too, from their loved Mother General, who forwarded the longed-for blessing of the Holy Father on the American Mission. This blessing Pius VII deigned to extend to all who would join Mother Philippine Duchesne in the years to come. This was indeed good news, and Mother Duchesne wrote enthusiastically:

S.C.J.M. . .   ST. CHARLES, OCTOBER 8, 1818.

Very Reverend Mother:

After we had long hungered and thirsted for news from our dear Society three packages of mail reached us at once. . . . Without doubt they came on different boats as far as New Orleans, but were sent at the same time to St. Louis, where they awaited the coming of our three pupils, who brought them to us last Saturday. Thus Our Lady on the day dedicated to her added to the many graces we owe her, the foundation of our first American boarding-school and the arrival of a copy of letters from Rome. Here we invoke Our Lady under the title of Prompt Succor, as we promised the Ursulines we should do.

We shed happy tears on learning that the Sovereign Pontiff has added his approbation and blessing to the many signs that our mission is God's Will. To-morrow we shall chant the Te Deum and a Mass of thanksgiving will be said. We rejoiced, too, in the hope of having some more foundresses, as well as in the news of our houses in France. It was good to hear of your journey to La Louvesc, of the conversion of that English lady, of our Sisters' vows, of the new wing at Paris, of the retreat and even of the death so precious in God's sight.

By this time you know that Providence has brought us to the most distant village of the United States. It is situated on the Missouri, which is frequented only by those trading with the Indians, who are not far away. In spite of this fact, I have not yet seen any small Indian girls, though a half-breed is promised us as a domestic or postulant, according to her capacity.

The Bishop is now at the Barrens, or Bois Brulé, not far from St. Genevieve. The Seminary is being built there by a colony from Kentucky. These people were instructed by Mgr. Flaget and the Trappists and live like the first Christians of Jerusalem or the Guarami of Paraguay. St. Charles is now showing some signs of piety.

Our parish school numbers twenty-two, which in proportion to the population equals a school of one hundred in France. The children had never heard of Our Lord, of His birth or His death, nor of hell, and listened agape to our instructions. All except two are learning the alphabet. When we complain that we have no savages Monseigneur says: "Indeed you have, and your work among these will be more lasting and wider because of the influence of the rich over the poor."

We are very inconveniently lodged and shall have to go elsewhere at the end of a year, for we are paying nearly 2,000 francs in rent for a house consisting of six very small rooms badly in need of repairs. The large garden and orchard are uncultivated and we have no one to work them. We need a French gardener. As we shall not be able to find a larger house, we shall have to build. There are here more English-speaking people than there are French or Creoles, but, as both languages are fairly well understood and the children are accustomed to hear both, Mother Octavie will do for the

English part of the school, at least for the present. Eugénie pleases everyone.

Our things have arrived in good condition. Monseigneur shows great interest in all that has to do with the chapel. The statue of Our Lady over the Tabernacle touches the ceiling of our tiny chapel, which is about the size of the sanctuary of our chapel in Paris; in our little nook all is devotional. There is a beautiful picture of the Sacred Heart with more than fifty figures—this came from Rome. The picture of Our Lord showing His Sacred Heart is also from the Eternal City. There is a ravishing painting of the Nativity and the Adoration by the Magi, a reliquary containing bits of the true Cross, of the sponge and a thorn; also many relics of saints, many devotional pictures and finally that one of St. Regis which I found in the garret at Grenoble and promised to have honored if he should bring us to America. We put it above the Tabernacle the day it was framed, and the Mass of St. Regis was said.

As I was finishing this letter we received a visit from a French Sulpician from Canada. For twenty-three years he has been pastor of Detroit, the largest town in the territory of Michigan, having nearly fifteen hundred inhabitants, American and French, Catholic and Protestant. Twelve years ago he instructed for their First Communion five young girls, whom he has directed ever since. The eldest, who is now thirty, has just been elected Superior of the little Congregation formed by them. The election was carried on in the presence of Mgr. Flaget, Bishop of Kentucky, who confirmed it. The good pastor of Detroit, Father Gabriel Richard, made them read Rodriguez ten times, gave them an Order of Day and allowed them to take vows, but only temporarily, since His Lordship wants them to make their noviceship under a Superior who knows religious life before they bind themselves more completely. His intention was to have them go to Kentucky to be trained by the Trappists and to join a penitential order there. They had not enough money to undertake this long journey, and besides, as Father Richard and his nuns are Canadians, they did not want to join the Americans, so nothing has come of it all. They want to be formed by French nuns, and Father Richard asks us to send them a Superior. I told him that for the present this is impossible and that we have to await your consent, Very Reverend Mother, and I promised to write to you. Detroit has a Canadian climate, and there one needs a fire in September. The country is poor and we should have but few boarders able to pay about 450 francs, and even few day pupils able to pay, but living is cheap and souls are abundant. It takes a month to get there from here and one goes by way of the Illinois River. A small conveyance brings one to another stream which empties into Lake Michigan, which one ascends in a larger vessel.

As winter came on the nuns were saddened by the sight of the poverty of the people around them. Of their own suffering they always made light, but they lamented that of the children who came barefoot to school and whose clothing seemed far too thin for the season. On All Saints' Day eleven of these poor children made their First Communion in the little log church of St. Charles; the altar was decorated with artificial flowers made by the nuns, who had also painted the Tabernacle for the occasion.

The good Bishop followed with interest the progress of the school. In November he spent a few days at St. Charles, and, finding the convent without bread, he disapproved of any arrangements for building in a village where, he said, the nuns would starve. He had bought a large farm at Florissant which he intended to put under cultivation. It would also be a good centre for the missionary activities he was seeking to further;

moreover, Florissant, he thought, had a future. Mr. John Mullanphy had offered to build a capitol there at his own expense if Missouri, on entering the Union, would choose this village as the state capital. His Lordship said but few St. Louisians would send their children to St. Charles, as each winter the river would be impassable. In the meantime the community must remain where they were, as the house had been leased for a year. It was probably at the Bishop's suggestion that arrangements were made to exchange for bread the great quantities of apples which they had, for Divine Providence had so protected them that the fruit, which ordinarily fell to the ground in August, had ripened that year only in October. Mother Duchesne's trust in Providence is shown in her letters:

S.C.J.M.   ST. CHARLES, NOVEMBER, 1818.

Dear Reverend Mother:

So remote are we in this corner of the world that we do not yet know if you have received a single one of our letters, but I have had the inexpressible consolation of getting several from you, from Mother Bigeu and from Father Barat, who seemed to know that the *Rebecca* had arrived in New Orleans. Perhaps God has allowed the letters written later to reach you at the same time as the earlier ones in order to save you anxiety, for so changeable is everything in life that much of what I said at first I afterwards had to take back. My first letter to France went off after we entered the Mississippi, my second was sent via George-town, Washington, my third through the French Consul at New Orleans, my fourth on the returning *Rebecca;* my fifth, written just before we left New Orleans, was sent through the Consul there; my sixth from St. Louis via Washington, my seventh on the

Franklin when it returned to New Orleans, my eighth from St. Charles via Washington and the ninth via Philadelphia. This is the tenth. I do not fear to repeat, because our situation has changed so completely. You will be most interested to hear how things are at this moment. They are just what we should have desired— thorny and difficult—but sweetened by grace and alleviated by a kind Providence Who will never desert us and Who makes His protection sensible at every moment. What has consoled me most has been the Cardinals' letters, the blessing of the Sovereign Pontiff, the two prospective foundations in France, the news that the noviceship is to remain in Paris, in spite of the increase in the school, and your journeys to La Louvesc and to Ste. Marie. The kindness of your brother, Very Reverend Mother, which pursues us even here, is another sign of the protection of God.

We were disappointed in opening our boxes to find no writing paper thinner than this, no Meditations by Nouet or Sermons of Bourdaloue, nothing except what is suited to Lent and retreat, no catechism of Constance or by Chancey, few books on religious life; but to make up we discovered a copy book of the first draft of Greek themes, a geography and some poems written by Mother Balastron, but even these will be useful. Of all that was wanting to us and all that I have already asked for, the most useful will be what will keep us alive, as here below one's soul depends on the body. A gardener or general workman and someone to do commissions for us are indispensable. The French laborers here are forgetful of favors received and are independent and lazy. One must have slaves in order to be sure of work being done; here there are few negroes and they will be of no use to us. A laborer gets at least ten francs a day, and our garden and orchard are so neglected that one can scarcely get through the tangle. We look upon potatoes and cabbage as you in France do upon rare delicacies. There is no market; a pound of butter and a dozen eggs would be a fortune, and, although we did not want to avail ourselves of the permission to eat meat on Saturdays, we have been obliged to do so. In the hunting season, in which we now are, one can procure deer and geese, but in spring and in summer one can get only salt fish and meat. Our cow only supplies enough milk for our three pupils and for Mother Octavie, who presides over their meal. The well in our garden is dried up, and it costs twelve cents every time we send someone down to the Missouri to get us two little buckets of water.

So many difficulties make one dream of building elsewhere than here, but the people have assembled and have appointed a committee with a president who inscribes the names of those willing to chop wood on the village common and to put up and roof a house for us. We should have only to finish it off and to put up partitions. It would be only thirty-six feet in length and twenty-five in width, which is thought large enough for anyone here, where there are only log cabins covered with mud, which easily comes off, letting in the light. (Sister) Marguerite (Manteau) sleeps in the kitchen; the other three nuns and I, surrounded by the children of the boarding school, which can never exceed ten in number, occupy the parish school class room. Our boarding school still counts but three—others are about to arrive. We have six day pupils who pay fifteen francs a month, and twenty in the parish school, where nothing is charged.

Experience confirms what faith teaches—that those who are lost have no one to blame but themselves. Why do not the Indians go to the priest for instruction with the same eagerness that they show when they flock around one who has whiskey to give, even though they have suffered from its effects? We sweetly dream of giving instruction to docile and innocent Indians, whereas the women, no less than the men, are afflicted with indolence and drunkenness. Jesuits are needed to make men of them before we attempt to make them good Christians. The only success that has fallen to the few priests is to gather and to sustain those already converted. So far we have had to deal only with half-breeds—born of one Indian and one white parent; there are many such at St. Charles. I am no less convinced that God has His designs in bringing us here. Already pictures of the Sacred Heart adorn several churches, for I have revived my old talent for painting and making flowers and we have decorated many tabernacles. Our parish school children now sing Benediction, and they have learned some of Father Barat's hymns, among them that to the Sacred Heart. They are zealous and easy to manage. Father Richard, our pastor and chaplain, showed his delight on the Feast of All Saints which marked the close of their retreat of three days. This holy priest, who was at Bellay, reminds one of Father X in his extraordinary efforts. He is not as scrupulous as was said, and gives us just what help we need, as we cannot be under the direction of Jesuits. The pastors of the neighboring villages have been very kind, especially the Trappist in Florissant, who eagerly urges the people in St. Charles to build for us so that they may keep us amongst them. We cannot stay where we are, and it will need much money to finish the house, the mere frame-work of which they will erect. Already I am sore taxed to provide for our household on what comes in from three boarders, for the cost of living is exorbitant. One must live from day to day and stint even drinking water, but daily privation and dependence are consoling because of the visible help which God gives. I have also found consolation in seeing myself getting weaker in soul and body. This decrease in God's sight warns me that death is near. I see to my joy that the other nuns are more liked than I am; I only help them. Octavie is in charge of our boarders, Eugénie assists her with the day scholars, and God blesses their work. We are making so many friends with our painting and flowers that we shall need much carmine and pink coloring, some green paper, needles, pins and thread, leaflets of the canon of the

Mass, which one can get at Grenoble for nothing, and two cinctures.

If the vocations we hear of are true ones, we shall need a special house of novitiate. My hope is that by the end of the year the new convent here at St. Charles will be built and ready for use and that the two younger nuns, who are successful and are winning the confidence of outsiders, may take possession of it, while I open a noviceship at Florissant. The good and distinguished pastor of St. Genevieve is to send us postulants; some will also be found in the parish school here.

In another letter written on November 20 to "the Mothers, Sisters and Children of the Society of the Sacred Heart," she says:

Though our New Year's greetings will reach you late, the Sacred Heart, Who annihilates both time and space, will have made up to you for these wishes, especially since we have already confided you to His Sacred Heart. We have not yet heard of your receiving any of our letters, but we have rejoiced over yours, especially that which forwarded to us copies of the messages of Cardinals Litta and Fontana. Father Barat has kindly written to us five times, but his last letter was far from consoling, as we had hoped he might be coming out here. Our Bishop is equally disappointed, as he does not dare to invite missionaries on account of the customs and the climate and the privation of so many things. But God, Who looks with mercy on this country, has inspired the Superior of Georgetown to buy in Upper Missouri land much in demand, and he daily sends here families of Americans, most of them from Kentucky, who are settling at Boonslick, where there are good salt mines, and they are establishing themselves also not far from Franklin, where the Jesuits will probably build their college, and from there settlements will extend to far regions where the faith is unknown. A religious order is needed for such an undertaking, and this will be the third Society of men to bedew this vast diocese with the sweat of their brow. The Lazarists are opening a Seminary at the Barrens or Bois Brulé, the most fervently Christian part of this country. Some young ecclesiastics are founding a college at St. Louis.

Again she wrote:

S.C.J.M.   ST. CHARLES, DECEMBER 16, 1818.

My very dear Mother Maillucheau:

All the news from France fills us with joy and lightens the pain of separation. Thank you for Aloysia's journal and, above all, for the detailed account of the two foundations. God is good in thus bringing about the growth of the seedling—His little Society. You see that Upper Louisiana will not be your rival—*we* were suited only to a land still in a state of early colonization. God, Who wanted us here, has allowed that we should see Indians but rarely. He sends us instead those who have the same needs and whose instruction will procure a greater good in bringing us postulants. We already see signs of vocation in several and we have just received our first postulant, Mary Mullen, who was brought up by nuns in Baltimore and in Kentucky. She understands only English, and I despair of speaking to her and of understanding her well; it is the pronunciation that staggers me. Mother Octavie is quite successful, Eugénie less so.

We have had the happiness of doing without bread and water. I had expected the former privation, but I never dreamed that on the bank of the Missouri we should lack water. We may not go down to the river and no one is willing to go there regularly for us. Sister

Marguerite came back to-day from the two springs nearby carrying her two buckets, one only half full of water and the other filled with ice. The Missouri is almost frozen over, and it is so cold that the water freezes beside the fire, as does the laundered linen hung there to dry. Neither doors nor windows close tight and there is no one to be found who knows how to make a foot-warmer. Our logs of wood are too large and there is no one to chop them for us and no saw with which we could cut them ourselves. The people work only for the need of the moment and are too proud to want to seem mercenary. As a result, we find only maize (Indian corn), pork and potatoes, but no eggs, butter, oil, fruit or vegetables. So, dear Mother, the things that could be bought more cheaply in France than here and those of which we are most in need are seeds of fruit trees, vegetables, grain and of shrubs that might form our enclosure, the tools that John Francis had packed for us, a small stove with its pipe jointed so as to save space, some English books on religious life, a history, etc. You would find these books at Bordeaux. We should also value a case of altar wine and olive oil—the only edible oil to be had is bear grease, which is revolting—but if you do send us some, please make sure that the vessel containing it will not leak on its way out here. I do not see how we shall survive Lent with fish cooked without either butter or oil, and not an egg to be had till the spring. We brought from France and from New Orleans not a single thing that has proved useless. We are content in the midst of privation.

I scarcely know what I write, but I do it to-night, as to-morrow will be too late. I cannot reply to all the kind letters received. Please make up for me, especially to Mother Bigeu, who should have heard from us more than once. I fear that several letters sent by way of the Jesuits at Washington have been lost, as I was given the address incorrectly. Fiat! The Sisters here are well. I have spoken of them more in detail to our

Mother. I am undoubtedly the one of least worth here.
Octavie and Eugénie are well.
Au revoir in C. J.,

PHILIPPINE.

On Christmas Eve the little day pupils were invited
to return to the convent at seven in the evening. There
they and the ten who now formed the boarding school
read stories which were not too distracting and sang
canticles in a way that delighted Mother Duchesne
until midnight Mass assembled them all in the little
chapel. For the rest of the night they camped out in
the convent, going to their homes in time to wish their
fathers and mothers a happy feast. The religious had
a Christmas not unlike that of Bethlehem; their only
possession was Jesus; but, as their sainted Foundress
used so often to say, "Avaricious indeed is the heart
which is not satisfied with God."

In crucial times such as these Divine Providence
always came to their help. They had been buying water
at an exorbitant price and had nothing with which to
pay their bill. A novena was begun to Our Lady of
Prompt Succor, a title which Mother Duchesne had
learned to love. The very next day Father Richard,
whose meals they furnished, insisted on paying his board
and in advance—surely, a great act of faith on his
part—but he knew from experience that the little community would starve rather than that he or Madame
Duquette or the children should suffer. It was without
doubt Our Lady of Prompt Succor who inspired the
Ursulines in New Orleans to send just then to St.
Charles a generous box of provisions.

In February either the Missouri must have been
frozen so hard that it could support the weight of a

cart or else an unusually early spring must have opened
it up for the ferry, for Bishop Du Bourg went out to
St. Charles to take two or three religious to see the
spot he had chosen for the house he was to build for
them at Florissant. It was not on his farm on the
heights, but on the low-lying land between two small
creeks. The house was to be built under the supervision
of the Trappist, Father Dunand. A month later a
letter from the Bishop told Mother Duchesne that he
had changed his plans—they had better stay in St.
Charles. This was not the swerving policy it might
seem. His one desire was the spiritual good of his
diocese. For this end he was bringing in missionaries,
building a seminary at the Barrens, preparing a centre
for missionary activity at Florissant and erecting a new
cathedral all at once when the treasury, if there was
one, was empty. "He was all liberality and schemes
from a long habit of expenditure," wrote Mother Seton,
and she added elsewhere, "This is not a defect of
mediocre men; silent suffering will undermine his
nerves." There were many, however, who frowned on
his plans. He did not want the new community to fall
under that frown, so he chose to postpone their coming
to St. Louis to stay, and Florissant was even nearer
his episcopal city than was St. Charles.

He continued to visit them there and showed his
admiration of the high spirit of the younger nuns. One
day he laughingly asked Mother Audé if it was at the
court of Napoleon that she had learned to milk cows.
He took Mother Duchesne into his confidence and often
asked for her intercession. On one occasion when her
prayers in his behalf had been granted she playfully
reminded him of his promise to give her a picture of St.
Francis Regis as a reward. The Bishop said that a large

case of pictures was about to arrive from Europe, and
that, if it contained one of St. Francis, he would send it
to her. What was his surprise to find in the box a large
and beautiful oil painting of Mother Duchesne's
patron! The Saint is at the point of death, a moun-
taineer holds him in his arms; in the face of the dying
Francis is reflected the peace and the radiance of the
Heaven that is opening for him. The thought of
Heaven was needed to encourage the nuns, as the following letter shows:

S.C.J.M.   ST. CHARLES, FEBRUARY 15, 1819.

Very Reverend Mother:

A few days ago I received from New Orleans a
letter dated May 4 and addressed to Father Martial,
who is coming to St. Louis, and one from the Bishop
written six months ago which describes so accurately
what one may expect in this country that I thought it
would be of interest to you. The second from Monseigneur was written quite lately and has to do with our
going to Florissant. One must spend here a winter—
even a mild one such as this—to realize that for the
time being at least we can only vegetate in St. Charles,
doing none of the good that is promised elsewhere. But
it would cost me too much to abandon so many interesting children, many of whom will one day belong to
the Sacred Heart, and I believe it essential to leave
Sister Eugénie here for the present. With Sister Marguerite to assist her, she could easily manage our day
school, especially if she had some young girls to help
with the teaching. Many are spoken of, and while
waiting for them to offer themselves we already have
our one postulant, who is adapting herself to religious
life and who can act as interpreter with English-speaking people. She still has six months to learn French,
the study of which is developing her. Mother Eugénie

is loved by her school; when at the close of her retreat she returned to them the children received her with such tears of joy that she herself wept. All cried, and since we have made known that we may be going to Florissant several of the older girls say: "I shall then pack up and go with you," and the younger ones ask to be taken along, saying that they are begging this of the Sacred Heart of Jesus. If we were only not so badly off we should be able to do very much good by taking some of the children with us, but what can we do without either lodging or provisions?

The Bishop was quite mistaken in thinking that we should be able to house here twenty-five pupils; there is not even room for sixteen, and, as it is, the beds have to be put up at night and removed in the morning. As the country beyond the Missouri River cannot furnish pupils able to pay, we can have only one day school. We see the poor children coming, famished and barefoot, to school along frozen roads and wearing only the lightest of dresses. You see, Reverend Mother, that, obliged as we are to give up our boarding school here, it would be dreadful to leave these poor children without anyone to give them instruction. In four months many have learned to read and to write. They now know the whole little catechism, a number of hymns and prayers for Benediction and they are able to do all the singing. I hope that you will approve of two of us staying here, as such is the wish of his Lordship. Yesterday was a happy day. Father Porter, a young priest who came up with us from New Orleans, paid us a visit, asking us to make room for several more pupils. He is being sent to New Madrid, the seat of the earthquakes, which are felt almost as far as St. Charles; no priest has been to that village for twenty years. Another young priest, Father De La Croix, a Fleming, and our extraordinary confessor, has just come back from a part of Missouri which no missionaries had yet visited. There are now two stations there, one at Côte Sans Dessein, which he has consecrated to the

Apostle, St. Paul, and where there are twenty-two families; the other, at Boonslick or Franklin, he has dedicated to St. Francis de Sales. There he gave a mission attended even by Protestants and fruitful for the Catholics. Some Protestants there are allowing their children to be instructed in the true faith by a catechist lately appointed.

Father De La Croix confirmed what the Bishop had told us—that the Jesuits of Georgetown are to buy land at Franklin and to labor there for the glory of God. I should long to go there if English were not the most difficult language to learn.

On the 14th four letters reached me, one from M. Pétry, the French Consul at Washington, who in a most gracious letter written three months ago offered to send on our European mail. I heard also from the Abbé Perreau, who wrote six months ago; the letter from Grenoble took but five months, that from Mother Bigeu four. Our joy was great as we read the letters which bind us to our Sisters in France and recall the graces that God has given us in the Society of His Heart. Mother Bigeu gives no details and alludes to previous letters, which we have not received. I hope that there is one from you in the package, as you would not leave us without this consolation. Père Perreau shows himself ever our father, and I shall be always his spiritual daughter, for I find no one, and have no hope of finding anyone, to take his place. This solitude of heart which finds nothing on earth to satisfy it is reason enough for throwing oneself upon the Heart of Our Lord. Please thank the good Father for his letter and for the joy given us by the Holy Father's third blessing, as also for the hope of obtaining the brief for the Confraternity of the Sacred Heart, which we shall prize.

All agree in saying that in order to succeed with Indian children one must get them at the age of four or five before they learn bad habits. There is much good to be done and, oh, such lack of means! As to enclosure, there is not a wall within one thousand miles of here; and wooden fences keep animals out—but not men. Our enclosure consists in remaining at home, but people come into our grounds as much as they like, making an entrance anywhere.

If our Sisters picture us surrounded by Indian children, they are mistaken. I have seen only old Indian women, who make their First Communion at fifty or sixty years of age. But in compensation I engage in new trades together with Mothers Eugénie and Octavie. We dig in the garden, carry manure, lead our cow to drink and clean out its tiny stable, the only one in the neighborhood, as here all the animals wander about as they please. We do all this with as much joy as though we were teaching, because God wills it thus and our penury prevents our engaging a workman.

At the end of March the Bishop went to make his retreat at St. Charles. Suddenly he interrupted it for a day to tell the religious that he had decided on Florissant for them and that he now agreed with the Mother General, who disapproved of dividing the community and of leaving one or two nuns at St. Charles to carry on the work among the poorer children. On a previous visit he had shown his desire that a few minor changes be made in the Rules of the Society of the Sacred Heart in a missionary country. Each one of the five religious had withheld her consent, so that he had said, with a laugh, that they had five heads in one cap. Afterwards he had acknowledged that they had been in the right. During this retreat he read the Constitutions and Rules, and thought them full of wisdom. When he returned to St. Louis he said that he was leaving his heart in the little house of St. Charles, which he had visited in search of rest and the spirit of the Heart of Jesus, and he had found both. On April 27 he wrote to Mgr. Maréchal of the nuns: "Three of them," he says, "have a rare talent for teaching. Their institute, based on that of the Jesuits, is in its first fervor, and I have never seen anything as beautiful as its Constitutions and Rules."

During Holy Week little Emélie Pratte became very ill, and Mother Duchesne sent for her mother, whom Madame Duquette invited to share her room, as there was no other vacant corner in the convent. There had been several times alarm by prairie fires that swept over Missouri during the years the emigrants were passing from the East to the West. Once, too, their chimney caught fire, threatening the poor wooden house. On Holy Thursday, as Mother Octavie and the Sisters prayed before the altar of repose, they saw that the draperies were ablaze, and, unable to put the fire out, they ran for Mother Duchesne. It had rained the day before and the gully in front of the house provided water with which the flames were soon extinguished. In the centre of the bare and scorched altar they saw a black square. It was the charred pall which covered the paten, both having fallen off the chalice. Lifting the pall, Mother Duchesne saw that the Sacred Species was intact. The pure white Host in the middle of the burned linen and wood was a sign to Philippine that, though all might abandon them, God would ever remain. Their confidence in Him was unshaken, and they wrote brightly to France; but the Mother General read between the lines, and her virile sympathy was expressed in letters which Mother Duchesne read on her knees and which she answered as follows:

S.C.J.M.   ST. CHARLES, JULY 29, 1819.

Very Reverend Mother:

After I received your recommendation I began to number my letters—the first was to Father Barat. We have never been so long without writing to or receiving letters from France. Our delay is due to the steamboat held back by low water. Moreover at this distance from St. Louis we probably lose many opportunities of sending letters by hand through cities other than New Orleans. We do not complain among ourselves of our privations in order to excite regrets, but so as to keep up the sacrificial fire. The Captain who brought us over from France is said to have just arrived in St. Louis, which makes me eager to write, and we hope he has brought letters from the Ursulines enclosing others from you which are of course those most desired. Since we last heard from you, our dear Lord has favored us with a share of His Cross. The greatest and most painful trial is our total lack of success in our labors. The thought that if a saint were in charge all would go well only makes my burden weigh the heavier. I see ever more clearly that I have not what is necessary for the guidance of others.

The house which is being built for us at Florissant is progressing and is supposed to be ready the first of December when the Bishop will scarcely be back from Bois Brulé where business concerning the Seminary detained him. They say that Father Martial has joined him there. I trust in Providence for the payment of the debts that this little house will have brought us and for our transportation to Florissant. One day I had almost nothing—several bank notes having proved worthless—and no other money is accepted. God will be our refuge. I am always more convinced that He wants us here, so too are the other four nuns, though at times we feel the thorns which press upon us from every side. We know that we are your daughters, that we have Fathers, Mothers, Sisters and children who are praying for us, and our courage cannot fail. There is little hope of our going to the Indians. In the time of Marie of the Incarnation, the Jesuits everywhere gathered the children together, appeased the parents, and interpreted the diverse languages scientifically by dictionaries and books which they composed. Their labors surpassed those possible to individual missionaries; to those on the spot this is evident. But my desire is no less ardent to sacrifice myself for these poor souls if God but opens a way. I am with deepest respect,

PHILIPPINE.

And again:

S.C.J.M.   ST. CHARLES, MO., AUGUST 28, 1919.

Very Reverend Mother:

The last letters from France were written in January so we must console and strengthen ourselves by re-reading old ones. I cannot say that letters bind us more closely to you, for the bonds could hardly be tightened, so you can guess my joy when the Bishop said in speaking of us *"O c'est bien de la race."* ("Oh, they have a family spirit.") Nevertheless, dear Mother, I feel that there must be slight differences due to the diversity of nationalities and climates,—the summer here has been as crushing as was that in New Orleans. Here windows are opened and no one minds draughts as in France.

You see how difficult it is to conduct classes. The children of the poor, unable to read, come to us for only three months and have to be taught catechism and other lessons word by word and with incredible slowness. Some read English but not French, some both languages, some only French.

The First Communion in the Academy took place on the feast of the Assumption. Mother Eugénie went with the children to the church, as I thought you would have intended some one to be with them to insure order and piety. When they saw her with her band of ten or twelve, people said, *"La voilà, cette bonne Vierge!"* The First Communion has led us to believe that many of the children are capable of great virtue. The Holy Spirit has inspired many acts of mortification; we had suggested that they make five every day. From time to time we question them to know if they have understood and find that some have gone too far.

About this time, Mother Barat received the following letter from the kind Superior of the Ursulines:

NEW ORLEANS, APRIL 29, 1819.

Dear Reverend Mother:

The lively interest which your dear nuns aroused in us was the cause of our esteem for them and of the sincere friendship which will last all through our lives. We were naturally drawn to one another, as our two Orders differ only in name. They tend to the same end, and should form but one because of the religious affection we bear each other.

I think, dear Madame, that your daughters gave you too flattering an account of our hospitality offered them last year. Our Community will always rejoice to have had them as guests. The days that they spent here passed all too quickly for us, and left us undying memories of the virtues of your religious. We hope to profit by their example of zeal for Our Master and of devotedness to the salvation of souls,—virtues which make them rise superior to the difficulties which encompass them. Their glorious enterprise, the spread of the Kingdom of Christ, brings with it much fatigue and anxiety, but their trust in Divine Providence will uphold them, and the strength of the Sacred Heart will sustain them. . . .

You may, dear Madame, feel quite free to confide to us any of your nuns whom you destine for the mission of Missouri. We shall be glad to welcome them, and to forward any parcels or letters you may send them through us.

The good Superior of the Ursulines knew well that Philippine's trust in Providence would have its reward —summer had come early that year and the apples ripened in August. Meanwhile the lease of the little log cabin in St. Charles was soon to expire and Mother Duchesne noted in the journal of the house:

We were impatiently awaiting a visit from the Bishop so as to learn where we might camp out until our new building at Florissant should be completed. Monseigneur came at the end of August (the 25th) just after having celebrated High Mass with great pomp in his cathedral. Fathers Martial and De La Croix accompanied him. As it was evening when the Bishop reached St. Charles, and he intended to leave the next day, he spoke at once of our future, saying that we should go to his farm (on an elevated site in the Valley of Florissant) until our new house should be ready. The children asked him to preside at the Prizes which were given the next morning at nine o'clock. The day pupils and boarders recited poems and fables sent me by Father Rivet, S. J. His Lordship thought them excellent as a means of instruction and several were well recited. Miss Odile DeLassus received the prize for Good Conduct and the ribbon of merit. The day pupils then went home and the Bishop left us on horseback at noon after having expressed himself well pleased with all that had been done. The next day we began to prepare for departure.

There was another ceremony of First Communion at St. Charles on the First Friday of September, and

a day or so later the last Mass was said in the little
house. Mother Duchesne's journal contains the quaint
item "Father Richard ate no breakfast," and continues:

Our baggage was taken down to the river in carts
and transferred to two little boats which towed them
ten miles to a landing-place opposite Florissant, where
they were put on the sand.   They were guarded by
Mother Eugénie who had come down by water together
with Sister Catherine Lamarre and three children who
remained hours in a burning sun.   The Pastor of St.
Ferdinand brought carts belonging to the Bishop's
farm. There were seventeen trips across the river; this
does not mean that we were very rich, because a one-
horse-cart can only carry three people or baggage in
proportion. This first setting out from St. Charles
was followed by a second when Mother Octavie and
two older girls left in a carriage belonging to the family
of one of the children. In the evening, I closed the
march with the cows, calves, chickens and Sister Marguerite. But our cows revolted when they found themselves tied and obliged to walk in the heat so that I
had to wait until early the next morning when the rest
of our furniture was packed into three small wagons.
We had to appease the cows with cabbages for they
were at first very obstinate. Finally worn out by their
ropes and fatigue they decided to follow along with
their calves. I perched on top of a cart dividing my
attention between the care of my relics and that of the
poultry. Then (having gone a drive of ten miles or
so) we crossed the Missouri opposite Florissant in a
small boat. When we landed, with motherly tenderness Marguerite lined up the chickens and gave them
food and water; I fed the cows with cabbages, and
Father De La Croix having appeared on horseback
led the way urging his steed into a gallop whenever
our cows, which we had let loose, tried to run to the
woods.

It was a glorious view that met their eyes as they reached the top of the Charbonnière, a bluff rising almost perpendicularly from the river. Looking back, they saw the Missouri with its wooded banks, islands and sandbars, and far away on the hillsides beyond, smoke arose from the log cabins of St. Charles. Just a year before Mother Duchesne had crossed that river and had written of it as the Jordan, for the Promised Land lay beyond it, and now as she looked back she thought she had failed in the place she had come to love in spite of—or rather because of—what she had suffered. It was only a glance, and then she looked forward to what lay before them. This was no Vale of Grésivaudan, flanked with mountains of snow-capped red granite, but the smiling Valley of Florissant, enclosed by steep terraces of the Missouri on one side and limestone bluffs of the Mississippi on the other. In the fields corn-stalks, pulled together and tied at the top, looked like miniature wigwams, and here and there a precocious tree had assumed the yellow and red tints of autumn.

The strange procession wended its way across rough, rolling slopes, through clumps of trees, where woodpeckers flickered, and across open spaces where elderberries were offering an early supper to the ever-starving bluejay. The quail called out "Bob-white" as they hurried across the cowpath, and rabbits scurried into the thicket. The sun was about to drop behind the Charbonnière when the nuns entered the Bishop's farmhouse. It was a log-cabin, compared with which the one at St. Charles seemed palatial; the one room, 18 feet by 18, would be the children's dormitory, parlor, class-room, refectory, according to the hour of the day or the night; it had but one door, one large

window without sash or glass, but with a heavy board
shutter, and two small windows with a few panes of
glass.   There was a fireplace made to hold logs eight
feet long—no wonder that the Americans laughed at
the dainty French fires that the nuns were accustomed
to make!   The floor was of puncheons—split logs with
their faces a little smoothed by an axe or a hatchet.
The door was made up of seven slabs, with a wooden
latch lifted by a string from the outside.   Happily,
there was also a low loft or attic, which would serve
not only for a kitchen, but for all the needs of the community.

Mother Duchesne notes in the journal:

I reached our tiny house in the evening and learned
to my distress that Father De La Croix, who lived
there as Monseigneur's treasurer, had left his cabin to
live in a hut open to the winds like a birdcage.   There
he contracted fever from which he suffered for several
days and we were not even able to force a chair through
the hole which served for both the door and the window
of his cabin.   When the Bishop had been informed of
his state he was told to build a log house with one room
for himself and one to serve as chapel.   This house
built by few hands was completed in eight days.   At
least the good Father was there under shelter, and the
Blessed Sacrament was left in the chapel.   Since then
we have been as we should wish, for he who has Jesus,
has all.

The farm people took fever and could do nothing
for themselves so Sister Marguerite cooked their meals.
Mother Eugénie had six cows to look after morning
and evening, of which two were our own, four belonged
to the farm.   This was only for a short time, but was
succeeded by a worse trial, for Mother Octavie and two
children succumbed to fever, and as there is only one
room for the school and one for us, we feared that the

disease would make the round of the house, but a kind Providence came to our aid and to-day all are well.

Yesterday the Bishop paid us a visit. He is going to give us as chaplain Father De La Croix, who was first his secretary and then his treasurer and whom he calls his good angel. He is a young Flemish priest and was in the Seminary at Ghent, when Napoleon drafted the ecclesiastical students. His is a strong character which shows itself in his painful mission life. He crosses rivers all but impassable by making his horse swim the flood, and he was the first priest to visit many parts of Missouri. He will stay at Florissant in a very small house to be put up on the same lot where ours is being built. We are to offer the hospitality of the convent to the Bishop whenever he comes out to visit his farm. His Lordship came to us from St. Charles, where he says we are much regretted and where tears still flow. They are for Mother Eugénie, whom the children loved dearly. The farewells on the river banks were like those made to St. Paul. I fear I gave them pain by arranging that she should be the first to leave, but even on the day before that fixed for our departure, they flocked to the boats, from which they could not be driven. It was the same with the mothers of some, for they would gladly have let their children come to assist us in spite of the national feeling that manual work is for the slaves, but of course we could not accept their offer.

So roughly had the new cabins been put together that no dustpan was needed; as Philippine said, "the sweepings went through the holes in the planks of the floor." The attic above was used as a storeroom; through the wide chinks of the ceiling dried beans and corn fell into the chapel. From an overhanging apple tree ripe fruit fell through the holes in the roof and was stored in the attic.

Classes began. Mathilda Hamilton came to join

the few children who had moved with the nuns from
St. Charles, two or three other new pupils arrived and
the school numbered nine. To-day it seems almost incredible that parents should have been willing to send
their daughters to such surroundings. The reason is
not far to seek. Some shared their Bishop's zeal and
were willing to make any sacrifices for the Christian
education of their little ones. Few were able to send
their children to Europe, not all could pay even the
moderate tuition and board asked by the nuns, and
then it was Mother Duchesne who made the sacrifice
and took these children for little or nothing rather than
refuse those whose parents wanted them at a convent
boarding-school. Many of the children came from
homes where conditions were no less primitive than at
the convents at St. Charles or Florissant; for their
mothers and grandmothers were the women of whom
Richard Elliot wrote: "Neither song nor story has
ever done justice to the women of the frontier. The
great world knows little or nothing of the faithful
pioneer women, but their obscure lives were often full
of what in man would be called heroism." The children of such women as these were glad to lend a helping hand to the nuns. They collected the wood for
the fire, picked wild berries and fruit, gathered nuts in
the hazel thickets, and shucked the corn. To Mother
Audé fell the care of the seven cows and their calves,
which took advantage of the absence of fences and constantly wandered away. Mother Duchesne had more
than one opportunity to put in practice what she had
learned in the infirmaries of Ste. Marie d'en Haut and
the Mother House in Paris, for colds and fever were
prevalent. It was nearly impossible to keep the snow
off the beds in the attic.

Yet Mother Duchesne wrote heroically:

We should do wrong to complain, for Divine Providence has shown Its power in our behalf. A small sack holding twenty or twenty-five pounds of rice lasted us all year, though we often made use of it. We have never had to buy coffee or brown sugar. The apples at St. Charles, which only ripened last year in October, were quite ripe this year at the beginning of August, and for some time they replaced both bread and vegetables without our suffering any harm thereby. We had an abundance of apples some of which we sold for bread. Here fruit and vegetables are no less abundant. We have salted some beef and we get bread from Florissant and meal on six months' credit. The débris of logs have been cut into small pieces for our winter fires. The frequent visits of the Bishop and his missionaries, the constant presence of Father De La Croix and of the pastor, who pays the builders in advance when this is necessary—all show us that we should be both ungrateful and unjust did we fail to trust in God for needs both temporal and spiritual.

A word written to her director, Father Barat, reveals her soul suffering:

I realize that my soul is alone, but I have too little feeling to be afflicted by this. I do not know in what state I am, and though unfaithful, I do not tremble; though impatient I taste but the sweetness of Jesus. I rarely yield to others and yet I am sure of God's love for me. Father Richard does not flatter me, for which I am thankful. My heart seems suspended and devoid of inclination save towards the Hearts of Jesus, Mary and St. Regis.

At about the same time she wrote to Mother Maillucheau:

S.C.J.M.   FLORISSANT, SEPTEMBER 26, 1819.

My dear Mother Thérèse:

We left St. Charles early this month upon the expiration of our lease, which we had no wish to renew as it cost far too dear. The pastor there offered us his house while we had to wait for the completion of our new one here. But before we could decide one way or the other, the Bishop paid us a visit, disapproved of this project, and wished that we come at once to Florissant, not indeed to our convent, but to a tiny house belonging to him. So here we are and shall be for another month, when it is hoped that our brick house will be ready for occupation.

I cannot now write to the nuns and children at Ste. Marie d'en Haut, for we are only camped out and constantly being upset, since a single room serves for parlor, portry, class-room, dormitory, refectory, pupils' infirmary, and we have nine children with us. The other room, a mere garret, is both kitchen and community room. All sleep on the floor and put away their mattress each morning. In this cabin I received a letter addressed to me at "Monseigneur's Chateau!"

Though I am writing only to you, please give my love to the others. Aloysia knows what I feel for her and how I long that her sisters may follow her into religion, above all my little Constance, whom I still seem to see as she walked so solemnly in the lower garden dressed as the religious which she always wanted to be. I give you no details, as I have written all to our Mother General in a sort of journal which she will share with you, as she knows well that our union in the Sacred Heart gives rise to a holy and kind curiosity for all that concerns us. In that lovable Heart I am your old friend and daughter,

PHILIPPINE.

And again:

S.C.J.M.   FLORISSANT, OCTOBER 10, 1819.

Very Reverend Mother:

I am profiting by the return of Father Martial to
give you news. His Lordship has put us in his farmhouse until our new convent is ready, which will be
only in December—a month already filled with loved
memories, since it was then that God brought me back
almost by miracle to that happy solitude where you
adopted me and where to my joy I saw you for the
first time, when together we celebrated the feast of St.
Francis Xavier. He whom we so love will give us
new proof of his interest if in his month we take possession of our convent. It is the first to belong to the
Sacred Heart in the New World. The Bishop will
increase our joy by sending us someone to give us a
retreat and animate us with courage for the work which
is about to increase, for we shall be able to take more
pupils.

On December third, the Trappist builder came to
say Mass, and told the religious that he thought the
new house would be ready for Christmas. There were
other visitors, among them Father Inglesi, who had
been one of the Papal pages present at the coronation
of Napoleon; he was to be the Vicar General of New
Orleans and later one of the founders of the Society
of the Propagation of the Faith. Of Father Dunand,
Mother Duchesne wrote:

This good Father before becoming a Trappist, had
been in the army during the Revolution and deserted
to enter La Trappe. His travels had taken him to
Russia with Father Augustin, his Superior General.
He built in Switzerland a religious house, and in Kentucky another which was destroyed by fire, while illness
put an end to their establishment near Cahokia, his
confrères returned to Europe, leaving him alone in

Missouri. He makes many conversions in the remotest parts of this diocese. In his journeys he has had to defend himself against prairie fires, mountain-lions and serpents; he has seen thunderbolts fall at his side, but his greatest cross is not to have conquered souls. His zeal has made him many an enemy, and he says that our coming has been his only consolation, nevertheless, we give him nothing but trouble. When money is needed to pay a workman, he advances it. This is enough to cause you to pray for him.

Father De La Croix being away on a mission to the Osage Indians, the Bishop brought out to Florissant the Vicar General of St. Louis, a young Lazarist, Venerable Félix De Andreis, who was to keep an eye on the farm and give a retreat to the little community. This venerable servant of God had been on the American Mission for about three years. He, with Father Rosati, his former pupil in the Seminary at Rome, and several other missionaries, had landed in Baltimore in 1816. They floated down the Ohio River in barges, delighting, one of them wrote, "to make the echoes repeat for the first time the sweet Names of Jesus and Mary." They left the Ohio at Louisville, and Father De Andreis went to Bardstown, where for nearly a year he taught theology and studied English at the Seminary of the holy Bishop Flaget. From that saintly prelate, the young missionary learned "tact in dealing with those whose customs were not European," a lesson which was to prove invaluable in the work for which God destined him. This fervent young priest, whose eloquence had thrilled large Roman audiences, and who had seemed so indispensable in the theological college at Rome that it required the intervention of the Pope to have him sent to the American Mission, was now to preach a retreat to the five re-

ligious in the shanty on the knoll at Florissant. In him
Mother Duchesne found the spiritual guide she had
longed for. His burning words inflamed her soul.
They had in common a love for the Indians and a
yearning for the missions of China. He had written
to Italy, "I write to you from the very ends of the
earth, on the banks of the Mississippi, only a few weeks
from the Pacific which separates us from China." His
words consoled her for the year at St. Charles: "Were
they but to save a single soul, to prevent one sin, the
toils, money and trials of a thousand missionaries would
be amply repaid." His doctrine: "God only is great,
and happy is the man that lives but for Him," helped
her in the trials of the farmhouse at Florissant. His
maxim: "We must follow Divine Providence, step by
step, without ever interrupting, anticipating, or de-
serting it," would be her inspiration in the still greater
sufferings to come. "All," says the journal, "were
touched by the solid doctrine and the sanctity of the
director." And he declared this week to have been the
happiest of those he had spent in America.

On the 14th of December, the community of Florissant celebrated at recreation, the anniversary of Mother
Barat's going to Grenoble in 1804. This was their last
little feast on the farm. A week later Mother Duchesne, at the request of Father Dunand, took with
her an orphan, who often acted as interpreter, and went
down to the village. Just then the bell of the little
church of St. Ferdinand rang for Holy Mass; the two
pilgrims needed no other invitation, and went in.
Mother Duchesne's apostolic heart thrilled at the
thought that, on the feast of an apostle, St. Thomas,
they were entering into possession of their new convent, which the kind Trappist builder gave over to her

after Mass. It was a two-story house, built of hand-made brick, and large enough to accommodate about twenty boarders. The community and school were to move on the 23d.

That was a very cold day. Mother Octavie, Sister Lamarre and six of the children started off wrapped in comforters, with stockings over their shoes, so as not to slip on the ice. They were followed by a wagon, which brought most of the earthly goods of the household. Mother Duchesne went back in the cart to get anything that might have been left behind, and to pack the things belonging to the sacristy. That evening another wagon appeared at St. Ferdinand; it brought the rest of the boarding school, escorted by Father De La Croix, who rode one of the farm horses. The next day, Sister Manteau drove over in a cart, bringing the sacristy furnishings and the altar. Mother Eugénie and her valiant Superior walked, driving the cattle or enticing them with an apronful of corn. One obstinate cow, no doubt the same one that had refused to leave St. Charles on that September day, three—was it only three?—months ago, now objected to a two-mile tramp in the snow and on ice. After many desperate efforts to catch the runaway, and after having been themselves caught by every bramble and briar, the two religious ceased their efforts, and the cow returned to the farm. Heavy sleet fell, it was impossible to to see more than a few steps ahead of them. The tracks left by their live-stock were the only clue to where the rough road to the village might lie. Their hands were so cold that the parcels they carried dropped into the snow; the strings broke and the scattered contents could only with difficulty and long patience be picked up by fingers that were almost frozen.

It was late on that Christmas Eve when the five religious were gathered together in St. Ferdinand. They set to work at once, throwing out the wood and other remnants of building material from the room to be prepared for a chapel. It had no door, and sheets were hung up as curtains; the altar was put in its place and decorated. Then they went to Confession, and, in the stillness of midnight, Father De La Croix said Mass and their Lord and Master took up His abode in their midst.

The next day the Bishop arrived. He was glad to find the little community in surroundings better adapted to prayer and to work, and he rejoiced that he had insisted on keeping for this house, and for it alone, the funds that the Superior General had sent him a year before for the use of the religious. Their poverty was evident; the only table they owned was given to the Bishop for his breakfast, and during the meal its legs broke and it fell to the ground. "His Lordship," wrote Philippine, "exhorted the parishioners to contribute to the erection of a parochial school. In the evening he returned to the convent accompanied by Fathers Inglesi, De La Croix and Dunand. The children were all in their uniforms, which are reddish purple with black velvet pipings. They were arranged in a semicircle in the parlor, where they sang of their gratitude in couplets, composed by Mother Octavie."

The good Bishop blessed the house, and then told the religious that Father De La Croix was to be the pastor of Florissant, as the Trappist builder was needed elsewhere, and Father De Andreis had gone back to the Barrens, or Bois Brulé, as Mother Duchesne generally called it. From there the saintly Lazarist was expecting to be sent to the Indians, and he wrote, "Deo Gratias! Alleluia! We are to begin a mission among savages at last." God, however, had other work in store for this zealous apostle.

Pleased with all he had seen at Florissant, Bishop Du Bourg wrote to tell Mother Barat of his plans and hopes for the Society, whose American foundations he now wished to see multiplied. It was hard for him to understand how impossible it was for her to send at once more religious from France. In closing he said: "Mother Duchesne is a saint; Mothers Octavie and Eugénie are angels of perfection." His appreciation of her house must have meant comfort for the poor Superior of Florissant, who was feeling isolation more than ever before in her life. "I have no consolation," she wrote; "my heart longs for support and finds none save in God." She, too, appreciated her little community, her letters ring with their praise. In writing to Mother Barat, she gave frequent bulletins of the progress in virtue of Mothers Eugénie and Octavie; both had needed formation, for when they left France neither had been in the Society for more than three years and a half. Mother Philippine was training them in her own school of heroism. She could not see in herself the substance of the virtue whose shadow she praised in her daughters. Mother Audé had her Superior's active ardor and attraction for self-imposed pain; Mother Berthold unconsciously imitated Mother Duchesne in patience in sufferings. The Sisters tried in vain to rival her in heroic labor for God. None of them prayed as she did. The chapel of Florissant could bear witness to that by night as well as by day.

It was her prayer that brought about an increase in the school in spite of the dire poverty and privation.

Before the altar Philippine grew in the courage, confidence and humility, which her letters allow us to glimpse. To Mother Barat she wrote:

Saints are needed for work among souls so little prepared. I am all the more distressed not to be one. As to Octavie and Eugénie, they are making great strides in the way of perfection and they do the little good that is done. In them you have two future superiors, and if you cannot replace me by an English one, Octavie would do. We shall soon have more Americans than French-speaking Creoles, and what good should I be, as I cannot speak English? I see this already with our postulant. For my own good as that of others, I would be delighted to have the lowest offices in the house.

And again she writes:

One day, when struggling to put a calf in the stable, I thought how better suited I am to such employment than to that of being superior. Ah, if God hearkens to my desires for the good of our mission, assist Him, I beg, by putting someone in my place.

In another letter she says:

Our watchword "God alone!" and "Ita Pater!" have a new meaning in my present situation, when I feel not only that Providence will never abandon me, but almost as if God were close and I could touch Him.

All consolation has gone. My heart yearns for someone to lean on. In my yearning for human comfort I hoped to find it in Monseigneur Flaget, but he did not come. I thought too of Father De Andreis, but he is always ill. I must lean upon God and on Him alone.

Her only consolation was the success of others. She wrote in 1820:

We are persevering in the hope of being well established one day; but now we foresee it only through darkness. We are learning by experience that happiness can be allied to very much pain. We are content with our abode, we have nothing to regret, and we are disposed to remain in peace in the midst of failure; poverty costs us nothing when it affects only ourselves, it is debts that afflict one. An abject, dependent, despised poverty we embrace as being that of Jesus, and as coming from Him. This is the one feeling of all your spiritual daughters in America.

In a letter wishing the saintly Foundress a happy feast, Philippine says:

"When I consider that I belong to the Society my soul seems to dilate; I shed tears of gratitude and see only happiness in our privations. Could God grant me any favor greater than this? There is nothing more to desire save His Cross and martyrdom."

Her confidence had its reward. In May, 1820, there were twenty-one in the boarding school, and Mother Duchesne wrote enthusiastically to her loved Mother General: "We can but admire Divine Providence, for, after several setbacks and light privations, God has found us a house, kept us in good health, established us so that we hope to pay the debts on our building, and provided us with spiritual helps, often in abundance. Say with us then that God is good."

Mother Barat read between the lines of these cheerful letters and answered: "What you have sown in tears will one day be harvested in joy." That day was not yet. The year 1820 ended in suffering. Mother

Octavie's delicate health gave due cause for alarm. Mother Eugénie too fell victim to fever, but recovered in time to care for Mother Duchesne, who was violently attacked by erysipelas and a malignant fever. The remedies given only made her worse; her face was swollen beyond recognition; her headaches were such as to make her delirious. She received the last Sacraments and prepared to meet the God she loved. The Bishop, warned that her life was in danger, went out to Florissant, taking with him his own physician, who, under God, was the cause of her restoration to health. "Monseigneur has ordered me to take care of myself," she wrote, "and I obey him simply."

While Mother Duchesne was still convalescent, she learned of the death of the Venerable Félix de Andreis. He had died on October 18, having fulfilled a long career in the short forty-two years of his life. The community recalled with emotion the evening in the little farmhouse on the knoll, when Bishop Du Bourg said that he liked the hymn that the religious had sung at his Mass; and he asked them to sing it again, that Father De Andreis might hear it. Sister Manteau's good voice was helped by Mother Duchesne and the others. As he listened to the hymn to Our Lady composed by Father Barat, the Lazarist grew pale, then flushed, and seemed to be oblivious of the song and the singers. They were reminded of the picture of St. John of the Cross in an ecstasy brought on by the singing of St. Theresa of Jesus. In Father De Andreis, Mother Duchesne had lost the one in America who best understood her. To the end of her life she treasured an Imitation of Christ which he had used, and which she looked upon as a relic, and in the void that his home-going left, she realized more and more what was meant by his words:

"Love is not satisfied until it measures itself with death."

No sooner was Mother Duchesne fit for work than Mother Octavie fell and broke her leg. Her suffering was great and brought on fever, and, while her Superior was caring for the invalid and replacing her in the school, and doing all her own work besides, a letter from France told Mother Duchesne that her niece, Mother Aloysia Jouve, had died at Ste. Marie d'en Haut on the Feast of St. Agnes. Mother Barat had promised to send this holy young religious to America if only God would see fit to restore her to health. Her mission was ended, however, and although she died in her twenty-fifth year, she has always been looked upon an accomplished type of what a religious of the Sacred Heart ought to be. Hers was "the habit of patience and prayer and endurance, and a holy tenacity of life, with the will to give to God its last drop, its very last flicker for love's sake." The death of this beloved niece was a great grief to Mother Duchesne. She wrote to Mother Thérèse Maillucheau, who had helped her in training Aloysia for God: "It was with tears that I saw the end of this career made perfect in so short a time, while my life, already long, has no real virtue to offer for that Eternity to which I have been so close. How true it is that we carry ourselves about everywhere. One is full of faults overseas as one was at home. I tell St. Francis Regis that he ought to have more spirit of rivalry, so as not to leave me so imperfect when St. Aloysius has made Aloysia so perfect."

St. Francis Regis was the one to whom Mother Duchesne turned in another trial that then came upon them. The workman who helped in the garden fell and dislocated his shoulder. Florissant and its doctor could do nothing to relieve him, and he was suffering intensely. Mother Philippine turned to her saint and began a novena. When the ninth day came, the poor man was suffering more than ever, and it was decided to send him to St. Louis to obtain medical aid. As he climbed into the cart, which was to take him to the city, he stumbled, fell and got up to find that his disjointed arm had been thrown into place. Philippine's prayers had been answered, and she was exultant.

She had long hoped that American postulants would ask admittance into the Society, and she had written to a religious in France: "Pray that God may send us subjects in this country, for if we were always to await them from France, the dangers and expense of the journey and the difficulties that foreigners meet with in bearing this climate would limit us to a small number."

She noted with joy that it was immediately after the deaths of Father De Andreis and Aloysia that American postulants offered themselves. Among the first to arrive was Mary Layton. This young girl came from the very fervent parish of the Barrens; she had had no opportunity of being educated, and delighted to hear of an order devoted to the Sacred Heart, where she might give her "beautiful service and co-operation in a kind of helpfulness other than teaching." Smilingly, in that long winter at Florissant, she drove the cows through snow, ice and rain, and once, at least, she was found in the kitchen cracking and cutting the hard-frozen milk with a hammer and knife.

On St. Cecilia's Day, November 22, 1820, she received the religious habit. Mother Duchesne notes the ceremony in the following words:

On this happy day those of our pupils who have a talent for music sang the Mass very well. The altar was still adorned with the decorations of the preceding day, the Feast of the Presentation in the Temple, on which we had all received Our Lord. We took advantage of this to celebrate in a becoming manner the first clothing that had taken place in Upper Louisiana since the beginning of the world, and great was our joy to see that Sister Layton's courage was an inspiration to others.

Mary Ann Summers came to join her humble labor; and in March, 1821, Emilie St. Cyr, one of the pupils of the boarding school, received the habit. She was then only in her fifteenth year. Eulalie Hamilton also passed straight from the school to the noviceship; and at her clothing took the name of Mother Duchesne's patron, St. Regis. Mother Regis Hamilton was to be her holy Superior's consolation and comfort to the end of her life. Mathilda, Eulalie Hamilton's elder sister, had passed a year at the Sacred Heart as a pupil, had shared the poverty of the log-cabin on the knoll, and had helped in the transfer of the convent to the bed of the Florissant Valley. With the religious, she had made the retreat given by Father De Andreis, and then and there she realized that her vocation was to give up all for Christ. She returned to her family at Kaskaskia, intending to bid them good-bye. A love of pleasure held her back, and she was on the point of embarking on a trip to Europe when her god-father, Father Dunand, went to Kaskaskia, reminded her of her high resolution, and persuaded her family to allow her to follow her younger sister into the novitiate. He accompanied her to Florissant. He described this visit in a letter to Father Rosati: "We arrived at the house of the Religious of the Sacred Heart on Thursday at half-past one in the afternoon. The welcome given my good daughter was a joyous one. Her pious sister had received the habit the day before. Mathilda is getting on famously. Madame Duchesne is very well pleased with her. I hope with the help of your holy prayers we shall have the happiness of seeing her persevere."

This postulant had a remarkable devotion and a certain resemblance to St. Francis Xavier, and Mother Duchesne gave her, at her clothing, the name dear to both of them, Xavier. These young women were types, not exceptions, for Father De Andreis had said of those whom he met in St. Louis and at the Barrens: "The young girls especially delight me by their candor and simplicity. They are lilies of purity, angels in human form, and their piety will do much good among the rising generation." Mother Duchesne was beginning to see that much of the impiety and apparent tepidity which had at first been such a shock to her zeal was due to the fact that villages and towns had been without priests for months and years at a time. The Christians of one of the isles of Japan, after their conversion by St. Xavier, did not see a priest for three hundred years, yet they kept the fire of faith burning—but they were the rare exception and not the rule. The signatures of the beadle and verger and sacristan, replacing that of the priest in the Baptismal and Burial Registers of both St. Charles and Florissant, show that in missionary countries, the title of resident pastor is little more than a name for a priest whose parish covers a thousand square miles and cannot often be found in any one place. The New World, Mother Duchesne saw, was not a barren desert, but a virgin forest or a field white for the harvest. Of the people she now wrote:

"When they are Catholics, they are more pious than we are, and more constant in their resolutions." She was beginning to acquire a better realization of American conditions and ways. It was in her fiftieth year that she came to the missions, and she probably never attained, in its perfection, "the tact in dealing with those whose customs are not European," the science which Bishop Flaget had taught the young missionary, Father De Andreis. This was to her a source of humiliation, and from the world's point of view the cause of her non-success. That she was learning new ways is evident, however, for she saw the necessity of shortening the hours in the parish school of Florissant. She had been accustomed in Europe to have the children come for Mass, and to keep them until well towards evening. Now she found that the distances between their homes and the school, and their objection to spending long hours in learning to sew and to embroider, made this impossible, and she wrote to the Mother General that, with another mistress they would be able to have an early dismissal.

Bishop Du Bourg now decided to build a new church at St. Ferdinand. It was to be next to the convent, in fact it was to adjoin it, so that from their cloister the religious would be able to follow the services. Philippine wrote on October 20, 1820:

Father De La Croix says his Mass in the parish church twice a week and the other five days in our chapel. We shall have daily Mass when they build a new church on the lot which adjoins ours and which belongs to the Bishop. Our chapel will then be like that of Grenoble—a choir looking into the sanctuary, and we shall profit by all the religious services in the parish, since priests are so few. . . . I should indeed

regret to die before having built in this country a public
oratory dedicated to the Sacred Heart, so I am hoping
to have such a shrine in the church opposite our choir.
I spoke of this to the Bishop, who has decided to dedicate the church itself to the Sacred Heart, to make St.
Ferdinand only the second patron, to have also a Lady
chapel and a shrine to St. Regis in an angle of our
part of the church for which I had asked. We shall
arrange suitably for our relics, we have four of the
True Cross and two sacred thorns. Thus we shall be
devoutly situated and it will be our own fault if we
are not fervent.

Mother Duchesne presented the cornerstone, which
was laid in February, 1821. In the stone was placed
a bottle containing a parchment with the following inscription in Latin: "On this February 19, 1821, I,
Charles De La Croix, by permission of the Right Reverend Bishop, Valentine Louis Du Bourg, laid the
cornerstone of this church, dedicated to the Sacred
Heart of Jesus, under the invocation of St. Ferdinand
and St. Francis Regis; Madame Duchesne, Superior,
having donated the said cornerstone, Madame Octavie
Berthold and Madame Eugénie Audé being present,
as also the pupils and many persons from the village."
The dedication of this church to the Sacred Heart
gave great joy to the religious. It was the first church
west of the Mississippi to be thus dedicated, and they
probably recalled Mother Barat's parting words: "If
you only establish one new tabernacle in Louisiana,
ought you not to consider yourselves greatly blest?"
At times these words seemed a warning; the school was
not prospering; of the twenty boarders very few paid
anything at all. The poverty became almost penury;
at one time there were not seven cents in the house.

The work in the apostolate too was discouraging. The missionaries were too humble to be even tempted by the thought: "To what purpose is this waste?" but the trial that had come to her Lord may at times have visited Mother Duchesne: *"Quae utilitas in sanguine meo?"* "Of what use is my blood?" She may have felt this; there is no proof that she did. On the contrary, her letters then show that her prayer in suffering must have been that of St. Francis Xavier: "Yet more." Her brother, who had heard how things stood at Florissant, sent word that he would supply the wherewithal for her return journey to France. She wrote to her sister, and her words sound like the battle-cry of the knight of Dauphiny, who knew neither reproach nor fear: "Tell him," she said, "to pay with that sum the passage of two more religious coming from France to America."

At that very time, Mother Barat was actually planning to send two or three more religious to Louisiana and Missouri. They were sorely needed, for a new foundation was about to be made. In his pastoral visits to Lower Louisiana, Bishop Du Bourg had gone to the Opelousas, a settlement about one hundred and fifty miles northwest of New Orleans. There, Mrs. Charles Smith called on him. She was a convert and the widow of a fervent and generous Catholic who had come from Maryland in 1805. Their only desire had been to build a church and a school at Grand Côteau, a hamlet situated about twelve miles from Opelousas. Bishop Du Bourg accepted her generous offer of land and of her house, which they decided would be used for a convent boarding school, where the benefactress would be able to live. He spoke of the Society of the Sacred Heart, and Mrs. Smith promised to furnish the house and to pay the travelling expenses of two religious if they would come from St. Louis at once.

When he returned to his episcopal city, the Bishop went out to see Mother Duchesne, who accepted the proposal, feeling sure that the Mother General would approve, as she was sending some nuns from France in the hope of a new American foundation. In the course of time the letter of approval arrived from the Mother House. Mother Duchesne had written to the saintly Foundress, "God made Eugénie to be a Superior." And so to Mother Audé was entrusted the care of this new foundation. It was characteristic of Mother Duchesne to offer the best that she had. Mother Audé was much loved by the children, her pleasing manner had won the parents' appreciation, and of the little community at Florissant she was the one on whom the Superior relied most. Sister Mary Layton was chosen to accompany Mother Audé; they would be alone at Grand Côteau until the arrival of the little colony expected from France. At seven o'clock in the morning of August 5, 1821, they set out for Louisiana.

Mother Duchesne felt this separation most keenly. In these three years she had been called upon to leave St. Louis where she had thought to succeed; to abandon St. Charles where she felt she had failed; to give to God Aloysia Jouve whom she loved, and Father De Andreis on whom her strong soul might have leaned. Furthermore she offered for the foundation of Grand Côteau the Mother and Sister who had been her most capable aids. Her great soul had grown greater in sacrifice, and she wrote to Mother Barat, "As for me, put me where you wish, all my desires save that of doing God's will are extinguished."

CHAPTER II

The Compassion of an Apostle

CHAPTER II

The Compassion of an Apostle—1821-1824

"Measure thy life by loss and not by gain,
Not by the wine drunk but by the wine poured out,
For love's strength standeth in love's sacrifice,
And he who hath suffered most hath most to give."

HARRIET ELEANOR KING.

The scholastic year of 1820-1821 closed in August, and in September classes began again. The new colony of religious from France had not arrived; they had not even sailed. These long delays were among Mother Duchesne's severest trials. She was slow to take advantage of the extraordinary permission given her to act with less dependence on the Mother House than did the convents of Europe. If she wrote to France to ask counsel or to beg for help, she knew that, even were the letter to be answered by return of post, she would get no reply for four or five long months. So expensive was the postage that parcels and even important letters were often held over until there was an opportunity of sending them by hand. The saintly Mother Foundress was far from being indifferent to the need for laborers in the American vineyard, but she was hard pressed for help at home, as her letters testify. In March she said, "More than a month ago I wrote to you, and did not expect to do so again until the departure of our travellers, but I am obliged, for reasons too numerous to men-

231

tion, to delay their going until the end of August, despite our desire to send you help. Your last letter, dated October, tells us of your illness and recovery. We should have been anxious had we known only of the first."

Among the reasons for delay to which Mother Barat alludes was the great poverty of the Mother House. A beggar refused the black bread given him at the door, until he was told that only the children of the boarding-school fared better. He opened eyes and mouth in surprise, took what was offered him and slunk off abashed.

Another reason for Mother Barat's hesitation in sending reinforcements was her fear that foundations in small villages would not succeed. When she had heard that her religious had been sent to St. Charles, she had written to Mother Duchesne:

"I am astonished that our friends have sent you to St. Charles instead of keeping you in St. Louis which seemed destined for you. I fear that set aside in a village you will languish slowly and that the school you will found will offer no hope for the future." And again a little later: "We cannot help regretting that His Lordship, the Bishop, has placed you in a spot so unsuited to the end proposed." When she heard of the transfer to St. Ferdinand's she wrote: "Why do you leave one village for another, and go to such expense for a foundation that can never succeed? Why does your good Bishop not put you in St. Louis itself? Even if you were to have there only a hole, the hope of soon hearing that you were well established would encourage me to send you some religious. As it is, I am waiting to see how things will turn out."

August, 1823, came and went and the nuns had not

left Paris. Again Mother Barat wrote to Florissant: "My brother will have told you the cause of our delay in sending reinforcements. Death is reaping on all sides; we scarcely have time to form subjects to replace the dying." So Mother Duchesne possessed her soul in patience and the work went on at Florissant. At last, the weekly post brought a longed-for letter from Mother Audé, and Philippine's heart went out to her in her new mission.

The travellers had left the Mississippi steamboat at Plaquemines, where they lodged in an inn, the walls of which were tapestried with spider-webs. An ox-cart took them to the Attakapas, whose bayous they traversed in a flat-boat.

Then leaving the bayous they drove out of the cypress forest into the open. They were on the edge of a vast prairie, its long grass undulating like the waves of the sea, its broad expanse dotted here and there by islands, clumps of trees, live-oaks, firs, locusts and figs. Grand Côteau is a ridge some twenty-five feet above the swamp land; on that plateau, in a clump of trees, was the house that Mrs. Smith had given the Society.

The log-house, Mother Audé wrote, was fifty-five feet square, well painted inside and out; the two or three one-story buildings behind it would serve for the kitchen, infirmary and refectory. Wolves prowled about at night, so that the religious and children would have to avoid going from one part of the convent to the other after sunset. Mrs. Smith wanted the religious to delay taking possession until some furniture should come, but Mother Audé had thought it better to move in on the day after their arrival in Grand Côteau, so she and Sister Layton had been there since August 28. In spite of Mrs. Smith's kindness and good will there were countless privations and there was everything to be done before the opening of school.

Mother Duchesne, in her compassionate love for Mother Audé, had sent to Côteau whatever she could possibly do without, and now Florissant was in need. The Ursulines of New Orleans again came to the rescue. There is a quaint note in the journal of the Convent of the Sacred Heart, St. Ferdinand, in 1821:

> Presents received from the Ursulines of New Orleans:
> A barrel of sugar for the third time,
> A barrel of rice for the second time,
> A case of cod for the third time,
> Two boxes of raisins for the third time,
> A case of preserves for the second time.

> We have also received from M. Chénier, during the past month, a large green cover for M. Leduc's piano, and some white wine for Mass.

Bishop Du Bourg's most cherished dream was to make of Florissant a missionary centre. There he sent his worn-out priests for a rest, and Mother Duchesne was not only the provider of food and drink, but often the doctor and the dispenser of remedies. To St. Ferdinand, too, came the priests from the outposts of the diocese on their way to and from St. Louis, where they had gone to visit their Bishop. No matter when they appeared, Mother Duchesne had a meal to offer; it might be frugal indeed, but it was far better than what she kept for herself. One day, just as Mgr. Du Bourg and some priests were leaving the convent, the Bishop espied on a bench in the corner some remnants of food. He asked what this meant, and had to be told that those leavings were to be the meal of the religious when their guests should have gone.

In giving an account of her spendings Mother Duchesne wrote to the Mother House: "Without doubt constant visitors cause expenditure of money and time and a loss of regularity. I am consoled for this only because these poor priests, worn out with work, find a little country air at Florissant where we make them at home. Besides, this is a part of my vocation; as I said to you before I left France, 'Even though I should do nothing but cook for priests, I shall be glad.' "

The Bishop delighted in calling attention to Mother Duchesne's virtue, even at the expense of her feelings. She slept in the parlor, and her poor mattress and the one cover she allowed herself all through the year were kept in a cupboard, or rather a curtained niche. One day, during Monseigneur's visit, the mattress and coverlet fell into the room, and His Lordship pointing to it said to his priests: "Behold the bed of a valiant woman." Mother Duchesne's choice of this sleeping-place was due partly to the lack of room, for when there were twenty boarders, several orphans and a growing novitiate, the little house was quite full; but its chief cause was her love for vigils. By sleeping downstairs she could spend long hours in the tiny chapel, and later on in the doorway leading into the sanctuary of St. Ferdinand's church. One who was parish priest there for several years declared that he never went to get the Blessed Sacrament at night without finding Mother Duchesne in her favorite haunt. It was thus that she won the grace of vocation for many. Her parting words to the Mother General, "I would rather die than fail to train for you religious worthy of you and of the Society," were the keynote of the training she gave in the noviceship. She asked much, very much, of others, but it was nothing compared to what she exacted of herself. If the community were poorly nourished, *her* only food was the scraps she could collect from the plates of the children. If the nuns had no cells and no privacy, *she* camped out in the parlor; if they had sacrificed the luxury of a second habit so that the cloth might be made into a cassock, *her* one habit was so patched and re-patched that it resembled a sack. The last thing at night she went round to see that all were taking the rest allowed by the rule, then she either crept to her place in the chapel or to the opening looking into the church, or she climbed the stairs to the attic to mend the stockings which she had collected in making the tour of the children's dormitory. Her complete abnegation won her the admiration of the clergy who were glad to give into her keeping the young girls they directed.

Father Dunand had recognized in several members of the fervent parish of the Barrens the signs of a religious vocation and spoke of these young girls to Mother Duchesne. On June 1, 1821, he wrote to Father Rosati: "I have written to Miss Manning to have her come to the convent. I hope she will do well here and form herself easily to the religious life. Miss Celeste Moor has also some desire of coming, but not knowing her character, I have spoken to her about the matter only slightly. She will do well to write to Madame Duchesne and to tell her all her interior dispositions, so that Madame may ascertain whether she is called to this kind of life." A little later he wrote again: "I have spoken to Mr. Moor in regard to his Miss; he ought to bring her here the first opportunity." Until his return to France, Father Dunand continued to encourage young women from the Barrens to enter at Florissant.

Father De La Croix was also able to appreciate Mother Duchesne, whose interest and prayers followed

him in his missions to the Osages; she provided silk for
a banner and taught the children how to embroider it,
and then gave it to the missionary to use for the May
devotions in the Indian village to which he was going.
While he was away on one of these trips, he was replaced at St. Ferdinand by Father Andrew Ferrari,
one of the Italian missionaries who had come over with
Fathers De Andreis, Rosati and Acquaroni. The fervor of this young priest appealed strongly to Florissant,
and of his sojourning there Father Dunand wrote to
Father Rosati: "He has been the consolation of the
religious, and they, as well as the entire parish, would
like to keep him."

It was in 1821 that the Confraternity of the Sacred
Heart was organized in the parish of St. Ferdinand
"under the auspices and by the authority of His Lordship, the Bishop." The old parish register records the
object and aim of the Confraternity as well as its regulations and rules, and the entry is in the handwriting of
the sacristan, Philippine Duchesne. She must have
noticed and loved the similarity between the purpose of
this association and that of the Society to which she
belonged. Both have as end "the glory of the Sacred
Heart of Jesus and the honor of the Blessed Virgin
Mary, the sanctification of its members and the propagation of the faith by the education of youth." Among
the spiritual exercises prescribed for those forming part
of the parochial congregation at Florissant was one
hour's adoration each year in the church of St. Ferdinand. The record contains the following data:

Charles De La Croix, on the great Feast of the Sacred
    Heart, from two o'clock until three.
Rev. Aristide Anduze, Pentecost Sunday, from four
    o'clock until five.

Emily Pratte, on the great Feast of the Sacred Heart, from three o'clock until four.

Emilie Chouteau, Good Friday, from two o'clock until three.

Jane Chambers, the 15th of August, from two o'clock until three.

Pélagie Chouteau, at Easter, from four o'clock until five.

Theresa Pratte, Holy Thursday, from three o'clock until four.

Louise Chénier, the 15th of August, from four o'clock until five.

Patrick McDowell, the 15th of August, from two o'clock until three.

Virginie Labbadie, the 24th of December, from four o'clock until five.

Among the names of this Confraternity occur those of: James Cummins, Hugh O'Neil, Mary McManus, Betty Miles, Lisette Clemens, etc.

The annual fee of one gourde (the Franco-American name for a dollar)˜ was used to buy books, paper and prizes for the Sunday school which was the chief work of the Confraternity. Every Sunday the teachers collected the children and brought them to the church. After Mass there were classes for two hours in the morning, and as many again in the afternoon. The pastor was the president of the Sunday school, he chose the teachers, fined them if they absented themselves without due warning, and punished the more serious faults in the children.

It seems unlikely that the religious had any part in the Sunday school, although they shared in many an enterprise of the parish. On November 21, 1821, several Masses were said in the convent chapel. The clergy then met in the parlor and in procession entered

the church which was blessed by Father De La Croix.
A High Mass was sung by Father Neil, the President
of the College of St. Louis, an institution which had
evolved from the Latin Academy started in 1818. After the last Mass the priests returned to the convent
for breakfast.

In some letters written during these first years
Mother Duchesne gives an account of the Missouri mis-
sion. One is directed to "my dear Sisters Aloysia,
Louise de Rambo, Josephine de Coriolis, Louise de
Vidaud, Julie Dussausois."

I have just received a letter by a steamboat long
delayed by ice in the Mississippi. I write to all col-
lectively in fulfilment of a promise. Do you remember
when we used to read letters from missionaries how we
longed to follow them and you made me promise that if
ever I went to the missions I should send you an account of them? It is time to keep my promise.

Louisiana has no large city except New Orleans.
Much of the country is fertile but uncultivated, However, it is being colonized by Spaniards, French and
Americans—the last name is that given to the subjects
of the United States. The climate of New Orleans and
its environs is less healthful than that of the country further north. St. Louis is the largest town of Missouri,
which is still only a territory. The passion for travelling is remarkable, especially among the youth of this
land. Some go as far as Philadelphia on business and
bring back all kinds of luxuries so that the poor people
here often seem to have more than have our pupils in
France—even those in the easiest circumstances.

I have been told that there is in this country a soil
which has all the properties of soap and is used as such
by the savages who wash and massage themselves with
it and exchange it for gunpowder, necklaces, blankets,
etc. Every householder here makes his own soap from

ashes steeped for several days in water and then slowly filtered, then they mix it with oil and boil it for several days and at the end they have a red and very good soap. Candles too are home-made and are used in church, for they cost less than would those made from yellow wax, which is easily procured here but is never refined.

The woods between St. Charles and Florissant are filled with trees which they tap for sugar, used as much as is that obtained from cane—most of these sugar trees are maples. There is also much honey in the wild nut trees, the nuts cannot be eaten as the shell is too hard. There are wild grape vines the fruit of which would make fairly good wine could it be picked, but the vines wind about tall trees to an inaccessible height. The fruit of the plaquemine or date-plum is nicer than that of our medlar tree, and is also eaten when over-ripe, so too is the papaw—a cucumber-shaped fruit with meat like that of the fig. You have seen the pecan, the national nut which is very much liked but never used to make oil.

There are very fine horses and these are more numerous than are the men who never go the least distance except on horseback. On Sunday the church is surrounded by horses, giving it the appearance of a horse fair. Cows wander about everywhere but come home night and morning. The oxen and horses also come home regularly, being enticed thither by salt and Indian corn. When they stray, men ride through the woods in search of them. It is often difficult to yoke oxen accustomed to freedom, so, to save time and trouble, they are left yoked together day and night for several months. To my mind the roe-deer is the prettiest animal to be seen in this country, it has a beautiful head and is so affectionate that when we approach it comes up to kiss us, it is as mild as a lamb and is easily tamed.

As to plants and grains the most common is Indian corn, from which bread is made. We often eat this sort of bread which many Americans prefer to that made from wheat, which grain also grows abundantly here.

There are beans, pumpkins, canteloupe, and water-melons. Potatoes are much in use; there are white, red, yellow and bluish or purple ones, and sweet ones that taste just like chestnuts which are not known here—but this kind does not keep. Lentils are unknown, rice comes from Louisiana and is expensive. The woods furnish besides the fruits named, many mulberries that are eaten with sugar like strawberries, which here grow wild, as does a small fruit having rather the shape and taste of a lemon; it is called citron in English. One finds everywhere a herb called belldame, prepared as is spin-ach, which it resembles in taste. Maize or Indian corn is eaten on the cob while it is tender.

This, my dear Sisters, is what has impressed me in the products of this country. My letter has often been interrupted for the love of God. May we have the happiness of making Him loved and of loving Him our-selves with an effective and generous love. I am in the Sacred Heart,

Your sister,

PHILIPPINE DUCHESNE.

In another letter she shows her interest in the good done by others:

My dear Mother and Sisters:

I often long to be with you to profit by your holy recreations. I should want to be only a listener, but you would say: "It is for you to do the talking, for you have crossed the sea and can tell us many a tale." But I am quite rusty, and without wanting to displease you, I should often be silent. While awaiting that meeting which I trust will be one day in Heaven I have put together some incidents to buy your prayers in return. What pleases us most is the deputation sent by the Osage Indians to Bishop Du Bourg. The chief came to St. Louis to ask Monseigneur to visit his tribe. His Lordship will go there next month with some traders from Missouri who have promised to help him in every possible way to win respect for his sacred character. These traders will prepare the way for him as did the Portuguese merchants for St. Francis Xavier. The Bishop gave the Indian chief a crucifix which he took with respect. Later when he entered one of the stores in St. Louis the shopkeeper, anxious to see if the crucifix were valued, offered to give in exchange a fine saddle, then liquor and finally a large sum of money. Each time the chief refused, saying that never would he give away what he had received from the "one who speaks to the Author of Life."

Yesterday we entertained at supper the two directors of the Seminary of St. Lazare at Bois Brulé or the Barrens. They are also parish priests of the primitive church there. There are about sixty communions on Sunday and about twenty on Saturdays and often more men than women in church. There are in the parish only eight persons who are not at least monthly communicants. If any one finds a coat or a cloak he hangs it on a tree near the church that the loser may claim it without delay, and if not claimed by the owner it is likely to stay there a month without being touched.

The Bishop has given me details of the foundation of the Sisters of Charity made by Mrs. Seton near Baltimore. He directed to New York this widow who had three daughters and no fortune. She told him that often after Holy Communion she felt the inspiration to found an educational establishment for young girls, and she followed him to Baltimore in the hope of succeeding there. One day she went to him and said: "You refused to found this school because of the lack of means, but after Communion I was told that Mr. X. would give $6,000 for such a good work. You must ask this of him." On the very day on which she visited the Bishop Mr. X called upon him and offered $6,000 for the establishment of a school. His Lordship refused to accept it at once, but the appointed delay having elapsed without the gentleman changing his mind the convent was built. It now houses fifty nuns and novices and sixty children. The religious have taken the rules of the Sisters of Charity and a habit something like ours. Mr. M., who has seen them, says that they are very capable women. Every year they are able to save a certain sum so that now they can add new buildings and they have founded houses in Philadelphia, New York and in Kentucky, where they have done much good.

There are very few priests in the dioceses of New York and Boston, in which respect Mgr. Du Bourg is the richest of all the Bishops in the States. He will soon have ten Lazarist priests and several brothers. The Lazarists have recruited their ranks from a Milanese society of Brothers. There are more than forty priests in this diocese, while in Canada there are over two hundred, also five or six well-established convents and a fine seminary. The British Government protects our holy faith in that land where the governor and army attend religious processions. A Methodist minister wished in good faith to win over some Catholics, and thought it best to begin with the Seminary. As a result he was converted to our holy religion, of which he had been in complete ignorance.

Father Anduze has spoken often to me of Father Barat, in whose school he was for eighteen months at Bordeaux. This young priest is very talented and teaches in the College of St. Louis. In Kentucky there are three or four convents of the Sisters of Charity and a Trappist monastery. In one of the convents they were so poor that there was nothing to eat. One day when the Sisters according to their custom had gone to cut wood a beautiful roe-deer came up to them, and allowed itself to be caught; it was killed and supplied them with meat for some time.

Bishop Flaget has lost three of his missionaries who returned to Europe, one was the founder of the Daughters of Penitence and a saint. We have four children from Prairie de Chien, a month's journey from here. That is where the Councils between the Indians and the representatives of the Government are most often held. They carpet the place of assembly with beaver skins. The most skilful Indian is the speaker and always begins: "The Author of Life has made all things and He has made the earth for all men to enjoy." He concludes with a request for liquor, gunpowder and bread.

Letters from Grand Côteau told Mother Duchesne that in spite of Mrs. Smith's good will and charity, privation was the order of the day. Mother Audé had been very ill, and had recovered so suddenly that she felt sure she had been favored by a miracle. Mass and Communion were often wanting, as the chaplain had gone, and the nearest parish was that of Opelousas, twelve miles away. School had opened with but five children, one of them, Mrs. Smith's niece, was a Protestant; but her aunt's piety and what the child had seen at the convent were having their effect, and she now longed to be received into the Church. A little cabin was built for the poorer children of the countryside. Mother Duchesne longed to go to Côteau, but she could not leave Florissant, where Mother Audé's place in the boarding school had not yet been filled.

At last the good news reached Mother Duchesne that two religious were about to leave France for America. They knew well what was in store for them, for one of the first colony had written to the Mother House: "Give them a true picture of our position. We enjoy every inconvenience in lodging, our food is often meagre and poor, the cold is rigorous and the heat excessive. We possess God alone and desire only His glory!" Mother Lucille Mathevon had been one of Mother Duchesne's pupils at Ste. Marie d'en Haut. She was

not unworthy of such a guide; they had in common untiring devotedness, unflinching courage, unflagging zeal.
Her faithful and generous service in France had won
for her Mother Barat's unstinted praise. The other
missionary, Mother Xavier Murphy, was Irish; she had
been educated by the Ursulines of Black Rock, and
Mother Barat felt that her knowledge of English and
French, her generosity, and her charming and lovable
character would make her a true missionary.

It was Mgr. Du Bourg's custom to visit New Orleans and the scattered parishes of Louisiana each year,
and he was at the Crescent City when, on February 2,
1822, the two religious landed in America. They enjoyed for several days the kind hospitality of the Ursuline convent in New Orleans, after which Mother Murphy left with two American postulants for Grand
Côteau, and some weeks later Mother Mathevon, under
the fatherly protection of the Bishop, made the long
journey up the Mississippi, arriving at Florissant on
Low Sunday. She had had ample time to ponder at
leisure Mother Barat's words to her: "My child, I have
always wanted to extend the Kingdom of Christ among
infidels and to teach them to love God. That does not
now seem to be in the designs of Providence for me.
I send you, dear Lucille, in my place. Be always entirely devoted to your mission." To take the place of a
saint was a high calling indeed, and Mother Mathevon
was to prove herself not unworthy. However, she was
to have twenty years more of waiting before being sent
to the Indians—the infidels of whom Mother Barat had
spoken.

The meeting of Mother Duchesne and her loved
child and novice was a great joy to both. Mother
Mathevon had much to say of the wonders that had been

wrought at the tomb of Mother Aloysia Jouve, of the conversion of the brother of this holy young religious, and of the entrance into religion of her sister, Amélie, to whom Aloysia had said: "You will replace me." Yet, even this meeting held disappointment for Mother Duchesne; she had asked the Mother General to send someone to take her place as Superior and she was certain that it was for this that Mother Lucille had been sent. To her dismay she learned that not only was she to continue to govern Florissant, but she was also to have Grand Côteau in her keeping.

It was the house of Louisiana that was giving her most anxiety just then. The very foundation had been threatened by the kind benefactress herself. Mrs. Smith had misunderstood the willing consent of Mother Duchesne to her spending the rest of her life in the house which she had given the Society. The good lady thought that she would be allowed to join in the exercises of the community without, however, binding herself either by vows or rule. Mother Audé had met this difficulty with firmness, saying that the religious would have to return to Florissant and to abandon the foundation if this were to be one of the conditions of accepting the benefactress' gift. At length Mrs. Smith yielded her point and Côteau was saved for the Society; but it was now menaced by another great obstacle. The isolation of the house made its inmates depend almost entirely on a resident chaplain for spiritual help. On the Feast of Corpus Christi they not only had Mass and Holy Communion, but a procession of the Blessed Sacrament in the wood behind the house. Ten days later, however, their chaplain, Father Jeanjean, embarked for France on business, and only occasionally could the pastor of Opelousas come the twelve miles for

Mass. Mother Audé was breaking under the strain of anxiety and work, and Mother Duchesne's compassionate heart could know no rest until she had given to Côteau all she could spare.

In July she left for the South, taking Mother St. Cyr, who had just made her vows, and a novice, as reinforcements for Côteau. Mrs. Pratte allowed her daughter, Theresa, to accompany the religious. The young girl would thus have a chance to see her loved Mother Audé and she would be Mother Duchesne's travelling companion on the return journey. The night in St. Louis was spent either with the Prattes or the Chouteaus, as both homes were always open to Mother Duchesne and her nuns, who could never be too grateful for the generous hospitality received whenever there was question of visiting the city. Mrs. Chouteau, knowing Mother Duchesne's love of solitude and mortification, would have sent the meals to the room occupied by the religious, but the Venerable Mother, fearing to give trouble, refused the kind offer and did her best to make herself at home at a sumptuous table. The travellers found that the new cathedral of brick was now in use. The unfinished interior was adorned with old masters which were the pride of St. Louis; the church itself was the boast of many citizens, but to those who had seen the cathedrals and minsters of Europe, the long narrow brick building resembled a "bowling alley." On the 20th of July the four travellers left St. Louis. The perils of a journey up the Mississippi were light when compared to those of a voyage down the river. So strong was the current at times that a boat was in constant danger of being stranded on a sandbar or hurled against the bank or against a rock in one of the sudden turns. Steam was still a novelty and not always managed. In consequence, there were explosions to which the accumulated wreckage of boats could bear witness. "Sugar Island" won its name from the boat-loads of sugar cast on its shore. To Mother St. Cyr, to the novice and the child this voyage was no less novel than terrifying. Mother Duchesne had outlived the age that finds delight in excitement afforded by danger. To her the voyage was the necessary means to an end. At Herculaneum, a tiny village not very far from St. Louis, the boat stopped to take on a load of lead from the famous mines of Missouri. As this would need some time, the religious disembarked and walked along the bank of the river. Two little girls and their father came up to speak to the travellers, and Mother Duchesne found out that the strangers were Catholics, but that the younger child was still unbaptized. At the desire of the father, she went back to the boat to get one of the three priests who were on their way South. There on the banks of the great river the child was baptized; Theresa Pratte adopted her as her god-child, and the missionary promised to put Herculaneum on his itinerary of annual visits to out-of-the-way stations.

On the 22nd the boat stopped at St. Genevieve. The religious heard Mass in the little church and offered their Holy Communion for the intention of their Mother Foundress, whose feast day it was. Just then Mother Xavier Murphy was writing in Côteau's journal which had been entrusted to her: "Sweet feast of *Notre Chère Mère Barat*. No Mass." To the end of her life she quaintly mingled French and English in her letters and notes; her spelling, constructions and idioms are those of the "language of the heart," as French has been called.

At Natchez the travellers disembarked and made
their way to the church. They found it to be a Presby-
terian house of worship beside which the small wooden
Catholic chapel seemed poor indeed. The young Flemish pastor was most kind to the visiting priests and
religious and all could share his sorrow in the little good
he seemed to be doing in Natchez.

The days between these disembarkations were passed
in prayer, in study and in watching the panorama on
the great moving river. The cumbrous "broadhorns" or
boats lashed together floated down on the current; keel
boats on the other hand were cordelled up the stream.
Swerving from their course they entered the bayou of
Plaquemine. There the travellers spent a week in the
inn described by Mother Audé, for their steamer needed
refitting before it could continue its journey through
the large bayous. The water was so low in that season
of drought that the steamer was abandoned for a flat
boat, even before they had crossed the larger bayous.
Yet, so shallow was the water that the boatmen were
soon wearied with rowing. Mother Duchesne wanted to
relieve them by walking for a time; but this was an
impossibility as the borders of the brackish streams and
stagnant pools were slimy marshes in which the oxen
sank deep at each step. The black, fetid waters could
hardly reflect the ghostly cypresses, many over a hundred feet high. These trees were draped with dark
streamers of moss, some twenty yards long. They
seemed in mourning for their leaves, for even the hardy
foliage of the cypress, like fringes of green silk, cannot
long survive, once the ravenous Spanish Beard moss has
entwined itself in the branches. As the voyagers went
on, they saw the green trunks of grape-vines which,
writhing upwards, clung like huge serpents to the limbs

of the trees. The waters of the bayous showed now black, now green, now yellow with the sap of decaying foliage, now radiantly pink, and golden and white, with water lilies. The noisy ouerang, or deep-throated bull-frog, croaked in the swamps; screech-owls called to one another from the tree-tops; and far-off and indistinctly could be heard "the whoop of the crane and the roar of the grim alligator." Night came on suddenly as it always does in the southland and Mother Duchesne was sure that they were lost in the primeval forest. She said to one of the four boatmen: "I think you have lost your way; wouldn't it be more prudent to turn back to the nearest place where we could land?" Though he seemed somewhat disturbed, he answered that he had not lost his way. Just then cries rang out over the waters. Mother Duchesne was so frightened that she thought they were being pursued. She did not dream that fear had robbed her of even the sense of direction. Suddenly a canoe swept upon their view. Half-naked Indians and negroes plied the oars and swiftly bore down on the party of eight in the flatboat. The pale-faced boatmen turned paler. Mother Duchesne promised to have nine Masses said in thanksgiving if they should be spared by "the cannibals"; she encouraged her companions by saying, "We have but one thing to do, and that is to pray to God, and to place ourselves under the protection of the Blessed Virgin." The canoe reached the barge. The Indians stared at the religious and looked curiously at their water-bottles; then the bark darted away, disappearing as swiftly as it had come. Suddenly dry land was seen and a friendly voice called from the shore, where an ox-cart awaited them. The travellers were not lost after all; the boatmen *had* known the way, and the "cannibals" had been well-

THE CONVENT IN ST. CHARLES AT THE TIME OF MOTHER DUCHESNE'S DEATH

meaning negroes and Indians who had been asked by the wagoner to tell the travellers from the North where he awaited them. The tired religious climbed into the wagon with its double yoke of oxen, whose great round eyes flashed back the light of the lantern. Even the names of these animals were not lost on Mother Duchesne, so often were Flambeau, Rousseau, Gaillard and Tout Blanc loudly exhorted to hasten their way through the swampland. A few hours of that night were passed in an inn. At two in the morning, the journey began again, for oxen, like Missouri cows, are averse to travel in the heat of the noonday, and they still had a seven hours' walk before them. They left the bayous and marshland behind them, and came out on the plain. In the cotton-fields little black children were gathering the snowy fluff from the bushes, their gay sunbonnets and bandannas looking like blossoms. At last, the ox driver pointed out a clump of trees as the orchard behind the convent. The hedgerows were bright with the violet clusters of the Spanish berry, the mockingbirds' favorite fare, and sweet with honeysuckle and jasmine. Quivering humming-birds glanced in the sunlight like emeralds and sapphires, and chameleons glided so swiftly about that they scarcely had time to change one bright hue for another. Giant live-oaks hid the house from view until the travellers had entered that garden of peace, the home of silence and prayer.

Mother Audé was with the children when word was brought her that Mother Duchesne was in the house. The news seemed almost too good to be true. She could hardly believe it at first, then she ran to the door crying: "It is my dear Mother," and she was in Mother Duchesne's arms. There was joy on all sides. Even Mother Eugénie and Sister Layton, who had grown so pallid from illness and heat, flushed with the gladness that this visit brought. Mother Xavier confided to the journal of the house: "What a memorable, what a happy day! With what delight we beheld the cherished *Mère,* and with what maternal affection she embraced us!"

The prizes had been given on August 3rd, and school had closed. Some of the children remained over for a few days. Mother Audé asked Mother Duchesne to see them, and a little address was read in the name of all by Mary Hardey, destined later to carry on Mother Duchesne's work in the United States. She and the other children went home on the 8th of August and during the two weeks' holiday the religious made their retreat. There was no priest to give the exercises, so Mother Duchesne read the points of the meditations and gave the instructions herself. In this outpouring of herself on others she must have felt even more than they did the want of the Sacraments, for their chaplain was still away. Mother Murphy, alluding in the journal to the privation of Mass, adds: "But the just man lives by faith which is indeed the only nourishment congenial to this climate." She found in Mother Duchesne one to whom she could say all, one whose replies calmed her fears, and she wrote to Mother Barat: "I have never been able to speak to any one with more facility and I have never felt greater peace than in accepting Mother Duchesne's decisions. She is a woman after my own heart." Mother Murphy's generosity, in turn, appealed to Philippine, for they both had a love of the cross and of suffering, which the little Irish nun was trying to put into words when she wrote: "Every privation has a *je ne sais quoi pour moi* in this cherished land of my adoption."

On the 22nd of August the summer holidays ended;
the school at Grand Côteau opened with eighteen boarders, Mother Duchesne gathered them around her, read
to them the Rule of the School and commented upon it.
It was the very same rule that was being explained to
the children in Paris, at Ste. Marie d'en Haut, at
Florissant, and wherever a Convent of the Sacred
Heart was to be found. The boarders at Côteau delighted Mother Duchesne, who humbly said that the
school there was already better established than was that
in Missouri. With enthusiasm she wrote to tell Mother
Barat of Mother Eugénie's devotedness, prudence, of
her pleasing manner, her talents, her courage—qualities
which were winning for her the hearts of the children.

The little community had, thanks to Mother Duchesne's generosity, increased to meet the needs of the
school that seemed destined to prosper. Mother Audé,
Mother Xavier Murphy and Sister Layton had been
joined by several postulants. At recreation they
gathered round Mother Duchesne who listened with
sympathetic interest to all they had to tell her of the
foundation. One day, when whitewashing a wall,
Mother Audé put her hand into a hole. Hearing a hiss-
ing sound, she quickly withdrew it, and out of the hole
glided a serpent. They managed to kill it and found
that it had swallowed whole several small chickens
which had mysteriously disappeared. Sister Layton
had to tell of Mother Audé's illness, of how in the height
of her fever she had dragged herself from room to room
urging on the negroes in their work, of how she had
gone for days without water rather than allow the good
Sister to go to the well which was half a mile's distance
from the house.

They had much to say of the visit of Bishop Du

Bourg who had received Mother Murphy's last vows, given the veil to a novice, and spoken of his real love for the little house of Grand Côteau. Mother Duchesne, in turn, could paint in glowing colors what she had heard of the Indians from the missionaries of Missouri. Sans Nerf, the leading chief of the Osages, had come to St. Louis to visit Bishop Du Bourg in the little stone cottage on Second Street. The object of his quest was to ask for missionaries—Blackrobes for his tribe.

> *"All our town in peace awaits you,*
> *All our doors stand open for you;*
> *You shall enter all our wigwams,*
> *For the heart's right hand we give you."*

The good Bishop said that he could never forget the emotion of the stern Indian as he gazed lovingly on the crucifix hung on the poor wall of the presbytery. There was an old squaw at the Barrens who remembered having seen a Jesuit before the suppression of the Society. This was probably the veteran, Father Sebastian Meurin, who from 1765 to 1768 was the only priest in the Upper Mississippi Valley. St. Genevieve was his residence but in name, for during all that time he did not spend four nights a year in the same bed. Mother Duchesne's enthusiastic admiration for the missionaries was revealed in her words as well as in her deeds, and her little audience of Côteau were delighted with all she had to tell them. Her simplicity, too, charmed them. Mother Murphy records: "August 29. Birthday of our dear Mother Duchesne. There was no Mass, but she passed the whole day at the foot of the sanctuary. At the evening recreation she told us she had accomplished her fifty-third year. May her valuable life be long, long preserved!" On the 2nd of September she confided to the journal: *"Notre chère Mère Duchesne left us. Judge of our feelings on the occasion, but it is unworthy of a daughter of the Sacred Heart to express them. Dieu seul, Dieu seul!!!"*

Mother Duchesne and Theresa Pratte left Côteau in a cart drawn by two horses. Of the one belonging to the convent Mother Philippine wrote: "This poor animal which reminded me of the Apocalypse resolutely refused to go on, and both he and his companion ended by falling into a quagmire. My pupil and I tried to draw them out but in vain. Finally a negro played the part of a horse, for after we had unloaded the cart he managed to draw it. We had recourse again to the oxen which pulled us through the miry roads, then we embarked on the steamer of the bayou, and at last took a carriage which brought us to Plaquemine." There in the inn the religious and the child waited five days for the boat to St. Louis. The river was low. The current would be less strong than usual; but the trip would be none the less dangerous, as some river bottoms had been changed to shallows and sandbars. A greater menace than this lay before them. From the rank verdure left exposed by the subsiding waters clouds of mosquitoes were rising; there were those with black and white stripes, malaria-carriers, and there were others which a later science would discover to be the means of spreading the dreaded yellow fever.

When Mother Duchesne learned that because of the fear of contagion no north-bound boat would be allowed to stop at Plaquemine, she decided to go to the fever-stricken city, New Orleans, whence she might be allowed to embark. Once again she would ask hospitality of the Ursuline convent, where she could always count on a

cordial welcome. On her way there from the landing
she saw the Place d'Armes with its serpentine and circular walks, its wild orange-trees, lemons, figs and
palmettos, their dark, shaggy trunks standing out black
against the emerald banners of the banana. On that
spot, nearly eighty years before, the Governor Périer
(might he claim Philippine as a descendant?) had assembled the citizens to offset an expected invasion of the
Indians. The Governor had more than ordinary claim
to obedience and gratitude, for he had built the first
levee along the city front. In the Place d'Armes the
French loyalists who had dared to resist the new régime
impersonated by the Spanish General, Alessandro
O'Reilly, had been shot. In 1803 the tricolor had
floated there again for full twenty days until it was
hauled down and the stars and stripes took its place.
All these varied events had taken place in that vast
quadrangle in the shadow of the Cathedral of New
Orleans, and not far from the old convent.

There Mother Duchesne received the same hospitality she had experienced nearly five years ago. The
good nuns thought her looking very ill, and the doctor
declared that, in her run-down condition, she had best
leave for the North at once, or she would surely succumb
to yellow fever. He little thought what advice he was
giving, any more than he and his medical colleagues
dreamed that the quinine with which they dosed their
yellow-fever patients killed far more than it cured.

His advice and the fear that she might be needed at
Florissant alarmed Mother Duchesne, and, ill as she
was, she set out with her young travelling companion.
They embarked on the *Hecla,* and a strange horror
came over the religious as she entered the boat; which to
her seemed like a grave. She grew worse and worse; all

the symptoms of yellow fever soon appeared. The epidemic was raging on that doomed ship. On the second day of the journey, the Captain, the first mate and a passenger died on board. A poor young Frenchman, who had been ill ever since he had left Lyons, was seized with such paroxysms that they put him ashore. A priest came out from the quarantined village, anointed him, and stayed with him till he died. On board the *Hecla* all was horror; men died like animals, while their comrades joked and sang songs close by them. Horrified by the sounds and the sights, Mother Duchesne ignored her own suffering. Though burning with fever, she watched beside the sick and the dying, speaking to them of the eternity of which they knew little or nothing. She baptized one man who had been forsaken by all save herself. Was it only five years before that she had heard Mother Barat tell of the missionary whose only apostolate had been the baptism of one, for he accompanied into eternity the soul he had saved? Was this to be true of her too? The fever was sapping her strength; she could not hold out any longer. When the boat reached Natchez she was so ill that she and Theresa Pratte were put off on shore. Mother Duchesne would have been grateful for shelter even in the squalid hovels of the boatmen on the bank of the river, if she were not able to reach the city set up on the hill; but both Upper and Lower Natchez were closed to anyone coming from New Orleans, the city of Death. Some good Samaritan rowed the sick religious across the river; one of the passengers of the *Hecla* went from house to house, asking for shelter, but no one would welcome a fever-stricken visitor. At last a kind man offered them lodging; his wife had died of yellow fever just two weeks before; and, in her bed, and between the very sheets she had used, Mother Duchesne was put to rest. During four days she sat bolt upright in bed, fighting disease, doctoring herself, praying for spiritual help. She longed for Our Lord as Viaticum on the journey to eternity, on which she thought she was embarking, and she sent for the Curé of Natchez, the young priest whom she had seen on her way down the river, and with whom she had sympathized in his apparently fruitless work. At his request two of his parishioners, who lived across the river from Natchez, brought Mother Duchesne and the child to their home and took the best possible care of them. What Philippine had really wanted was Holy Communion; the curé had planned to take the Blessed Sacrament to her, but he was too poor to pay the ferryman's fee, and they refused to take him for nothing, though he was another Christopher, carrying Christ. Her plea to be allowed to go to Mass on Sunday was firmly refused by the doctor for she was still too ill, and besides, Natchez was naturally afraid of contagion. The disappointment that this refusal caused her brought back her fever; but she got better in time to embark with Theresa Pratte on the *Cincinnati* bound for St. Louis. The voyage up stream was slower than ever; it would have seemed so in any case to one weakened with long suffering; but the summer droughts had narrowed the deeper parts of the river and the pilot had almost to feel his way. On the spot on which Cairo now stands, where the Ohio enters the Mississippi, they saw a dismantled steamer drawn up on the shore. Three men seemed to be guarding its ruins. One of them called to those on the *Cincinnati.* He was none other than the pilot of the *Hecla,* the boat which had refused to carry Mother Duchesne beyond Natchez. Its boiler had burst, and two of the crew had been most dreadfully burned. Yellow fever had carried off many of the passengers as well as of the crew; thirteen were buried on a little island hard by. How providential the enforced sojourn at Natchez now seemed! Mother Duchesne thought her long journey practically over, but it was not. At New Madrid the *Cincinnati* ran aground on a sandbank. There was no hope of getting her off until the Mississippi should rise. It was then November. If the cold weather should come early there would be no flood until spring. As they were only one hundred miles from St. Louis, Mother Duchesne wanted to go the rest of the way by land; they would probably be able to hire two horses in New Madrid, or to get someone to take them in an ox-cart to Florissant. But Theresa Pratte would not hear of another land journey, and Mother Duchesne yielded. She made her retreat on the stranded boat, her only helps were her Bible and her small office-book; but in the Heart of Christ, to Whom she had drawn nearer in suffering, she had an open book in which she read secrets unknown to many masters of the spiritual life. At the end of the retreat she gratefully accepted the kind invitation of Mr. and Mrs. Kay, who had heard that there was a religious on the boat and who asked her and her companion to stay with them in New Madrid. Suddenly, the longed-for rain fell; the river rose, the *Cincinnati* was lifted off the shoal and the voyage was resumed. On the 28th of November, Mother Duchesne reached St. Louis; she had left New Orleans on the 14th of September. Her errand of mercy had been for her a prolonged martyrdom, but she had shown compassion for those at Grand Côteau and she asked nothing more.

Suffering awaited her at Florissant. She had left

Mother Berthold in charge of the house, and she found that the gentle Mother had not the firmness necessary for her difficult post. The pupils and the orphans were in an alarming state of insubordination. Mother Duchesne's firm hand soon restored order; but the cause of the disturbance and ill-feeling lay deeper than she had at first thought. Financial depression had driven away from St. Louis some of the citizens who had been most interested in paying off the debt on the new cathedral. The hard times prevented others from giving their share of the subscription. Creditors demanded from the State the right to sell the Bishop's house and other church property in order to meet the obligations. This permission was granted and the sale was effected on condition that the property of the church might still be redeemed if the debts were paid within a stipulated time. The odium thus brought on religion was a great trial to the noble-hearted Bishop who felt that the sympathy of many of his flock had been withdrawn from him. The Religious of the Sacred Heart were known to be utterly loyal to him and this was the reason given by many parents for withdrawing their children from the boarding school at Florissant. At last there were only two left who were able to pay for their board and tuition. Mother Duchesne offered to keep any of the others whose parents were in need and were willing to leave them. Thus in those very hard times she shared with eighteen boarders and six orphans the potatoes and hominy on which the community lived. In explanation, she wrote to Mother Barat: "I thought at first of sending home those who cannot pay, but they would soon lose the faith. We prefer to be deprived of all and to keep them. We must be a providence for others as God is for us." She was becoming ingenious in converting old garments into habits for the little community. In March, 1823, Mothers Xavier and Regis Hamilton made their first vows; one of them wore a choir cloak made by Mother Duchesne out of a cassock left by the young nuns' god-father, Father Dunand. A novice received that day as her white veil a piece of crepe taken from a discarded dress of one of the children.

One of the sources of suffering at Florissant was the menace of floods in the spring. The beautiful valley is protected from the Mississippi and the Missouri Rivers by the gentle slopes that encompass it, but the Church of St. Ferdinand and the convent are similarly situated between two creeks which in flood times meet at and even within their very doors. The water has been known to rise as high as the top of the communion railing in the church and equally high in the convent. The suffering and inconvenience resulting from this can easily be imagined.

It was not the great flood of 1822, however, but the calumnies brought against the convent that robbed it of even the pupils it was receiving merely for love. The school was reduced to five, and Mother Duchesne wrote in heart-broken terms to the Mother House, blaming herself for the failure and begging to be allowed to give the government of the house to someone who she thought would be far more fit to meet the situation. She hoped Octavie Berthold would replace her; but that Mother's delicate health was growing ever more and more frail. Her courage, like that of Mother Duchesne, was unflagging. She wrote to Mother Barat, (it must have been in the *winter*): "If there were question of starting again for the icy land of Missouri or the burning Opelousas, I should fly; nothing would stop me.

If I had to leave you once again, to say good-bye to my Mothers and Sisters, I should again find courage in Him Who strengthens me."

In the meantime an event was brewing that was to mean much for Florissant. Since 1815, Bishop Du Bourg had been trying to secure Jesuits for his diocese. He had been most anxious to have Father Louis Barat, who was equally desirous to come to the missions. However, the Society of Jesus was then unable to spare anyone from Europe, so the Bishop turned to the Jesuit novitiate in Maryland; and in 1823 he obtained the transfer of the noviceship from White Marsh to Florissant. Seven novices and three lay-brothers left for the West under the guidance of two missionary priests, Father Van Quickenborne, the Master of Novices, and Father Timmermans. They reached St. Louis on May 31, the very day that the Bishop was rejoicing over the arrival of twelve Sisters of Loretto who were to make a foundation at the Barrens.

The Jesuits took part in the procession of the Blessed Sacrament on that Corpus Christi, and then they followed Father Van Quickenborne to Florissant. The Bishop had given the Society of Jesus his farm on the knoll for a noviceship and an Indian school which when once organized would receive some financial help from the United States Government—Mgr. Du Bourg had so arranged matters during his last visit to Washington. The Jesuits would be the parish priests of St. Ferdinand, of St. Charles, Portage des Sioux, Dardennes and Côte sans Dessein. The Bishop was enthusiastic over their arrival and wrote: "Seven young men full of talent and of the spirit of St. Francis Xavier, very forward in their studies, varying in age from twenty-two to twenty-seven, with their two masters and some excellent lay-brothers—this is what Providence has at last sent me in answer to my prayers."

The arrival of the Jesuits meant very much to the nuns at St. Ferdinand, not only because of the spiritual help they were to receive, but because of what they were to be allowed to give. As the little farm house on the knoll needed repairs and Father Van Quickenborne wanted to begin another building at once, Mother Duchesne offered the parochial school as a temporary home for the new arrivals. With them she shared the house linen and her scanty provisions. Whatever gifts of money she received went to them; for them she begged from the few friends of the convent who lived in St. Louis. They began to repair and to build. So as not to rob the valley of any of its foliage they brought their logs from the trees which they cut down on an island in the Missouri, just off the Charbonnière. They were strong—those Flemish novices—among them, for instance, was Peter de Smet, who it was said could bend a coin between his fingers and carry logs that others were hardly able to stir. The house was at last built and the next morning the builders saw from the Charbonnière that the little island from which they had taken their logs had disappeared. It had been washed away during the night.

On July 31, the Feast of St. Ignatius was celebrated with due pomp. There was a High Mass in the church in the valley, and Mother Duchesne had a feast dinner prepared for her twelve revered guests.

As time went on, she saw that the Jesuits were in need of more help, for the drippings and Indian corn on which they lived were not keeping up their strength.

She became a mother to them, leaving nothing undone
to provide what was wanting. Any black material that
came from France was made into cassocks for the
priests and scholastics. St. Francis stripped himself
of his one garment to clothe a poor man, for, said he,
"If I should not give what I have to him who is more
needy than I, I should be accounted guilty of theft by
the Giver of all things." This was also Mother Duchesne's policy; and, "thanks to her," as the Jesuits of
the twentieth century say: "the Province of Missouri
was saved." They were a delight to her—this band of
generous men——

> "*Recruited late, a century ago,*
> *To form new outposts near the setting sun,*
> *On mountain range and unexplored plateau,*
>
> "*To lose themselves on unmapped stream and trail*
> *In leagues of wilderness with savage bands,*
> *Sleeping with all the stars for counterpane,*
> *Or in such sheds as that of Bethlehem.*
>
> "*They husbanded their grace and found the time*
> *To pray and study and keep their purpose whole,*
> *To be concerned about the savage soul,*
> *To mark out empires for the reign of grace.*"

CHAPTER III

How an Apostle Gives

CHAPTER III

How an Apostle Gives.—1824-1830

"The world waits
For help. Beloved, let us love so well,
Our work shall still be better for our love,
And still our love be sweeter for our work."

E. B. BROWNING.

Mother Duchesne found real joy in ministering to the Jesuits. "It would be a greater happiness," she wrote, "to clean the boots of these good missionaries than to be Queen of France." What she and her religious could give in material help was returned a hundred-fold in the spiritual assistance which Father Van Quickenborne and Father Timmermans gave the little community in the Valley. The Novice Master of the Jesuit Seminary became the confessor and director of the nuns, and all from the youngest postulant to Mother Duchesne profited by his rigorous training. In Father Van Quickenborne's sternness, Mother Duchesne saw, or thought she saw, the rigor of her good Father Barat, and certainly the placid, phlegmatic Fleming put her through much the same treatment as his Burgundian confrère had his own little sister, Sophie. Louis Barat threw into the fire a gift prepared for him by Madeleine Sophie. Father Van Quickenborne sent back to the convent the dinner which Mother Duchesne had prepared for the novices whom she had seen at work in the

267

fields.   She had made the meal as elaborate as her
meagre larder would allow; the Jesuits must need something better than usual, she had thought—their
morning's work had been so strenuous.   A message
accompanied the rejected gift: "Father Van Quickenborne does not want Mother Duchesne's alms."
Humbled by this, Mother Philippine thought neither
of resentment nor of taking the good Father at his
word.   Food and clothing found their way from St.
Ferdinand after the reprimand as before, and her letters still described the Jesuit Novitiate as "a nursery
of Saints and Apostles."

Father Barat had publicly held up to ridicule the
timid Sophie's qualms of conscience and unwarranted
scruples.   Father Van Quickenborne took another
means to try Mother Duchesne, refusing to grant her
absolution.   Once this trial lasted so long that she
thought it necessary to seek someone who would absolve
her.   She revolved to go to St. Genevieve, a distance of
about ninety miles from Florissant.   It is scarcely
likely that Father Van Quickenborne put at her disposal
his famous roan steed, so the long lonely ride was probably made on the convent cart-horse.   At St. Genevieve
the kind hospitality of the Vallé home was generously
given her.   Then, having received absolution, she rode
back through the forest, past the flinty knoblike hills,
across the desolate valley of the Meramec.

At last she reached Florissant, which a traveller,
Timothy Flint, described as the most beautiful
valley he had ever seen.   He added that in 1824
the village had a "convent, a building of considerable size and beauty."   Another traveller, of
the same period, says that "this monastery was
the largest house in the town."   This little con-

vent, which is still standing, is of handmade brick
and to the right of the front door is a small room with
two windows, to the left a room with but one. In Mother
Duchesne's time the chapel was behind these two rooms.
The basement was entirely under ground and often
under water, and in it was the kitchen with the bake
oven which every house in Florissant possessed. A
Spanish custom prevailed in the village—each family
took turns sending bread to the presbytery on Saturday. At the last Mass on Sunday, the bread was
blessed, and part of it, cut in small pieces, was handed
round to the congregation by the sexton. The remainder of the *"Pain beni"* was an offering to the pastor.
Whether Father Van Quickenborne long continued
this custom introduced by Father Dunand, it is impossible to say; be that as it may, bread often went to the
presbytery from the convent bake oven. As Father
Van Assche said in 1873, just fifty years after he had
come to Florissant, "Mother Duchesne imitated the
raven of old, carrying bread to the hermitage of Paul
in the desert; with the exception that she and her religious gave food three times a day and not bread alone,
as did the raven to Paul the Hermit, but several things
besides, both wholesome and palatable."

Louis Barat reproached himself in his later
years for his severity to his sister, but if Father
Van Quickenborne entertained any such sentiments,
he has not left them on record. He had a sterner
nature with which to deal, and Mother Duchesne
remained grateful to the end for all he made her
suffer. Yet Sophie was but in her teens when
Father Barat so treated her, whereas Mother Duchesne
was nearly sixty; rough training she had had
in her early years, gentle handling she had experi-

enced from her loving Mother General, and it was not yesterday that Our Lord had Himself taken up the chisel.

Occasionally, however, Mother Duchesne's old fault reasserted itself. Once she and Father Van Quickenborne disagreed about the placing of a rug in the sanctuary of the Church of St. Ferdinand, of which the nuns were the custodians, and their Superior was sacristan.

"Very well," said the Pastor, "I will remove the altar, which belongs to the parish."

Mother Duchesne answered impulsively that to do so would avail nothing, since the tabernacle was the possession of the convent. Neither would yield the point and Father Van Quickenborne told Mother Philippine that he withdrew his consent to her receiving Holy Communion the following day. And that day was the Feast of the Sacred Heart when the nuns were to renew their vows aloud at the altar-rail! The Superior, debarred from the renovation and fearing to scandalize the novices, remained in bed, letting it be supposed that she was too ill to go to Mass. But when all were safely in the chapel she rose, crept to the door, and kneeling on the floor outside, like one of the public penitents of the Ages of Faith, she cried as though her heart would break. "The tears of the saints," says Father Faber, "are more significant than words;" so too are the sobs of one who at leisure atones a hundredfold for a fault of impulse. Ryder compares Newman and Manning to "the sea and rocks confronting it," which, as Shane Leslie says, "might, while the storm lasted, combine against a hostile armada, but their eventual condition was one of settled opposition of sentiment, method, aspiration." Father Van Quickenborne and Mother Duchesne, on the contrary, were at one in sentiment, in aspiration; they differed in method. Each had what Newman attributes to Manning; an iron will and a resolve to have his own way. An iron soul is tempered to steel by fire and tears; and Mother Duchesne, knowing herself, wrote, "To live in the neighborhood of saints and to profit by their direction are such blessings that I prefer our poor country home to the most wealthy establishment in a town."

On the eighteenth of February, 1824, she wrote to a priest who had befriended the convent: "I was tempted to reproach you with calumny since you say that you are forgotten at Florissant where your memory is held in veneration, and always will be, not only by us who have known you, but by everyone. . . . The Jesuits have had their tribulations, but they know how to suffer; nothing has come to them from Maryland."

A new establishment was just then being prepared for the Sacred Heart in the Parish of St. James, about sixty miles from New Orleans. The pastor of this place was Father De La Croix, who had proved himself a true friend of the Religious of the Sacred Heart from the day that he had met them on the Charbonnière to welcome them to Florissant until, on the arrival of the Jesuits, he had been sent to Louisiana. There he had kept up a correspondence with Mother Audé asking her to intercede with Mother Duchesne and Mother Barat to obtain a foundation of the Sacred Heart in his new parish. Towards the end of 1823, Bishop Du Bourg sent Mother Audé a document in which the trustees of Father De La Croix's parish of St. Michael's, offered a piece of land and pledged themselves to set afoot a subscription for a building fund. Mother Audé referred the matter to

Mother Barat, who wanted to have a convent nearer New Orleans than was Grand Côteau. It seemed unwise to try to open a boarding school in the metropolis itself, as the Ursulines had just been obliged to abandon theirs in the Rue des Chartres and to move further out where there would be less danger of yellow fever, which had claimed victims from both the community and the school.

Replying in 1824 Mother Barat urged Mother Audé to go to Florissant and consult Mother Duchesne upon the projected foundation at St. Michael's. The Mother Foundress said that she would suggest that the boarding school at Florissant, which was now reduced to five children, should be closed, and that Mother Lucille Mathevon should remain there in charge of the more prosperous parochial school. This would set Mother Duchesne free to be the Superior of the promising foundation of St. Michael's.

It was indeed true that good work was being done in the parish school of St. Ferdinand. "I see," wrote Mother Duchesne, "that, as in the days of Our Lord, the poor are chosen to accomplish His work." Her appreciation of this apostolate was increased by what she heard of Father Nerinckx, the apostle of Kentucky and the founder of the Congregation of the Sisters of Loretto at the Foot of the Cross. Having come to Missouri with the intention of devoting the remainder of his life to the Indians, then more numerous here than in Kentucky, he died at St. Genevieve, at which village he had stopped while on his way to Florissant.

Death seemed at that time to be near one of Mother Duchesne's religious daughters for Mother Octavie Berthold, often so suffering, grew steadily worse. However, the prayers of the nuns and children were heard, and again she recovered. To their great consolation the religious learned that their Protestant doctor had been so much impressed by the peace, neatness and regularity of the convent that he had decided to study Catholic Doctrine, with the result that he and his family entered the Church.

Father Rosati, a fervent Lazarist who had come from Italy with Venerable Félix De Andreis, had been named coadjutor of Mgr. Du Bourg. The new Bishop was charged with Missouri, and would live either in St. Louis or at the Seminary which he had helped to build at the Barrens. Several of the secular priests had accompanied Bishop Du Bourg to his new episcopal city of New Orleans, and the greater part of the service of mission stations and village churches in Upper Louisiana fell to the Jesuits. After the sudden death of Father Timmermans, S. J., on May 31, 1824, Father Van Quickenborne's already arduous labors were doubled and the spiritual privations of the religious increased. Mass was said alternately in the Church of St. Ferdinand and in the Novitiate on the knoll; thus the nuns were frequently deprived of what they loved most, while the Jesuit scholastics walked the two miles and a half to Mass whenever it was said in the village. Father Van Quickenborne also served St. Charles and other stations, so that during the months before the number of his priests was increased by ordination he was hard pressed indeed. Yet nothing could hold back the zealous missionary. When the Church of St. Ferdinand and the convent formed an island in the midst of the swollen creeks, he would let his horse swim or he would cross on a floating log. One day the horse appeared riderless, and the nuns took alarm lest the good Father should have been drowned in Coldwater

Creek. However, he shortly appeared, mud to his ears, for his famous roan charger had thrown him.

Mother Duchesne appreciated to the full the untiring devoted work of Father Van Quickenborne, which increased on the death of Father Timmermans, who, to use her own words, "fell a victim to the hard labor he went through for the missions and in travelling across countries either submerged in water or quite barren, where he was obliged to lodge in wretched huts, drink nothing but water, eat only salted meats, and lie on the bare ground at night." She goes on to say, "Poor Father Rector, since he is now the only priest in this region, has more to do than he can manage. Feeble as he is in health,.he has four parishes to look after and other distant missions divided by rivers. On Sundays he says two Masses, preaches three times in the morning, teaches catechism, and during every interval hears Confessions."

In the South there had been a flood and a cyclone besides, with the result that Mother Audé's visit to Florissant had been put off more than once. At last she was able to leave Grand Côteau, and on the 27th of February, 1825, she wrote to Mother Barat: "Here I am at New Orleans, waiting to take passage on a steamboat. I have seen the plan of the house for the projected foundation (at St. Michael). It is to be sixty feet square, not counting two rooms at the end of a gallery, which if needed will make a good dormitory. The property is two arpents wide by forty long in a very fine location."

Mother Audé was much impressed by what she found at Florissant. More than once she had told Mother Duchesne that that house was useless and should be suppressed. To Mother Barat she now wrote of her joy in being free for the moment from responsibility and in having no title save that of one of Mother Duchesne's daughters. "I have arrived in this dear and holy house," she added, "at a very interesting time and one calculated to convince me that, far from being almost useless, as I had thought, this establishment is one of the most useful that we can have in America. I base my opinion on the spiritual direction received here, on the numerous vocations that will allow us to have a noviceship large enough to sustain our other houses, and finally, on the good done here by our Mothers and Sisters." Mother Audé gave a detailed and glowing account of what had been accomplished by retreats, by the Sodality of Married Women, by the school for little boys. The one regret of her visit, she said, was to see Mother Duchesne looking so far from well. In spite of her physical sufferings this valiant Mother was working so hard and with such results that Father Van Quickenborne said that to send her to make the foundation at St. Michael would be to put a stop to the good being done at Florissant. Mother Duchesne was equally anxious not to be made Superior of a new house. To the Mother General she now wrote: "Mother Eugénie is well known in the South and would give a name to the house, which she will uphold by her zeal, her prudence, and her talent for governing children. I am becoming daily more ugly. Even in the village they call me, in a friendly way, 'the old witch'. If I were to speak of what is lacking to me spiritually, I should have even more deficiencies to acknowledge. So I think that Mother Eugénie should be Superior of St. Michael's and Mother Xavier Murphy of Côteau where she is loved. As for Florissant, I should be the last of the three Mothers here, nevertheless, Father Rector says that a change would destroy the house. Fearing that Monseigneur is in haste for a decision, I ask it of you, Very Reverend Mother, begging you to keep in mind my age, at which death must be near, as well as my faults and my incapacity."

The good Mother's attraction for Florissant was explained by her words: "It is true that the house is abject and poor. That is why I love it. Since according to rule we should love the poor more than the rich, we need envy our religious at the Opelousas nothing. We come in contact with as many souls as they do, and we shall soon have a larger novitiate." The boarding school at Florissant was indeed a failure, and it was in the parochial school that the chief apostolate lay. A third work—perhaps the dearest of all to Mother Duchesne—was about to be inaugurated. One day Father Van Quickenborne appeared at the convent in his large black cloak. Throwing it back he revealed two real Babes of the Wood, little Indian girls, the nucleus of the mission for which she had come to America. The building devoted to them and to the others who came later was Mother Philippine's favorite haunt; but as she could not isolate herself from the community, she was obliged to put the little savages in charge of one of her religious. On this score she wrote: "I have destined for them an Irish aspirant who is about forty years old. Her age and her solid virtue fit her for this work which keeps her a part of the day and all night away from us. These Indian children call her Mamma, and jump around her wherever she takes them—to the cows, the chickens, the garden—we leave the active occupations to them, as they are unable to lead a sedentary life."

The Jesuits opened at the same time a school for

Indian boys. It was for the evangelization of the Indians that Bishop Du Bourg had brought the Fathers of the Society of Jesus to Missouri, but the tribes were being gradually pushed westward, and though the Government gave a small subsidy for the upkeep of the boys, they never exceeded fourteen in number and the school at Florissant was shortlived.

However, even after the red men had no longer a home in Missouri, they continued to come from time to time to St. Louis to negotiate with the civil authorities. Those from the Great Lakes drifted down the Mississippi in canoes of white birchbark, others made the more dangerous descent of the Missouri River in pirogues—rough boats hewn from single logs. The Northern Indians brought buffalo hides for the wigwams in which they camped outside the city. The Southern ones made tents of rushes. The chiefs of these tribes wore their blankets flung in graceful folds, and left their right arms bare to the shoulder. With impressive dignity they conferred with the white man regarding the reservations, or land left to their use in the Great West. Some few brought their children and confided them to the care of the Jesuits or of the religious of the Sacred Heart at Florissant. The Baptismal Register of St. Ferdinand has Mother Duchesne's signature as the god-mother of more than one Indian child. Her love for these children of the forest is shown in the following letter:

Kaskaskia was once a more populous town with a church built of stone—a rare thing here—it was also a Jesuit Mission. When the Fathers were expelled, the Indians, hearing that the last priest had left, threw themselves into their canoes to follow him and bring him back by force, saying that they wanted their father and would keep him among them. After that, the only travellers who could safely stop at Kaskaskia were those wearing black robes, in consequence many donned the ecclesiastical costume so as to be sure of their safety. This village was nearly destroyed by a flood. The Mississippi rose constantly until a holy priest having organized a procession planted a cross at the edge of the water and said: "Thou shalt come no further."

This love of the "Blackrobes" is general among the Indians everywhere, even among the Sioux, a most savage tribe. A priest who has been among them and who often comes here tells me that they would supply all his needs were he willing to accept it, but that he does not want to be indebted to them lest they ask him for fire-water. An Indian had a striking conversion. As he lay on his death-bed he spoke of a previous illness during which he had thought he was dying, and he said aloud "I then saw the Author of Life and He said to me: 'Go back, your hour is not yet!' But I know that *this* time I *shall* go to the Author of Life." Francis, a Christian Iroquois present, said to him: "The Author of Life probably sent you back so that you might have water poured on your head." The dying Sioux made answer: "Indeed, I think it was just for that I was told to return to life." Francis replied: "Do you want me to go and get a Blackrobe to pour water upon you?" The Sioux answered: "Go quickly. There is need of haste." The priest who came at once was quite satisfied with the dying man's answers and baptized him, a few moments later he died. He was solemnly buried by the priest who also baptized the dead Sioux' son who was very ill. These happy events took place not far from here. The priest was Father Acquaroni, a Lazarist from Rome and one of our most zealous friends. Another, a Trappist, has told us similar incidents showing how the Indians loved him. He goes from place to place and often encounters them but with no unpleasant results. At Prairie du Chien—so called because the Indians there live in deer skin cabins which are carried from one camping place to another by dogs—all the women came out of their wigwams and gathered the children so that he might touch them. Men and women flocked to hear Mass, but not understanding their language he could do nothing for them.

I am sending you a writing portfolio and some Indian slippers which will show you the handiwork of the savages. They give the names of animals to those who go among them, calling the Pastor of St. Genevieve "the son of a white fish". One day as they greeted him they noticed that he was accompanied by the Bishop, and they asked who he was. "He," the priest answered, "is the Father of the Blackrobes." At once the throng approached to salute His Lordship.

A Canadian Iroquois who had been in Florissant returned home and died at a season when journeys are impossible. His father hollowed out a tree-trunk with one of his weapons, put the body inside and tied it to a tree. When spring came he was told by other Indians that the dead boy was crying out: "Let us go to Florissant!" The father then brought the body of his son these eighteen hundred miles and gave the pastor of Florissant two hundred francs to bury him in consecrated ground.

The expense of conducting the Indian School at Florissant, the first of its kind founded under Catholic auspices in the United States, was a drain on the thin purse of the religious. Five hundred dollars for the first year was a vast sum to them. Father Van Quickenborne wrote on this subject: "For the expenses incurred by them, I have offered and given them: (1) Corn for the year, (2) potatoes for the year, (3) firewood for the year. I doubt whether they will receive these things gratis. They help us much in working and in repairing clothes for us and the Indians." The Government at Washington refused Father Van Quickenborne's appeal for an annual subsidy of $800 for this school for Indian girls. This fact, and the ever-increasing distance of Florissant from the Indian settlements, militated against the prosperity of this work of zeal, and after a struggle of five or six years the school had to be closed. Then Mother Duchesne followed the missionaries in spirit across the state and even beyond the Rockies. "Send word to my nephew Henry," she wrote, "that the fields are ripening for the harvest and that it is time that he should come and seek souls in the land which his patron, St. Francis Regis, longed so much to cultivate. We constantly invoke this Saint for the conversion of the Indians, and we are making a forty days' prayer to obtain speedily an increase of laborers, but they must be dead to earthly things, for nothing gratifies nature in this ministry in which faith and love of our suffering Lord alone can find satisfaction."

While on her way to St. Ferdinand in 1824 Mother Audé had met in New Orleans the nephew of Mother Barat, Father Dussaussois, who had just come from France. He wanted to be chaplain of one of the convents of the Sacred Heart in the New World, and after some months spent at Grand Côteau and a visit to St. Michael, where he laid the cornerstone of the house destined for a convent, he came on to Florissant. In confiding his nephew to the care of Bishop Rosati, Father Barat told the American prelate that the young priest suffered "from a painful indisposition of a melancholic nature which troubled him and made him seem inconstant, and demanded the compassion no less than the indulgence of his superiors." It was hoped that the change of climate would complete his cure. At St. Ferdinand's the young priest made himself at home, and frequently visited the classes unannounced. The little

Indians could not accustom themselves to these sudden apparitions of the blackrobe, and as soon as he appeared they would take flight through the windows into the neighboring trees, where they played like squirrels, while a poor novice, Mother Anne Shannon, was left to make her excuses to the Reverend Father. After one such adventure, she went in tears to ask Mother Duchesne what she should do the next time the Father came. With a flash of her old impetuosity, the Superior said, "Does the Father think that his being our Mother General's nephew entitles him to upset our school?"

A little later, Mother Duchesne, realizing what she had said, sent for the novice and told her that each must impose upon herself a severe penance, she for having spoken disrespectfully of a priest, and the other for having listened. Hers was the "ingrained instinct of old reverence," and her habitual respect for the priesthood amounted to veneration.

This same novice recounts another sally of Mother Duchesne's old self. One morning the Superior went to the kitchen and told Sister Shannon to warn her when a certain tradesman should come. Then leaving a two-dollar bill on the table she went back to her work elsewhere. When the man arrived, Mother Duchesne returned to the kitchen, but the money had disappeared. Consternation reigned. Impulsively Mother Duchesne turned to the novice and asked what she had done with the bill; the novice burst into tears. Mother Duchesne confronted the man and asked whether he had not picked up the money, whereupon he protested indignantly. The kitchen was searched, but in vain. Suddenly the tradesman had an inspiration. He left the house and returned a few moments later with the two-dollar bill. A cow had put its head through the kitchen window and had taken the greenback with a mouthful of greens off the table, then had contemptuously dropped it not far from the house. Sister Shannon and the man laughed over the adventure—not so Mother Duchesne, who showed true distress and sorrow for her hastiness and for misjudging others.

At last word came from Mother Barat, who had accepted Philippine's judgments about all things save those relating to herself. Mother Audé was to undertake the new foundation of St. Michael's and would be replaced at Côteau by Mother Xavier Murphy, while Mother Duchesne remained at Florissant as Superior. Mother Eugénie left Missouri for the South, her heart torn, as she said, over the prospect of leaving Grand Côteau. She took with her Mother Duchesne's two loves, Mother Xavier Hamilton, who would be Assistant at St. Michael's, and Sister Marguerite Manteau, one of the original colony who had come to America in 1818.

The religious who remained in Missouri found true consolation in seeing the good which the Jesuits were doing in Florissant, as a letter from Mother Duchesne bears witness: "The 'revival' preached by the Fathers brings into the Church and then to the Sacraments almost all the village. One hundred and sixty men have received their Easter Communion. On the Feast of Corpus Christi, the procession followed by all the parishioners went along the street and through the fields. The Blessed Sacrament rested on an altar erected in our grounds. These Fathers would convert a kingdom." Father Van Assche, then a scholastic, gave the following account of the Corpus Christi procession of 1825:

One of the Indian boys carried the cross, then came

four of them in surplices carrying little bells, and after them the rest. The Indians were followed by the boys of the Sunday school and these by the women; next came the girls conducted by the nuns, then the children of the boarding school followed by their teachers and the other nuns; then the clergy, our Father Superior carrying the Blessed Sacrament and attended by deacon, sub-deacon, two chanters in copes and a master of ceremonies. After these marched the men with a bodyguard of soldiers. To enhance the beauty of the procession, statues were carried by the children who scattered flowers along the way while sacred hymns were sung alternately by the nuns and the scholastics. In the midst of a field adjoining the church an altar was fitted out with the finest decorations we could procure. It was guarded by more than twenty soldiers, several of them Protestants, who discharged their muskets before, during, and after the Benediction. During the High Mass, Reverend Father Superior explained the significance of the ceremonies and proved the doctrine of the Real Presence, at the same time exhorting the Catholics to show by their conduct the reality of their faith in the Blessed Sacrament. That day our church was altogether too small. Some of the Protestants were so captivated by our ceremonies that they assured one of the Fathers they would never fail to be present on similar occasions. The procession would have marched through the village were it not that we feared some act of irreverence; for this reason it took place on the property of the Religious of the Sacred Heart.

At the end of the year 1825 news reached Florissant of the foundation of St. Michael's. Mother Audé had left Grand Côteau with Mothers Xavier Hamilton and Aloysia Hardey at three o'clock in the morning so as to spare the community she was leaving a painful farewell. When the caller made the rounds of the house at five she missed her Superior and the two other religious.

Mother Xavier Murphy, the new Superior, alone knew that the departure was to take place that morning. The journey, which was made in an ox-cart across country, lasted a full week. The nuns found their new home not yet under roof, but kind Father De La Croix did as he had done on the knoll at Florissant six years before: he gave up his own house for their use. There they stayed for three weeks and then moved into the convent very near the Church of St. Michael. The brick house was one hundred feet long, with green shutters and a shingled roof; there was as yet no stove and no fireplace, and the religious suffered much from the chilling December dampness, all the greater because they were only a few hundred yards from the Mississippi River. Mother Audé wrote her letters in the kitchen, resting her sheet of paper on the cover of an iron pot. It was thus that Bishop Du Bourg found her one day.

"Mother Eugénie," he said, with the graceful gesture and in the mellow organ-like tones for which he was famous, "Mother Eugénie, this is not the place for you."

"Monseigneur," she replied, "allow me to take the liberty of saying that neither is it the place for you!"

They both laughed, and she led him to the room that served as a parlor. "A Religious of the Sacred Heart should be ready for anything and satisfied anywhere," she afterwards said.

This was one of Bishop Du Bourg's few visits to St. Michael's. He suffered much in New Orleans where "he showed himself reluctant to enforce his authority against the cathedral trustees who continually opposed him." So, during a visit to Europe in 1836, "he tendered his resignation to the See of New Orleans, thinking that another incumbent would be more successful," and became Bishop of Montauban, France.

His failure to return to America was a cause of sorrow
to the Religious of the Sacred Heart in Louisiana and
in Missouri, where he had proved himself a true father
and friend. He was succeeded by Bishop Rosati, who
made his residence in St. Louis and rarely failed to call
at both convents in his yearly visits to Louisiana.

The work at St. Michael's prospered beyond the
most sanguine hopes of Father De La Croix, but the
prosperity of the southern houses was bought at the
price of hardship and difficulties in Missouri. The
floods at Florissant were putting an obstacle in the way
of the good being done there, and Mother Duchesne
wrote to Mr. Auguste Chouteau, who owned the land
next to that of the convent:

Sir:

When there was question of our establishment here,
Mr. Mullanphy assured me that you would place no
obstacle in the way of our having a bridge over our
brook for those coming on foot. Since our arrival he
has told me that you had formally given your consent
and that you would put it in writing when the time
should come.

I come, Sir, to thank you for these kind dispositions
in our regard. We should not feel at liberty to begin
this work without consulting you and without soliciting
anew your written permission.

The permission came and the work was begun, two
bridges were built, the one for wagons cost $100, and
that for pedestrians $110. This was one of Mother
Duchesne's last benefits to the house of Florissant before she left there to make a new foundation. Mother
Barat had learned from Father Niel, then in France, of
Bishop Rosati's desire to have a house of the Society in

St. Louis. As soon as Philippine heard that her Mother
General wished this foundation made without delay, she
set aside her own fears and began to make plans. Never
had the time seemed less opportune for branching forth.
Florissant was in great poverty, Mother Octavie Berthold was ill, St. Michael's was calling for more subjects
for Mother Xavier Hamilton had died there, and there
was no one to take her place. Mother Duchesne herself
was suffering from a painful lameness. Obedience had
spoken, however, so she valiantly wrote to ask the advice and assistance of Mr. Mullanphy, who then offered
the Society a house in St. Louis on condition that
twenty orphans should be kept in perpetuity. The
building, Mother Duchesne learned, which was at about
fifteen minutes' walk from the church, was of brick, and
was most probably the home of John Mullanphy, described by Brackenbridge after he had supped there in
1821 as "the largest house in the city." Its location on
the terraces above the Mississippi River and its outlook
over the little city reminded Philippine of her loved Ste.
Marie d'en Haut, though she said that the American
view was less "smiling."

Accompanied by a young religious and an orphan,
Mother Duchesne went in 1827 to take possession. The
house had been practically uninhabited for years, and
needed much preparation for the school. There were no
class-mistresses, yet almost at once a flood of children
appeared clamoring to be taught. The reputation of a
"haunted house" had not frightened them, and Mother
Duchesne soon laid the ghost, or rather ghosts, for the
attic was inhabited by cats that slid down the chimneys
at inopportune moments. The largest room was in the
basement, so, despite its location, it had to be the chapel,
although it was so low that one could touch the ceiling

with one's hand. The altar was in front of the fireplace. When Philippine prayed there at night she often found toads hopping about on the floor, and her devotion was not increased by the crickets and locusts, which she described as "huge spiders that sang like birds." Even to those accustomed to Florissant, the house seemed remote and solitary. This feeling was accentuated when the religious realized that for the time being they could not have daily Mass regularly. Sometimes one of the Jesuits would ride in from Florissant to give the religious this greatest of benefits, and often Mother Duchesne would fast until noon in the hope that a priest would come and that she might receive Holy Communion. The curé of St. Louis was kind to the convent, but his parish and missions claimed his first care. He visited the nuns on their arrival, presented them with a cow, and sent over tables and benches for the school.

The overburdened life of the community was sweetened by the news from France that on December 22nd, 1826, the Holy Father had signed the Brief of Approbation of the Society of the Sacred Heart. Mother Duchesne wrote of her joy:

S.C.J.M.   ST. LOUIS, OCTOBER 7, 1827

With you we thank the Heart of Jesus for the grace of our approbation, and we want you to know of the pure happiness it brings us. It gives us courage to suffer in upholding by our labors, as far as we can, the work which God Himself has accomplished, and one in which, in His mercy, He allows us to share. Each succeeding foundation gives us new happiness since it spreads the glory of the Heart of Jesus, and draws to Him souls seeking to embrace religious life. The house of St. Louis is the latest to be founded, but it was here that we were meant to be from the beginning; it was here that our Mother General thought we should be, and it was to St. Louis that priests have repeatedly asked us to come.

Mother Duchesne did not forget Florissant and the noviceship there. A postulant, Adeline Boilvin, wrote to ask leave to change her Christian name for that of Aloysia. She was probably in ignorance of the fact that Mary Hardey, who had entered the noviceship of Grand Côteau in 1825, had asked for and had been given the name which the virtues of Mother Jouve had endeared to the Society. Mother Philippine's answer was as follows:

S.J.C.M.

My Dear Adeline:

It is with great pleasure that I shall see you bear the name of a Saint whose virtues I hope you will imitate. Choose, therefore, Louis, Louisa, or Gonzaga, since Aloysia is already taken.

I hope that the illness of Mère Octavie, instead of harming the regularity of the novitiate, will bring her in her suffering the sweet consolation of seeing you and your Sisters working courageously to merit the title of spouses of a Heart, the Most Tender and the Most Perfect. Since you, dear Adeline, have the joy of bearing the yoke of Christ from your youth, you are well adapted to acquire religious virtue and to walk steadily under His standard on which are inscribed only humility, simplicity, recollection, obedience, regularity, silence and sacrifice.

May it be said of you, as of your patron, Aloysius, of Berchmans, and of many religious whom I have known, that never have you wilfully broken the smallest rule. This is the happiness I wish you as I sign myself in the Sacred Heart,

Your devoted

PHILLIPINE.

A few months later Mother Duchesne wrote to thank the novice, Sister Gonzaga Boilvin, for some religious emblems which she had painted:

My very dear Sister,

I appreciate your kindness and charity in making for me gifts which will remind me of the Heart of Jesus and of His cross. Your last emblem seemed to me to be better made than the others—perhaps because of the finer material on which it is painted. You will please your two pupils by giving them two little pieces as they wish to make copies. They both have talent for this artistic work which is likely to arouse devotion; they will send you some of their models.

Your letter consoled me because I saw in it the unction with which the Divine Child has perfumed your heart at His Crib. The manger and Calvary are the two dearest homes to the lovers of Jesus. Pray for me that I may never leave them.

On New Year's day the choir from St. Stanislaus, accompanied by the organ, sang for us a beautiful Mass. They came also to wish us a happy New Year. They are twenty brothers united as one.

As soon as the house of St. Louis was in order, the Bishop came to bless it. The little community had slightly increased; Mother Berthold was able to come in from Florissant, but her work-day was drawing to a close. A gift made it possible to build a small chapel with a dormitory above. Then a new colony of religious left France, travelling west from New York to the Ohio River, down which they floated as far as Cairo. One of them continued her journey down the Mississippi to Louisiana. Among those who came to St. Louis was Mother Dutour, whom Mother Barat had sent over to be the Superior of a new convent of the Sacred Heart in the South.

The Order of Loretto at the Foot of the Cross, founded by Father Nerinckx in Kentucky, had done splendid pioneer work at the Barrens, and these nuns were the admiration of Bishop Rosati, who could not say enough in their praise. Mother Duchesne wrote of these Sisters: "Their life is very austere. In a few years their number has increased to one hundred. They teach the poor and form them to work, and do much good." These religious had made a foundation at Bayou La Fourche in Louisiana. The foundresses were Americans who happened not to speak French. The people of La Fourche knew nothing but French. In consequence the school did not prosper. Bishop Du Bourg had wanted the Sisters of La Fourche to unite with the Religious of the Sacred Heart. Knowing that Mgr. Rosati had the same hope, the Bishop of Montauban went to see Mother Barat to consult her on the subject. She gave her consent on condition that the Sisters should be received individually, and only after a noviceship, and she sent Mother Dutour from France to take charge of the house of La Fourche. Some of the Sisters from there went either to Florissant or to St. Michael's for their noviceship, and their place in the school was taken by professed and aspirants from the two houses.

Mother Duchesne notes these comings and goings in the journal of the house of St. Louis. There she mentions whatever was of interest to her little community. Of their privations and sufferings she says little or nothing. When she speaks of herself, it is only historically, and in the third person, as the Jesuit missionaries were accustomed to keep their diaries. On May 6, 1827, she notes that they had just heard that Bishop

Du Bourg had preached at St. Denys before the king on January 21, the anniversary of the execution of Louis XVIII's brother, Louis XVI. These names brought back to Mother Duchesne memories of the Revolution, of the refusal of the humble Foundress to accept the imperial school in the old monastery, and of her first meeting with the pioneer Bishop of St. Louis.

She never fails to record the success and prosperity of the southern houses, which she attributes to Mother Audé's tact and amiability. The good being done by other religious orders is always set down. Hers was the true zeal that rejoices to see God's work well done and to know that another succeeds even where one has met only failure. Intercourse with religious of other orders always gave her joy. In November, 1827, she lent the sacristy, the only free room in the house, to Mother Xavier, the Superior of the Sisters of Charity of Emmitsburg. There this admirable religious with several of her Sisters spent three weeks. Mother Duchesne's own room was a cubby-hole under the stairs; her meals were the scraps left by the children; her dentist, when intense suffering drove her to seek solace, was the workman, who pulled out the aching tooth with one of his tools. When the house grew too poor to have even this workman, she became her own janitor. On the day of the Prizes, 1829, she was in the garden at four in the morning putting the lawn and the walk in order for the Bishop. The "Commencement Exercises" that day proved a failure, and humiliation fell on the Superior.

Other humiliations were forthcoming. As Mother Berthold grew weaker, all work was taken from her except the care of a few plants in window boxes in the chapel. One day the extraordinary confessor asked Mother Berthold if she did any work. She smilingly said she was the gardener. In all probability the Father had seen a nun digging and weeding, and not knowing her to be the Superior, thought that Mother Berthold was being harshly treated. So he sent for Mother Duchesne and upbraided her for her neglect of the sick, but she said not a word. As a matter of fact, the good Mother spent night after night by the bedside of the suffering.

A joy to the community in St. Louis was the coming of the Jesuits to that city. The St. Louis College, opened in 1818 by Bishop Du Bourg, had been carried on by the secular clergy; in 1828 other work seemed more imperative, and the college was closed. Meanwhile, the Jesuits at Florissant were preparing to open a college in St. Louis on property donated to Bishop Du Bourg for school purposes by its owner, Mr. Jeremiah Connor, and deeded over by the prelate to Father Van Quickenborne. Aided liberally by popular subscriptions, the Father erected on this property, situated at Ninth Street and Washington Avenue, a three-story brick building in which the new college began its career in November, 1829. Father Verhaegen was to come from Florissant to be the first president of what is to-day the oldest university in the territory of the Louisiana Purchase.

His labors at St. Charles had been blest with success. When, in 1824, Father Van Quickenborne had replaced Father Timmermans in serving this station from his residence at Florissant, he was distressed at what he found there. The old church on Jackson Street was in ruins, it was indeed "the relic of prolonged struggle with frontierism, poverty and religious indifference." The zealous Jesuit determined to build another church in St. Charles. Funds were lacking; and the new build-

ing seemed only a hope, but Providence came to his rescue; in a year he not only bought ground for a new
church and a convent of the Sacred Heart, but he and
his religious brothers erected what was then the finest
church in the diocese of St. Louis. "The Jesuits," wrote
Mother Duchesne, "were their own architects, masons
and carpenters."

Since the Religious of the Sacred Heart had left
St. Charles in 1819 there had been no Catholic school in
the place, and no one to teach the children catechism.
The Jesuits and Bishop Rosati asked for the return of
the nuns. Gratitude and charity seemed to demand
compliance at no matter what cost, and Mother Barat
wrote to Mother Duchesne to arrange for three religious
to go to St. Charles, which would be the fourth American
foundation made in these four years. She went out to
Florissant, taking Mother Octavie Berthold as her companion and Mother O'Connor for the foundation. She
spent a day or two arranging for the new house of St.
Charles, of which Mother Lucille Mathevon would be
Superior. On October 10, at four in the morning, these
religious left St. Ferdinand, and walked across the fields
to the Jesuit Novitiate on the hill. The weather was
superb, for October is Missouri's most beautiful month.
Then the sycamore, "king of the forest," is gorgeous in
scarlet and gold; fields with their stubble and stacked
straw tell of the end of the harvest; vine-leaves no longer
hide grapes which the vintage has claimed.

The religious reached St. Stanislaus Seminary at
five o'clock. Bishop Rosati had arrived there the night
before from St. Louis on an old horse that he procured
with difficulty. Nine Jesuits and three secular priests
were to accompany him to St. Charles for the dedication
of the new church. The Father Rector took the nuns in

a carriage, while the Bishop and some of the priests rode, and others walked as far as the ferry-landing opposite St. Charles. At eight in the morning the nuns crossed the Missouri River and the strange procession entered the town which, although the population had doubled since 1818, could still boast of only one street. "All the ladies of the city," an old manuscript relates, "were at their windows to see us pass, and each one expressed her joy in her own way. One danced, clapped her hands and called enthusiastically to her daughter, 'Marie, see the nuns.' "

So generous were the good people that on that day they vied with one another in preparing dinner for the religious and their revered guests, and as they could only guess at what hour it would be convenient for the nuns to receive the meal, hot roasts kept coming to the convent all day long, so that there was enough meat left for a week. The convent was the old log-house on the gully which to-day is Decatur Street—the same house in which they had spent their first year at St. Charles; but now the church stood directly between it and the river. The log-cabin, vacant for years, was locked when the nuns arrived. One of the men of the village climbed in through a window and drew the bolt on the door. The Father Superior went in first and looked back saying, "Courage! come on."

"O Father," said Mother O'Connor, as she saw the condition of the place, "we shall certainly need courage."

She had never seen this poor little house, built of boards badly joined; but Mother Duchesne and Mother Octavie knew it well. There were six rooms, or rather holes, no floors and no inner doors, no panes of glass in the windows. Ste. Marie d'en Haut had looked like this after the Revolution. A basement, the length of the cabin, had been for some years the lodging of all the domestic animals of the village; sheep and pigs came there regularly for shelter. The atmosphere of the place is better imagined than described. The religious cleaned the part of the house in which they were to say Office, then little by little they got the whole cabin in order. It did not take them long to arrange the furniture, for there was not even one bed. An old carpet from the church was their only cover the first night. Rats, cheated of their accustomed abode, gave them no rest.

The eleventh of September was spent in preparation for the ceremony of the dedication of the church, and in preparing the convent for the priests whom Mother Duchesne invited to breakfast. Two little cupboards, one bench, three chairs, one stove and an empty barrel, and six dinner-napkins constituted the house furniture and linen. A small sack of sugar, one of coffee, one of rice, two bottles of altar wine and one of vinegar with the cooked meat left by the ladies of St. Charles, made up the larder. That evening at six o'clock the Bishop and twelve priests came to the convent, where they sang Office with as much dignity and piety as though they had been in a vast cathedral instead of being crowded into a poor little hovel,—this religious service might not be carried out in the church before it was blessed.

On the twelfth, nine Masses were said. Mother O'Connor, for want of acolytes, answered the prayers of the Mass. At ten, all the Catholics in the village assembled in the courtyard of the church to await the opening of the doors. The new building was of stone, the façade of cut stone surmounted by a pretty cornice resting upon four fine pilasters. The structure boasted eighty feet in length, forty in width, and twenty-nine in height, and was the only church in the diocese which was plastered. Besides the nine priests present that day, there were several seminarians and six lay-brothers.

After Mass, the Bishop went to the convent for breakfast. To receive him well the nuns offered him coffee, which was almost a luxury to the poor in those days. Monseigneur was presented with a large cup, into which Mother Duchesne hastened to put two generous spoonfuls of sugar. The Bishop raised the cup to his lips, then put it down quickly and said: "O Mother, how salty it is!" It was only too true. Mother Duchesne had put salt in the coffee, having forgotten that the only sugar they had was brown.

She and Mother Berthold remained two days longer at St. Charles. On the 14th they said good-bye to Mother Mathevon and Mother O'Connor, who for a year were the only religious who could be spared for that house, where the school grew and where much good was accomplished in a silent hidden way.

On her return to St. Louis Mother Duchesne wrote to Bishop Du Bourg:

On the 12th of October, the day Your Lordship appointed for the honoring of the Holy Angels, I assisted for the first time in my life at the dedication of a church. It was that of St. Charles, built by the Jesuits who have used in its erection all the funds which they had received for their own support. It looks upon the Missouri, and is built on the site of your former garden and just over the spot from which you helped with your episcopal hands to pull up a sapling.

Monseigneur Rosati performed the ceremony, and was assisted by all the Jesuits, two Lazarists and several young seminarians. Fathers Detroux and Dussaussois preached, the one in English, the other in French, to a vast concourse before the church door. I never saw so grand a spectacle. Your beautiful dalmatics were used for the occasion. The following day His Lordship confirmed sixty-six persons and preached with wonderful fruit among the Protestants who listened to him.

In order to unite the six convents of the Sacred Heart in America still more closely, Mother Barat wished the Superiors of Louisiana and Missouri to meet in a Provincial Council to confer regarding any minor modifications of customs, manner of living and school management that the climate and other conditions seemed to demand. There were points for decision, and problems for discussion as well. When there had been question of the establishment at La Fourche, Mother Audé had written to Bishop Rosati: "If you wish that the novices of the Sisters of Loretto at the Foot of the Cross, who have an attraction for our mode of life and who desire to embrace it, should be received in our house, they may come whenever they wish. We shall be charmed to receive them, and we are disposed to love them tenderly in the Heart of Our Lord. I fear, however, that they will miss and regret the edifying example and holy counsels of their good Mothers Xavier and Regina, which they will be far from finding in your poor servant, Eugénie." The problem lay, not with the novices who went to St. Michael's, but with the school at La Fourche. The curriculum of the new school was simpler and less extensive, yet the parents either could not afford or did not wish to send their children away to St. Michael's. Pupils were withdrawn and the house was in distress and in debt.

There was question, too, of a new building at Grand Côteau, and on this subject Mother Xavier Murphy had written to Bishop Rosati, who was not able to pre-

side at the Prizes as he had promised. Mother Murphy
says in her quaint English:

Immediately on the reception of the *sad* letter, the
medallions and ribbons were simply distributed without
crowns, for I really had not the spirit to place them
on their *disappointed heads.* Madame Louvillier recom-
mends my addressing General Jackson on the subject
(raising a subscription for a new brick school building), having a niece of the President in our boarding
school.

Yes, Father, our delicious solitude has charms and
advantages peculiarly advantageous to the peace of
mind and interior spirit of the Spouses of the Heart of
Jesus. I have not heard from Mother Duchesne for
three months, a silence unusual on her part. It also
appears that our letters have been opened. This is
annoying, as I have been accustomed to think aloud with
this *bonne Mère.*

Until the receipt of your letter I had no information
of the nomination of our Holy Father, nor of the final
sweep of the *now free* sons of Irin. The inviting words
of the Prophet in Psalm 44, *"Audi, filia, et vide"* which
I have endeavored to reduce to practice in this dear
land of my adoption, cause this intelligence to convey
less joy than the assurance you give us of our once
more possessing Fathers De Neckère and De La Croix.

In the meantime, Mother Barat had written to
Mother Duchesne from Paris on March 5, 1829:

We have received several letters from you and your
accounts. What poverty! My heart is affected by it.
I have worked so hard to collect the twenty-five hundred
francs for you that Monsieur X owes us, and I have
also collected the same amount promised by the Association of the Faith to you and to the Jesuits.

Go down to Louisiana. Assemble Mothers Xavier,
Eugénie and Dutour at St. Michael. I name you to

preside over this little gathering, and you will keep me in touch with your deliberations.

Mother Duchesne took alarm when she heard she was to preside at the Council, and wrote to Mother Barat: "Do consent to whatever the Mothers of Louisiana will regulate among themselves. I am only a worn-out old staff, good for nothing but to be thrown away. I look on myself as an old lion with no strength to act, and one overwhelmed and irritated by everything."

The Mother General knew her Philippine too well to believe what she said of herself, and she wrote to tell Mother Audé that Mother Duchesne would preside: "She has a right to it both as your senior and as the one to whom God originally entrusted the mission. And, moreover, she has both experience and virtue."

Mother Duchesne yielded. It was suggested that the Mothers come north, but she insisted on making the journey south, preferring, she said: "to risk the health of an old creature like herself than to expose to so much fatigue two persons still of an age to render great services to the Society."

She left St. Louis on November 7, 1829, and found her kind hostesses, the Ursulines of New Orleans, in their new convent two miles beyond the city limits. The house stood in a grove of pecans, the cloisters and terraces overlooked the Mississippi, and the gardens were shaded by live oaks and bordered by palms. Her stay there was short, for Mother Murphy and Mother Dutour were to meet her at St. Michael's, as she wanted them to be back in their own houses by Christmas, if possible.

The time of the Council was a painful one for Mother Duchesne. Individual houses were then more directly dependent on the Mother House than they are to-day, and Mother Duchesne, feeling the position a delicate one, did not assert herself freely. Moreover, Mother Audé said that she sought the advice of this good Mother in spiritual matters, in which she was an adept, but that in other affairs she did not consult her at all, but wrote to France, and during the long interim between question and answer she did what she thought best. Mother Duchesne found it her unpleasant duty to request the suppression of public examinations, entertainments and distributions of prizes, of which she knew well that the Mother General would not approve. Time was to prove the correctness of her decision, but meanwhile she suffered at having to preside where she felt she was considered a stumbling block to progress. Except for this she would have enjoyed her visit to St. Michael's. The community, including the novices, numbered twenty-two, the school counted ninety-two children, and all were happy under the guidance of Mother Audé, who was as loved there as at Florissant and Côteau, and of whose true attachment and loyal devotion to the Society no one could doubt. Among the Sisters was one of whom Mother Eugénie had written to Mgr. Rosati two years before: " I have received Mrs. Boudreau, who will draw down God's blessing on this house." The only desire of this holy lady was to enter as a coadjutrix Sister, and to give the remainder of her life to the hidden labor of Nazareth. Her daughter followed her mother to St. Michael's, and as a novice was charged with certain work of the Sisters. When she gently called her mother's attention to a counterpane badly put on, the humble Sister fell on her knees. Mother Audé never had a talk with this religious without being moved to tears by her unbounded confidence in God, her charity, humility and utter simplicity. This last virtue she tested in the presence of Mother Duchesne, who gave the community extra recreation on the day of her arrival at St. Michael's. At one of the gay reunions Mother Audé begged old Sister Boudreau to sing for Mother Duchesne. Without any hesitation the good simple nun did as she was asked. "Could you dance for us?" said the Superior, and Sister Boudreau did as she was requested. The Mother Visitor was as charmed with her simplicity as was St. Francis with that of his Brother Juniper. The very next day this good simple Sister went suddenly to her eternal reward.

Mother Aloysia Hardey was giving promise of the virtue and ability that were to make her a power later on in founding the houses in the eastern part of the United States; and Mother Duchesne, seeing her worth, did not hesitate to find fault with her grand and dignified manner and poise.

The house of St. Michael's was finely situated on the Mississippi. There the river broadens out like a lake which at sunset shines as molten gold over which gleam banners of red, purple, amethyst and green. For "league after league the river pours its tide along between its almost untenanted shores, with seldom a sail or a moving object of any kind to disturb the surface or break the monotony of the blank watery solitude, and so the day goes, the night comes, and again the day, and still the same, night after night, and day after day, majestic, unchanging sameness of serenity, repose, tranquillity."

From St. Michael's Mother Duchesne went to Bayou La Fourche, where she found six nuns and about twenty-six children. She did what she could to arrange matters, but on leaving felt that her visit had not done much towards pleasing the parents. Her next journey was towards Grand Côteau, across country, where at night "the moon diffuses a great secret melancholy over the ancient forests." Christmas Day was passed on the way through that semi-tropical country. On the 26th of December the children of Côteau, having heard that Mothers Duchesne and Murphy had reached Portage, went to meet them. These two religious were a joy to each other, and Mother Duchesne wrote: "Mother Xavier is the *one* of our Mothers with whom I can converse most intimately. We could not help wishing that we might be together in St. Louis, but who could fill her place at the Opelousas?" Yet with all the work that she accomplished, the Superior of Côteau was often as ill as she was during Mother Duchesne's visit, for she suffered almost constantly from fever. "My soul is stronger than my body, I think," she said simply, "for my mind is always at peace. It seems to me that the more imperfect I am, the more God loves me."

Under her care the school prospered. So anxious were the parents to have their daughters with Mother Murphy and at the Sacred Heart, that they would bring them a fortnight's journey in a caravan, even when they knew that the children might have to sleep all winter on the floor in a garret or in an outbuilding. The religious were still more poorly accommodated, and Mother Duchesne made arrangements for erecting a new wing. She sent to France for approval some regulations restricting the number of non-Catholic children to be taken as boarders, as she thought the atmosphere of the school less conventual than she would have wished. Yet on the whole, the visit to Grand Côteau brought her true joy. There, all speaks to the

Heavenly-minded of God, there she was awakened by the "songs of the cardinals and mocking-birds nestling in the acacias" surrounding the house. The garden was radiant with December roses and the snowy bushes were mammoth bouquets of camelias.

Yet all days are not radiant, even at Côteau: on January 19, 1830, in a torrent of rain Mother Duchesne left there, accompanied by a priest and guided by a negro. "Look at that green spot, Mother," the priest would assure her, "that is a dangerous quagmire." "There is the place where I saw a wagon stuck for five hours in the mud." "This is the wood where I was attacked in the night by a negro."

In spite of these warnings no misadventure occurred, and they safely reached St. Michael's, where Mother Duchesne was delayed for three weeks awaiting a boat to St. Louis. At last on February 5 she left Louisiana. The journey up the Mississippi was uneventful as far as the junction with the Ohio, but for the last hundred miles the boat was stranded time and again on sandbars or in shallows. So Mother Duchesne continued her journey in an ox-cart, stopping at the Barrens, where she saw the Bishop and was hospitably and kindly received by the Sisters of Loretto at the Foot of the Cross. At St. Genevieve she also spent a few hours, and at last arrived in St. Louis on February 27. To Mother Barat she wrote: "I do not know if God will look favorably on my journey, which I liked only because it was your will that I should undertake it, for my heart always inclines towards the poorest country and that is Missouri."

Her visit to the South was to bring on the three Louisiana houses God's dearest blessing, a blessing not often appreciated, the blessing with which He begins every work that is truly His own, a blessing that inevitably, if slowly and through pain, brings true success. That blessing is the cross.

CHAPTER IV

In Love with the Cross

CHAPTER IV

In Love with the Cross.—1830-1840

"Soul, soul of mine, be not unworthy found
Her slavery whom Calvary crowned,
A Queen, compassion-throned,
Be moulded, Jesus-shape, in her embrace;
Be crucified, and on thy face,
The Passion's hall-mark trace."

T. GAVAN DUFFY.

Mother Duchesne returned to St. Louis more convinced than ever that she was an obstacle to good in her houses of Missouri. She had contrasted the promise and success of Grand Côteau with the dismal failure of the convents founded directly by herself, and she blamed only herself. She could not know that she had sown seed on running water, and that her prayer and labor and suffering on the flinty bluffs of the Missouri at St. Charles, on the limestone terraces overlooking the Mississippi in St. Louis, and in the Valley of Florissant—within the embrace of the two streams— were to bear fruit in the vast delta a thousand miles further south. She could not know this, and she wept over the thought that she stood in the way of God's work. "It is my misfortune," she wrote to Mother Barat, "that I have not always before my eyes the description you gave me at Grenoble of the exterior

of Jesus Christ. Oh, that there were not such a complete
contrast between me and my Master and Model, and
also between me and my dear Mother who never breaks
the bruised reed." The contrast was not all she thought
it to be. The Master and Model had uttered a strong
cry: "I have a baptism wherewith I am to be baptized." Yet, when "heard for His reverence," He murmured, "If it be possible, remove this from Me." So
too, His servant, who thought she followed but afar
off. She had tried to convince Mother Barat that she
was a worn-out staff, good for nothing but to be thrown
away—and she meant every word that she uttered.
Yet when she felt the confidence of that venerated
Mother waning, she must have suffered soul-agony.

The holy Foundress never doubted the loyalty and
high virtue of this cherished Mother, but she feared that
her love of humility and mortification were standing in
the way of her gaining the confidence of the parents
of the pupils, that she had not asserted herself in the
Council at St. Michael's, and was becoming unpractical
in the management and upbuilding of a house.

The establishment at St. Louis, now four years old,
seemed to offer proof of this. Woods surrounded the
house, and so country-like was the neighborhood that
the chaplain could reach the convent in snowy weather
only by sliding down the banks of ravines. Within,
there was abject poverty. One room served for infirmary, community room and the children's recreation hall.
The refectory was a dark hole under the stair; and the
cups, which were of tin, held only sugarless coffee. One
could only guess what color the faded and patched
habits of the religious had originally been.

The saintly Foundress wrote to Mother Duchesne
in 1831:

Perhaps you would do well to get Mother Eugénie Audé to spend six weeks in St. Louis drawing up the plan of a building to be put up little by little—one that would place your house on the same footing as hers. I think, my daughter, that at your age and after so much suffering this American boarding school, requiring so much care and perfection, is beyond your strength. God forbid that I should blame you. I know too well what you have done and suffered, but times are changing; we too must make changes and modifications. Moreover, I have learned by experience that Superiors should not be left too long in the same house.

Mother Duchesne felt relieved as well as pained at this letter, for she longed to lay down her burden of authority; but just as Father Van Quickenborne had stood out against her removal from Florissant in 1825, so now, Bishop Rosati, appreciating her virtues, interposed and insisted that she be left in her office and in St. Louis. Mother Barat yielded all the more readily that she had not wanted to withdraw her Philippine from a position in which she had been a model of abnegation, and she wrote to Mother Duchesne: "I was yielding to the desires which you have so often and so energetically expressed, and because some others thought as you did. I am glad that they were mistaken and that humility alone made you ask for this change."

So Philippine, who always read Mother Barat's letters on her knees, knelt to receive anew the burden she had thought about to be lifted. This burden was becoming daily heavier. A letter from Mother Audé announced that, as the Superior General had written to her to suppress the house at La Fourche, she had done so at once. There was now one tabernacle less in Louisiana, the children there might thus be deprived of religious instruction and training, while it devolved upon St. Michael's and Grand Côteau to pay the debts left by that foundation, and the heart of Mother Duchesne had to suffer the aftermath of an apparent abandonment of a convent.

It was about this time that she wrote to a novice, Gonzaga Boilvin:

Profit by moments of trial. This is the time to make progress. I always remember the words said to me by a man of God when I was situated much as you are: "Unless the grain of wheat fall to the ground and die, it remaineth alone; but if it dies, it brings forth much fruit."

The wish to die sometimes springs from laziness. One can but say the words of the Canticle: "After death there will still be suffering." And what suffering! In Purgatory! One is appalled by the thought of the last farthing for which one must render account. Let us bear our cross and leave it to God to determine the length and the weight.

As the time for this novice to make her first vows drew near, Mother Duchesne wrote to her:

S.C.J.M.

My dear Sister:

I wish I had all the unction of your good Father so as to be able to express my wishes and feelings at the approach of the day on which you will contract your sacred, and, I hope, your eternal alliance. One month, and the happy day will be here! We shall try to give you more time for prayer and for recollection. In the calm of solitude your Beloved will speak to you of the conditions of His union with you, of all He will do for you and of the ornaments which he presents to you. They are the cross, the thorns, the bonds; such are the jewels of Calvary. Have courage! Others before us have worn them and have exchanged them at the last for joys not given to the heart of man to conceive.

The religious at St. Charles were still in the log-cabin behind the church. Father Verhaegen wrote: "Mother Lucille's building is going to rack and ruin, but Father Van Quickenborne is determined not to prop it up. He will have another house for this very useful community. He has $300. He will get the rest, though he will have to wear out six pairs of shoes running through St. Louis on begging expeditions."

So cramped were the nuns for space that in 1833 Mother Mathevon had to refuse refuge to a poor little half-breed whom the Bishop wished her to harbor. On this subject she writes to His Lordship: "We have one room for religious, boarders, day-pupils and an orphan. She would be lonely in the kitchen. May she go to Florissant where there is an Indian girl?"

In the early thirties there was in St. Louis a fad for raising mulberry trees, the leaves of which furnished food for silk-worms imported from France. Even St. Charles was not immune from this hobby, and Mother Lucille Mathevon in writing to Bishop Rosati alludes to the matter: "I have been promised mulberry trees; I hope that some small ones will come to-morrow. I shall in all probability not be able to send for silk-worms this year." Three weeks later she writes again to the Bishop: "I have planted six mulberry trees, some of which are eight feet high, and I hope to have some leaves. If I succeed, I shall send you some silk." It is not likely that Bishop Rosati engaged an embroiderer to make vestments of the silk here offered, unless Mother

Lucille's venture proved more successful than did that of many another.

Mulberry trees, silk, new buildings, and all were forgotten in what now took place. In 1832 Asiatic cholera came to North America, being brought to Canada by immigrants. It swept the shores of the St. Lawrence and of the Great Lakes, then followed the course of the Mississippi south to the Gulf, ever increasing in virulence. At New Orleans, Bishop de Neckère and the Abbé Martial were its victims, and altogether, twenty priests died, struck down in ministering to the thousands afflicted by this most frightful malady. Mother Duchesne mourned over the death of all these priests who had lived "seeking not praise for their labor, forgetting the deed in the doing."

Then word reached Mother Philippine of what had happened at St. Michael's. The house sheltered about two hundred persons, including religious, children and slaves. Cholera appeared in the community. The sick nuns were immediately isolated, and the school was dispersed. The kind planters were so distressed to see Mother Audé and her community remain in the stricken convent, that they went so far as to rent and furnish a house at Donaldsonville where the plague had not appeared, and they hired a steamboat which stopped at the convent-landing to take the religious away. Mother Audé, in the name of the whole community, absolutely refused to leave a house where one of her daughters lay dead, where two were dying and where several others and two orphans were attacked by the cruel malady. Three more nuns died. Mother Audé dragged herself from room to room, and during two weeks allowed herself not a moment of sleep, and ate only enough to keep herself alive. As soon as the danger seemed over she fell ill, and thought her last hour had come. She grew better, however, only to attend the deaths of four other religious. In a long letter to Mother Barat Mother Audé described the painful experiences of St. Michael's. She ended by saying: "Some time spent with you would strengthen me, would revive my poor soul and would dispose me to suffer anew. Mother, dear Mother, will you not allow me to come? But, forgive me, this request is contrary to abandonment—do what you wish with your Eugénie. Her will shall be yours to her very last sigh; if this sigh expresses suffering, it also speaks of submission, and of the happiness of dying in obeying you." This letter was not the first in which Mother Audé had poured out her longing to see her loved Mother General, and it crossed one in which Mother Barat said that she indeed hoped to bring her daughter shortly to France.

Mother Duchesne's solicitude had not been concentrated on St. Michael's. One morning when she made the call, as was her wont, she found that every nun in the house in St. Louis was ill. Their illness proved to be cholerine—a mild form of cholera. The orphans were also attacked by this disease, and Mother Duchesne made herself all things to all. For nearly two months the invalids had repeated relapses, so that the strength of the Superior was exhausted in ministering to others. That strength must have been upheld by Heaven, for in November, 1832, she had written:

S.C.J.M.

My dear Sister:

I have always answered your letters, and I have never been displeased with you, except perhaps when you showed anxiety about my health, which should not concern you. I am at an age when, as David said, one has only miseries. One's poor carcass falls to ruins, in some cases suddenly, in others little by little. I think that the latter lot will be mine, and I expect to be ill often this winter, but this will be a means of expiation for the past. One must look upon it as a gain and not as a misfortune, since nothing tarnished can enter Heaven.

As to what pains you, believe that I have the same trial; but let us take up our cross without cowardice, looking upon Jesus reduced to the extremity of anguish and asking us if we wish to let Him suffer alone. Have we the courage to refuse Him this solace? It is at the foot of the cross with our desolate Mother that I am in C. J.

PHILIPPINE.

P. S. There is nothing serious in my state of health.

The isolation of the house at Grand Côteau saved it from cholera. The journal shows the anxiety of those there for the other convents and for the families of the children, and their well-founded fear that the plague would reach even the "Eden of Louisiana." Florissant and St. Charles were attacked by the disease, but there were no deaths at the convents. On August 7, 1833, Mother Lucille Mathevon wrote to congratulate Bishop Rosati on his recovery. She says in conclusion: "The town of St. Charles has been struck; several of the best citizens have died. Three of our religious have been ill, there was only one left to care for the rest. Mother Eulalie suffered the most, and she has not recovered her strength. Mother Duchesne thinks that a journey would do her good, and she has told me to send her to another of our houses at the first opportunity." In August, 1833, Mr. Mullanphy died. The orphans who owed their refuge to his initiative went dressed in black and white to his funeral. Regarding this Catholic philanthropist, Mother Xavier Murphy had written to Bishop Rosati: " I have been so completely American-ized (the English of some of her letters makes us doubt her word) that, for some time back, I nearly forgot that I ever had any claim on the Emerald Isle. But on hearing of all the *noble, dignified* acts of Mr. Mul-lanphy and of his co-operation with you in all your undertakings A.M.D.G., my national pride felt awakened, and I exclaimed: 'Ah, I cannot forget that I am Irish when I have such a man to claim as com-patriot.' You have also, dear Father, the Sons of Loy-ola. What powerful auxiliaries for your Godlike mis-sion. Poor Louisiana, *you* have nothing!!"

A death keenly felt by Mother Duchesne was that of her beloved Octavie Berthold, from whom she had not been parted a year since their coming to America in 1818. Mother Octavie had been most charming and winning, and gifted with unusual beauty. Fearing that she attracted others to herself instead of leading them to God, she begged Him to take away what He had given. It was in 1821 that she made this prayer, and two or three years later she felt the first symptoms of the strange illness which for eight years disfigured her with the most hideous abscesses and ulcers. When she was able to be with the children or to see visitors whom she had once overheard remarking her beauty, she would cover her face lest the repulsion caused by looking at her should keep them away from the convent. Yet, with all this physical suffering and humiliation "God tried her severely. Loneliness, solitude and the weari-ness of a long illness afflicted her successively. Satan tormented her interiorly, but she pressed the bitter cross to her heart and offered herself to the Eternal Father as a victim with Our Lord."

Her suffering drew her ever nearer to God, and she wrote to Mother Barat: "I feel drawn to a closer union with Him. During the last six months especially, He has attracted me very much towards a life of intimacy with Him. Sometimes the sense of His greatness and infinite sanctity overwhelms me, for it shows me the loathsomeness of my own soul; at other times when I am near the tabernacle or even with the children or in the refectory or in the room where I sleep, I feel an almost sensible consciousness of the Presence of God which lasts four or five days, and this state almost always precedes new bodily sufferings." Her example was an inspiration not only to the novices, with whom she was charged for a time, but to all who knew her. Little by little she grew worse, until the remnant of life became a lingering breath, a prolonged agony, yet her soul was in peace. To herself she seemed like a ship becalmed at sea: "I have nothing more to suffer," she said to her Superior: "Our Lord treats me like a tepid soul to whom He does not even send temptations."

"Do not be afraid, my child," answered Mother Duchesne: "Our Lord will see to that."

These words have the ring of prophecy. Three hours before Mother Octavie died, a cold sweat covered her body, her limbs stiffened, her hair stood on end. Terror could be read on her face eaten away by disease. The dying religious moaned: "Alas! all is lost! Our Lord has cast me off!" In vain Father Van Quickenborne and Mother Duchesne tried to comfort her. "O, my Jesus," she sobbed, "allow me to love You a little longer in this life!" Mother Duchesne knelt beside the bed, shuddering with compassion. With his face on the

ground, Father Van Quickenborne prayed for her
relief. Suddenly, peace shone on the countenance of
the dying Mother; smiling and radiant, she stretched
out her arms to Mother Duchesne, and whispered: "Let
us rejoice, the struggle is over. Now there is only
Jesus." The Jesuit rose and intoned the Magnificat,
and Mother Duchesne said it with him, for Octavie's
suffering was over. Hers had been:

> *"One last keen glance of Faith through shadows dim,*
> *One last brave cry of Hope 'mid shuddering fears,*
> *One last deep throb of Love to God unseen;*
> *Then flashed for 'her' the dawn of endless years."*

Two days after the death of Mother Berthold the
Prizes were given in the new building, although it was
far from complete. It was of brick, and measured fifty
feet in length by thirty in width. The basement was to
be the children's refectory, and the first floor was to be
devoted to classrooms, above which would be dor-
mitories.

To her great relief, Mother Duchesne learned that,
though she had been confirmed in her office as Superior,
she was now released from the supervision and general
responsibility of the two houses in the far south, the
government of which Mother Barat reserved to herself, until such time as a Council should name an Assistant General for America and appoint Provincials in
charge of certain portions of the Society. It was in
November, while the Council General of 1833 was in
session in France, that Mother Duchesne went out to
St. Charles to see the plan of the new brick house, for
which Father Van Quickenborne had already succeeded
in raising $1,500. A month later Mother Lucille

Mathevon wrote to Bishop Rosati: "We shall ask Your Lordship to come to choose the place for our new building if the Reverend Father succeeds in his project of beginning it in the spring, counting on the funds of Divine Providence, which has helped us so much since coming here that I do not doubt that we shall be so assisted in the future."

The Council named Mother Eugénie Audé Assistant General and deputed her to visit the houses of Grand Côteau, Florissant, St. Charles and St. Louis before sailing for France. She wrote to Mother Duchesne announcing her appointment and her visit. Before her letter reached Missouri the visit to Côteau had been made, and Mother Audé was on her way north.

The annals of the house of St. Louis, of which Mother Duchesne was chronicler, speak of what the Mother Visitatrix told them of the southern convents; of the new building at Grand Côteau and at St. Michael's, and of the beautiful church which had replaced that of Father De La Croix on the bank of the Mississippi. Enthusiastically, too, Mother Duchesne notes the generosity of her dear Mother Eugénie. She says not a word of the pang her own heart must have experienced each time that she heard her old daughter say: "In a few weeks I shall see Mother Barat." A biographer of the sainted Foundress says: Mother Eugénie Audé arrived (in Paris) on the 26th of June. She gave her venerated Mother General an account of her mission, and near her she forgot the bitterness of the chalice of which the Lord had given long draughts." A chalice, even more bitter, Mother Duchesne was appointed to drink—and to the dregs.

The Council General of 1833 decreed the suppres-

sion of that house of the Sacred Heart which was, perhaps, dearer to Mother Duchesne than any other. The
monastery of Ste. Marie d'en Haut in Grenoble, redo-
lent with memories of her childhood, of her vocation,
her gift of self to God and of His gifts to her—this
dearest of houses was closed. Mother Barat had written
to warn her dear Philippine of the impending suppression required by change of surroundings, for Ste. Marie
was now overlooked and disturbed by works of fortifi-
cation carried on by artillery engineers. The sympathetic Foundress wrote again to tell her daughter
that the closing had been effected. In reply, Philippine
said: "I should sooner forget my right hand than that
delightful place, and I have more reason to lament over
it than Jeremias over Jerusalem. Tell my dear old
Sisters of Grenoble who have gone through the pangs
of separation how much I feel for them." She made
a sketch of her old monastery, and wrote under it the
words of the prophet of desolation: "The ways of Sion
mourn because there are none that come to the feasts."
But when she heard that the Ursulines had taken the
house and were there carrying on the work of education
with signal success she added to her drawing the verse
of the prophet of peace: "For thither did the tribes
go up, the tribes of the Lord, to praise the Name of
the Lord."

The convent in St. Louis was still in the Valley
of the Shadow. Cholerine had been followed by other
epidemics, and the school was closed; the invalids were
sent to Florissant for a change of air; the house was
in great need. The new building stood unfinished, for
in the financial crisis that followed on the plague the
cost of living was so high and wages and building
material so expensive that the generous sum sent from

France for the new wing did not suffice to complete it. With the orphans who remained and who were not ill Mother Duchesne formed an expiatory procession about the garden. She walked behind the children barefoot and with a rope around her neck and a candle in her hand, a mediæval symbol of a penitent who acknowledges that her sins have brought calamity upon her people. Her humble prayers, her fastings, her austerities were a strong cry which pierced the clouds. Her sick nuns and children recovered and the well did not starve.

Two months later, on October 11, 1834, the post brought a letter addressed in the loved hand of the holy Foundress. Mother Duchesne opened the envelope and knelt to read the contents: "My dear Philippine," it ran, "you need rest, and on that account an easier house to govern. You will, therefore, appoint Mother Thiéffry Superior at St. Louis, and you will take her place at Florissant." The next morning, Mother Duchesne gave Bishop Rosati the letter which had told her of Mother Barat's decision. The carriage which took him back to the episcopal residence returned to take her away, and before noon she was on her way to the convent which a Jesuit has called "the Valley Forge of the Society." The change was made calmly, simply, strongly, though it may have been through tears that she looked back on the dingy brick house, on the Indian Mound, on the ill-kept garden with its picket fence, on Chouteau's Pond where colored laundresses were rubbing snowy linen on the rocks and stones, where a lone fisherman patiently watched his line, and on the kaleidoscopic views seen as one winds along the old road to the Valley of Flowers, her Valley Forge. Her motto then, as always, was:

"With thee take
Only what none else would keep.
Learn to dream when thou dost wake,
Learn to wake when thou dost sleep;
Learn to water joy with tears,
Learn from fear to vanquish fears,
For thou else couldst not believe;
Lose, that the lost thou may'st receive."

Mother Duchesne reached Florissant at two in the afternoon, and found Mother Thiéffry preparing for her departure, which took place the next morning, to the great regret—says the one who succeeded her—of both religious and children.

The circular letter written to all the houses of the Society after the Council of 1833, the decrees, notes, recommendations and the answers to questions sent to France by Mother Duchesne were received by her just before she left St. Louis. One of her first acts after reaching Florissant was to continue the copying of these papers, so as to send duplicates to the other houses of Missouri. On the back of one of the manuscripts which she then sent to Mother Lucille Mathevon at St. Charles is this note:

My dear Mother:

If it were not for my change of house, you would have had this sooner. There remains much to be copied. The most pressing was the circular which I hope you have received—and these permissions. All yours in C.J.

PH. D.

On New Year's Day, 1835, Philippine wrote to thank a young religious for a gift she had sent—a picture of the Sacred Heart:

My dear Sister:

I have received your two letters, and though you did not tell me that what you were sending was your own work, I easily recognized it as such. Thank you for all, but especially for that which is the Symbol of our union, the Object of our devotion, the Mirror in which we should see both our own faults and the virtues that are wanting to us.

My wish for you this New Year is that you obtain the virtues one draws from the study of the Heart of Christ. I do not need His charity to forgive your faults against me, for I recall none. If you have displeased God, He has forgiven you seventy times seven times. So, as I have the same confidence with regard to my own failings, I hope that the Sacred Heart will unite us. In Him I am all yours,

PHILIPPINE.

This same young religious wrote to tell Mother Duchesne of her eagerness to make her final vows. The answer was as follows:

My dear Sister:

Your letter gives me much consolation because it expresses your desires, your love for your vocation, and your longings to contract the alliance which will make your union with Our Lord more entire. Your perseverance will help to make up to Him and to us for the falling away of several. If the love and yearning of His Adorable Heart are to be fully satisfied, you who wish to give yourself to Him must prepare for the Divine union by becoming like unto Him. Like Him in what way? He Himself has told us "Learn of Me meekness and humility."

It is the latter virtue that you will have to work upon, and since you wish to prune the vine before inviting the Spouse to eat of its fruits, I must advise you to be constant in cutting off useless branches. I remind you of your self-esteem, your tone of self-assurance, your astonishment when you are found fault with, your coolness if a request causes you a slight inconvenience, your occasional carelessness in conducting your class and in watching over the children.

As to penances, they are not for you. The only one I ask of you is to speak English always in public. This is a very good mortification and one that will give more glory to God and do more for the house than fasting on bread and water. These then are your penances:

1st—Speak English,
2nd—Study English more or less every day,
3rd—Learn English hymns,
4th—Make every day two acts of humility, avoiding quick answers, excuses and other like faults.

These years at Florissant present little matter for history, but open up wide vistas for thought and prayer and study. There were but few events to mark the flight of time. Mother Duchesne as chronicler of the house notes that Father Barat sent some money gained by selling the jewels of a generous benefactress, and she took $300 from this sum to St. Charles one day to give it to Mother Lucille for the new building. The munificent mite helped much.

On October 28, 1835, the Superior of St. Charles wrote to remind Bishop Rosati of his promise to visit them on the feast of the patron of the parish. She adds: "Will you be so good as to bless our house which though not quite finished is nevertheless habitable, and we hope soon to occupy it. You will admire the designs of Providence on this convent, built, I hope, for the greater glory of God."

Meanwhile the house at Florissant was threatened.

Father De Theux, Rector of the Jesuits there, wrote to Mother Barat on this subject from the "Novitiate of St. Stanislaus, near St. Ferdinand," on December 31, 1835: "Having learned from Madame Thiéffry and Madame Duchesne that you are thinking of suppressing the house of St. Ferdinand, I hasten to tell you how much this step will be felt, or rather how much it will detract from the good done to religion in this parish. Your nuns keep the church so well."

Father De Theux concluded his letter by suggesting that Florissant be made the general noviceship for America, and that the orphans from St. Louis be sent there. However, Mr. Mullanphy's wish that the twenty children remain in the house he had helped to establish was respected by the Superior General, who did not see fit to transfer the novices from Louisiana to St. Ferdinand, but who acceded to Father De Theux' more important request, and the convent at Florissant was saved for the moment. The journal of that house notes the illness of the Superior; for several weeks Mother Duchesne lay between life and death. The heroic endurance with which she had borne so much pain in the years gone by had hidden from others what she suffered, but now the body she scorned took its revenge. Calmly she prepared for death, whether it were to be a peaceful passing from this life to the next, or a struggle such as that of Octavie. But God had other work for Mother Philippine. During her illness she had offered the convent side of the sacristy to the Jesuits, and there Brother De Meyer of famous memory opened his little school for the boys of the village.

At this time, Mother Xavier, Superior of the Sisters of Charity in St. Louis, was taking a much needed rest and change of air at the Convent of the Sacred Heart near Opelousas. Mother Xavier Murphy wrote of this religious: "What a holy soul! What a treasure for the Institute to which she is attached!" The Sister of Charity described her visit to Côteau in a letter to Bishop Rosati:

I write to you from the white cottage situated west of the convent. The institution here far exceeds anything I could have expected to find in this country. They have eighty-five boarders, all in good health. In a word, it is a little heaven on earth; the garden and the surrounding country charm the eye; the warbling of the little birds enchants the ear, while the innocent gaiety of interesting youth, the solid and cheerful piety of these admirable nuns rejoice the heart yet cannot content it, for I greatly prefer my Dolor Hospital filled with human miseries and my little orphan boys. Have the goodness to tell Mother Duchesne how very kindly I am treated here.

Building was going on at Côteau, and the house soon had room for its one hundred boarders. In the midst of success the cross came to Grand Côteau in the death of its loved Superior, Mother Xavier Murphy. In her grief, Mother Duchesne wrote to the Mother House: "If it had been the Will of God, I should have wished to disappear from the world instead of good Mother Xavier. My death would have affected no one, but how will she be replaced?"

The Superior of St. Michael's, Mother Bazire, was succeeded by Mother Aloysia Hardey, and was herself sent to Grand Côteau to take the place left vacant by Mother Murphy, a place which, to Mother Duchesne's way of thinking, none could ever quite fill.

In 1836, Father Van Quickenborne with three other

Jesuits came to ask good Mother Philippine's prayers for the mission to the Kickapoos which they were about to begin. With holy envy she saw them go, for even at sixty-seven years of age and worn out with labor and pain, she had not given up all hope of going to those for whom especially she had come to America, her Indians in the backwoods. In the following year she heard with sorrow of the death of her rigorous director, Father Van Quickenborne.

When Mother Audé had been summoned to France, she expected to be allowed to return to America for—as Assistant General—she had been given charge over the convents here, but her health seemed in such a precarious state that Mother Barat sent her instead to Marseilles. Mother Duchesne notes this fact and alludes to the great good her Eugénie accomplished in Europe as in this country.

The chief item in the annals of Florissant in 1837 is the departure of a negro slave and her little girl, who left to Mother Anne Shannon the care of the cows. These slaves returned to the convent the following year, and when the child became very ill, Mother Duchesne nursed her with the tenderness of a mother and placed her in a cot in the convent parlor where she received her first and last Communion. The Blessed Sacrament was accompanied from the church to the deathbed by four children of the Academy, who, fired by the example of the zeal and charity of Mother Duchesne, also carried to the cemetery the box containing the body of the poor little negress.

Thus run the events of the time from 1834 to 1841. Between the lines of the journal and in notes left by contemporaries of Philippine Duchesne we glimpse a little of what those years really meant. The life of the religious was one of hardship, labor, self-sacrifice, and prayer. When in December, 1819, they had moved into this house, Mother Duchesne looked at the swollen creeks and said with grim humor: "At least we shall have enough water." The next morning the streams were frozen and remained ice-bound for several weeks that winter—and this proved a yearly occurrence.

On New Year's Day, 1839, there were so many calls on the devotedness of the religious, so much work to be done in feeding the cows, in all but creating meals in the kitchen, that the little community could only meet for a moment to wish one another happiness in the opening year. Their recreations at this time were passed in the kitchen where the half-frozen nuns recalled memories of New Year's Day in far away France.

The question of suppressing the house at Florissant came up again. Frequent floods, extreme poverty, the poor prospects of the boarding school—all seemed to justify closing this convent in order to branch out in another more promising direction, but Mother Duchesne was distressed at the idea of leaving the poor children of the village without religious training, and in silent anguish she prayed. While she invoked the intercession of "the whole court of Heaven" in behalf of this house, Father De Theux, the Rector of the Jesuits, again sought the intervention of "the just on earth," this time by writing to Bishop Rosati:

I believe it to be my duty, seeing that the village is committed to the care of our Society, to observe to you that the suppression of this house would work very serious harm to the village of St. Ferdinand, unfortunately, bad enough already, and yet destined by its situation to develop shortly into a place of importance.

We should lose besides the prayers and good example of these religious, the day-school which they had decided to maintain and which, together with the boys' school that I opened last September, ought to give the Father Missioner a great ascendency over the whole parish. In fine, who will keep up the church as neatly as they do? And what will become of the house? I will not insist further. *Fiat voluntas Dei et Superiorum!!*

His intercession prevailed, and the convent was again saved for Mother Duchesne and the Society. Of the work done there during these years, someone has written: "Though scoring no great educational success within its own walls, the Florissant house of the Society of the Sacred Heart became a dynamic centre from which uplifting influences were dispensed over a great range of territory."

Mother Duchesne kept her old post of sacristan, and when there were too few for Office and she could not spare the time to go to her stall, she would say it aloud while working in the sanctuary. She was still the night-visitor, and once awoke early in the morning to find that sleep had overcome her on her rounds the night before, and that she was still standing before a shrine at which she had paused. She would slip up to the attic used as a linen room to finish the sewing left undone by another. One day, the religious charged with this work suddenly remembered that she had been told to leave the door of the linen room locked. Quietly she hurried upstairs and turned the key in the door. No one dreamed that Mother Duchesne had been locked in until the Bishop came to see her and the rest of the house had been searched in vain. At last she was found and set free, but she said not a word of reproach.

She tried to hide her mortification by reading in the refectory so as to make her own meal afterwards of scraps left by the children. Her strong, tender letters showed that she never forgot the souls whom she had initiated in the practices of virtue. To one of these, Mother Boilvin, she wrote:

Rest assured that you do not cause me suffering but rather consolation, since I see in you one who can render great service to the Society of the Sacred Heart. It was because I feared that you were yourself conscious of this fact, and because I know that good qualities are seldom without their corresponding defects, that I intended to deal a blow to your self-love. Thus I hoped to make room for the love of God and of others. It would be the greatest pity to think oneself without blame. On the other hand, sadness over our faults may spring from humiliated pride. We must be like the Sister Hospitalier who, when reproached for fifty-two faults, only plunged herself the more deeply in confidence in the Heart of Our Lord.

I am sorry that you did not say sooner that you were suffering. You should not have fasted on Wednesday. You must make it known as soon as you feel the need of relief. Our Mothers cannot always guess our needs just by a glance. It will be a real pleasure for me to care for you.

PHILIPPINE.

In the summer time Mother Duchesne worked in the garden, not like the other women of Florissant to supply the St. Louis market, but in order to keep her daughters from starving. The Jesuits sent vegetables from their more prosperous farm on the knoll when they knew she was in distress; and she sometimes appealed to them for what she needed for her kitchen-garden. Thus Mother Anne Shannon writes to Father Schoenmakers: "Respected Father: Madame Duchesne wishes to know if any of your negroes could prune our fruit-trees; 2d; if you could let us have some cabbage-seed or plants like those you gave us last year; 3rd; if you would please to tell Rev. Fr. De Theux that there is a person here who wishes to see him when he can make it convenient to come."

Mother Duchesne's letters to Mother Barat tell of her farm work: "I have been so strong that since Easter I have been caller, night visitor, gardener, and also mistress of dormitory on Saturdays. I have sown and gathered in the garden and my pride has had nothing to feed on but beans and cabbages. I was quite proud of one plant which produced more than six hundred beans, and of another with over three hundred. My cabbages and apples were as large as an armchair!!! Several cabbage-leaves are two feet in length. As to the more delicate things—no success. The birds have eaten up all the peas and gooseberries. There were no strawberries."

Heroic as Mother Duchesne was, she was far from being callous. Oppressed by suffering, feeling herself an obstacle to God's work, lonely as only those close to Him can be lonely, she went on in her labor. One day someone was sent to the garden in search of her. She had put down her shovel and rake, and she sat on the edge of the cabbage-patch saying her beads. At first she did not see the one who drew near, for there alone, and as she thought unseen, she was weeping: "In her eyes were discerned the trace of tears, on her brow the furrows wrought by her sufferings. Because of these she will only appear the more worthy of the homage and veneration of those, who, like her, have suffered."

CHAPTER V

JOY IN THE APOSTOLATE

CHAPTER V

Joy in the Apostolate—1840-1842

"Give me, Thou Giver of all good,
A heart of joy that can sing songs to Thee
E'en in the night, or when life's tedious ways
Seem to press heavily through the days;
Joys that will lie deeper than the tears
That rise above unuttered fears,
Or like a fathomless abyss is still
And silent, wrapt in a more perfect will
Which suffers not a lesser need to break
The peace which God alone can give or take."

AUBREY DE VERE.

The office of Secretary General of the Society of the Sacred Heart, which post Mother Duchesne had been the first to fill, had been entrusted by the Council of 1833 to Mother Elizabeth Galitzin. This remarkable woman was a convert from the Russian schismatic church. During four years she daily renewed her vow never to abandon the faith of her Russian forefathers. At the age of nineteen, she followed her mother into the true fold; and ten years later left her to enter the Society of the Sacred Heart. Under stern, harsh tutors she had become proficient in Latin, French, English and Italian, but these teachers had neither bent nor broken her strong overbearing autocratic nature. She had certain characteristics in common with Philippine

333

Duchesne, but her iron nature had not been tempered by fire and tears.

Generously, fervently, Elizabeth Galitzin gave herself to God, to her Order, to obedience. Yet she retained much of her old desire to carry things through with a high hand, and in the Sixth General Congregation held in Rome in 1839 she showed that she looked upon Mother Barat's conciliatory spirit as pure weakness. They were contrasts—the autocratic, dogmatic, pragmatic Russian princess, and the humble, gentle, courteous Burgundian peasant Saint. Mother Galitzin, in that Congregation, held much the same position towards her Superior General that Mother Audé had assumed towards Mother Duchesne in the local Council at St. Michael's in 1829. Mother Galitzin wrote: "It was in vain that the Assistants implored the Superior General to act with firmness. It was not possible to persuade her, so much did she fear to extinguish the still smoking flax." Such was the criticism of an autocrat on the dilatoriness of a saint, and saints, like God, can afford to wait. At St. Michael's, it was the affable, winning Mother Audé who found fault with the virile firmness of a Duchesne. One of the fathers of the Church tells us that God leaves the wicked in life that they may either amend their ways or try the good. Yet it is a notable fact, and one made much of by the Church in her processes of Beatification and Canonization, that the hardest trials of her holiest children come for the most part, not from the wicked, but from those who are called to be saints, from the Eugénies and Elizabeths who, but for the "little more" or the "little less," might have been even as Saint Madeleine Sophie. There have been more religious canonized than secular priests and lay-folk, not only because of the shelter of the cloister and of the rule,

not only for the high graces of a life with God, but for
the lowlier grace of the daily, hourly contact with those
of different temperament, a contact which either lowers
to mediocrity or raises to sanctity. Saint Francis de
Sales says that self-love expires fifteen minutes after
our death, by which he means that we carry to the grave
and even into Purgatory the rough edges of dispositions
which cry out for mutual forbearance and mutual love.

It was ever Mother Barat's way, as it has been that
of many saints, to show special confidence in those who
held views opposed to her own. This holy rashness often
gave the death-blow to nascent disloyalty and inspired
vigorous fidelity to the Society. The Mother Foundress
wished to send someone to America to explain the new
Decrees, to visit the houses, to report on the mission,
and to see whether the time was not ripe for a foundation asked for in New York. This mission she entrusted
to Mother Elizabeth Galitzin. She knew well her
whom she sent, for she wrote to her: "In order to lead
others to perfection, one must be perfect oneself. Example and the spirit of God can alone dominate nature,
which, as you know, resists human methods. In America, above all, you will do nothing if you are not meek,
patient and calm; the national character is reason personified and will not put up with passion or what seems
to flow from it."

From New York, where she promised to make a
foundation the following year, the Mother Visitor went
on to Missouri and made the formal visit of the houses
of St. Louis, St. Charles and Florissant. She was con-
scientious and thorough, and nothing escaped her vigi-
lant eye. She saw the needs of the sacristy in each
house, and what was lacking in the infirmaries, the need
of a lantern to light the steep stone stairs at Florissant,

the holes through which the mice entered the kitchen. What strikes one most in the notes of her visit to St. Charles is the characteristic item repeated more than once: "Such and such a piece of furniture needs painting. Paint it *red!*"

At Florissant Mother Galitzin saw fit to remove from the church the picture of St. Francis Regis which Mother Duchesne had placed there in fulfilment of the vow made before she left France in 1818. The Mother Visitor replaced it by a picture of the Sacred Heart, the object of Philippine's dearest devotion, but the change caused the dear old Mother uneasiness and anguish, and for months she remained in a state of fear that she had been unfaithful to the vow she had made.

Mother Galitzin readily granted Mother Duchesne's petition to be removed from office, and without any delay she sent her to St. Louis, where the dear Mother returned to her hole under the stairs, to her long watch in the chapel, to the last place, which had always been hers. But the Superior, one of her former novices, Mother Eleanor Grey, insisted on her having a room, and lavished tender care on the one who had never thought of herself. At the first opportunity, however, Mother Philippine found an excuse to return to her old haunts and ways, and Mother Lucille Mathevon, then at St. Louis, could write thus to the Superior General: "Mother Duchesne is a grand example to this house, obedient to a religious who was her novice, mortified in everything and everywhere. The sight of her room would make you weep; she says that there she is quieter; besides there are few places available. Her bed is in a cupboard under a stair; she is an Alexis. With blisters on her legs she drags herself about to ask a permission. There are few canonized saints who have done as much

as this good Mother." Mother Duchesne expected to
pass the rest of her life in St. Louis, but God had other
plans for her. He was, at last, to fulfil the hope of sixty
years.

Mother Barat had been asked to make a foundation
at an Indian mission post. With the hope that it might
be made at the mouth of the Kansas River where he had
organized a parish, Father Roux had written to Bishop
Rosati in 1834: "If you could get me some religious of
the Sacred Heart, two Americans and one French, they
would be able to do more good than a priest, although a
priest would find plenty of work." Mother Duchesne
had to refuse in the name of the Society. Mother
Galitzin's visit to Missouri in 1840 providentially coincided with one of Father De Smet's begging tours in
behalf of the Indian mission he was to begin in the
Rocky Mountains. He had come in 1823 as a novice
from White Marsh to Florissant and had thus been one
of the founders of the Missouri Province of the Society
of Jesus. He never forgot that their coming to the
Middle West was due to an arrangement made by Mon-
roe, Calhoun and Bishop Du Bourg regarding the chris-
tianizing and education of the red man; and as soon as
he was allowed, he threw himself into this apostolic
work. In 1838 he founded with Father Verreydt a
mission among the Potawatomi at Council Bluffs, and
he made peace between that tribe and the Sioux. Then
appeals reached him from the tribes further west, appeals such as this from a chief: "At the Council our
Great Father told us that some Blackrobe would come
and live among us in the course of four or five years.
Blackrobe, five years are long to wait. In this interval
I, and many of my children, may have entered the land
of spirits. Take pity on us! I am growing old! Be-

fore I die I should like to begin the work, and then I could depart satisfied."

It was at one of the Missouri houses, probably at St. Charles, that this valiant missionary found Mother Galitzin, who listneed with interest to the account of his work. "My garden," he said, "is the immense forest of Chateaubriand, bordering the largest river in the world."

She in turn spoke of the little progress the houses of Missouri had made in the exterior apostolate.

"Believe me," he answered vigorously, "you will never succeed in this country unless you call down the blessing of Heaven by founding schools for the Indians."

"Such is my earnest wish, Father, but we have neither money nor teachers."

"Nevertheless, Reverend Mother, it must be done."

Determined to push the matter to a happy conclusion, he called on Mother Duchesne, who encouraged him to make another appeal and offered for the work what was left of her life, saying:

"How good it is to serve God gratuitously and at His expense!"

Mother Galitzin knew the saintly Foundress' mind on the subject, and when appealed to again by Father De Smet, she said: "If we can obtain $400 to begin, we shall leave this spring."

In a short time the Jesuit had collected $500, which he presented to the Mother Visitatrix. Nothing then remained but to choose the missionaries. Mother Duchesne had at once made known her desire to Mother Galitzin, and wrote:

Yesterday a visit of Father De Smet so revived my ardor that I feel renewed by the hope of taking part in the mission which is now offered us under the

most favorable circumstances. On the border of the
State of Missouri lives a good tribe originally from
Canada and partly converted, that of the Potawatomi.
A holy Breton priest, Father Petit, devoted his life to
them, and left his dear flock as a legacy to a Jesuit
who has been here to see us. He has the same privations as his people, but he enjoys the consolation
of his ministry. The Government has helped him to
build a church and might also aid us in putting up a
house. Yesterday I showed Father De Smet the letter
from Bishop Rosati in which he positively says: "Follow your call." Weighed down when I received it by
the thought that everything was against my desires, I
had paid little heed to it, but now I believe it to be the
voice of God Who is going to cure me. I shall be over
and above the number asked for, and I shall help with
the sewing and house work and thus allow a novice to
complete her novitiate at Florissant.

Father De Smet had given details to Mother Galitzin of the mission for which the Religious of the Sacred
Heart were destined. It had been established princi-
pally through the efforts of Father Christian Hoecken
on tributaries of the Marais de Cygnes or Upper Osage,
first on Potawatomi Creek, later on Sugar Creek, so
called from the sugar maples found along its banks.
The Indians there were joined in 1837 by one hundred
and fifty other Potawatomi who had been driven westward from Indiana by the flood of white immigration.
Bryant puts into words the feeling of these Indians in
their inevitable banishment from the land that had been
theirs:

> "They waste us, ay, like April snow
> In the warm noon, we melt away.
> And fast they follow as we go
> Toward the setting day,
> Till they shall fill the land, and we
> Are driven into the Western Sea."

Their chief, Nesfwawke, hearing that there was a priest at the Kickapoo settlement, sent a trader to ask that this missionary come to Sugar Creek to preach the Gospel to the pagan Indians and give the consolations of the Church to those baptized by Father Stephen Badin. Father Hoecken went at once and promised to return and remain with these children of the forest who seemed so eager to receive what the Kickapoos had rejected. The succeeding years were marked only by the addition of other bands of the Potawatomi tribe, by the change of pastors as one missionary after another was called elsewhere or broke under the strain of being Father, doctor, farmer, hunter, teacher, all at once. To relieve this strain Father Verhaegen, Superior of the Jesuit Vice-Province of Missouri, was now about to bring to the mission four religious who would teach and tend the Indian girls and women.

Mother Lucille Mathevon was named to lead the band of missionaries, and was to be ably seconded by Mother O'Connor, who had also had some experience in the Indian school at Florissant. Sister Louise Amiotte was to share the labor of the mission, and Mother Duchesne would join the little colony if able to travel. When the time came for departure the holy Mother was so weak that there was question of leaving her behind, but Father Verhaegen insisted: "Let her come; if she cannot work, she will forward the success of the mission by her prayers." This priest, gifted as poet, philosopher, historian, had as his better gift a childlike faith which prompted his insistence that Mother Duchesne, old, broken, ill, should go on the mission. "Learning," Father Faber says, "makes children of its professors when their minds are humble and their hearts are pure."

The steamboat in which they embarked went up the Missouri past St. Charles. Perhaps the children in their pink gingham uniforms with their white capes were allowed to wave a last farewell from the hill or even from the river side to Mother Lucille Mathevon whom they had known and loved so well. A river-voyage of but four days seemed little to her and to Mother Duchesne, who had experienced Mississippi journeys from New Orleans. However, they knew that the Missouri offered no fewer dangers in 1841 than had the greater river in the preceding years. When Mark Twain described the boats as "all whistle and no boat," he did not expect to be taken in earnest, but his fiction is founded on fact, and so when he asserts that the ships came to a standstill of necessity every time the whistle blew, we have some idea of the vicissitudes of a river voyage. Father De Smet himself spoke of it as one of the most dangerous enterprises of a western traveller. The scenery leaves little to be desired. "Majestic bluffs charm one with the variety of their forms, and the soft beauty of their adornment: the steep verdant slope, whose base is at the water's edge, is topped by a lofty rampart of broken, turreted rocks, exquisitely rich and mellow in color." The turbid ash-colored river winds "here and there and yonder its rapid sweep interrupted at intervals by clusters of wooded islands."

The travellers finally landed at Westport, which probably displayed then the same scene which Francis Parkman described five years later: "It was full of Indians whose shaggy ponies were tied by dozens along the houses and fences. Sacs and Foxes with shaved heads and painted faces, Shawnees and Delawares in calico frocks and turbans, Wyandots dressed like white men, and a few wretched Kanzas wrapped in old blankets were strolling along the streets or lounging in and out of the shops and houses." Mother Duchesne had kept fairly well on the river, but she found the eight days' journey by ox-cart most trying. When they were still eighteen miles from the Sugar Creek settlement, two Indians suddenly appeared, knelt at Father Verhaegen's feet and asked his blessing. They told how all the evening before the tribe had awaited the coming of the Blackrobe and the Blackgowns.

"Go tell them," said the Jesuit, "that to-morrow, by the first light of the sun, we shall be with them." The couriers departed and gave the good tidings of great joy to the tribe, who could not wait for the arrival, but came out in bands, with horses bedecked, their own horses plumed and streamers in their hands. Round the carriage of the religious they swept, now in circles, now forming a vast crescent, now going before as heralds, now dropping into the rear. Thus the cavalcade reached the village. The Indians brought benches on which the newcomers sat while the chief said a formal word of welcome. Father Verhaegen presented Mother Duchesne as one who for thirty-five years had been longing to come to the Indians. To show their appreciation of this venerable religious all the women and girls of the village arranged themselves in a long line to embrace her; then all the men came forward to shake hands. Seven hundred times the greeting was repeated. The Superior of the Jesuit missionaries who had come out to meet Father Verhaegen expressed the joy he too felt, and the ceremony was at an end.

The religious lodged in the hut of a savage while their log convent was being built. Father Aelen gave them two cows, a horse and a yoke of oxen, and doubtless inspired the generous gifts of the Indians to the convent. The savages brought the booty of the hunt, and as they were being taught by the Jesuits the new science of agriculture, they sometimes had vegetables to offer. To Mother Duchesne they brought eggs, for their sympathetic hearts read her suffering and her need of nourishing food. On July 19, school opened in a house near the church; fifty young girls were soon in attendance, and the elder women learned to sew, to wash clothes and to sweep.

The customs of the Indians became in turn the study of the nuns. The men of the tribe wore a colored shirt, a red, blue or white woolen blanket, a pair of leggins of red or blue cloth adorned with silk ribbons, and moccasins or slippers of tanned deerskin. They delighted in gaudy necklaces, in many bracelets, in their crown of tanned hide and gaily colored feathers, in their paint, and in their bedecked braids, one before, one behind. The women would have been glad to dress like "Miss Pack-up and Get," a Potawatomi whom Father De Smet described as wearing a shirt of crimson cloth fastened at the neck with a deer's foot, a blue petticoat, gaiters adorned with figures worked in porcupine quills and embroidered with sky-blue silk, a blue blanket, moccasins with toad-shaped bead ornaments, a bandeau of blue beads, vermilion on her face, Venetian red on her hair, and she was perfumed with nothing less than the essence of the skunk. However, this was her gala attire.

The Indians rose early, washed in the creek, using bears' grease for facial soap and white clay for cleaning their fringes. For drinking vessels they made use of the women's straw hats, whether the beverage was dog-soup or water from the stream. The men thought themselves destined merely to hunt and to fight. It was for the women to do everything else. In consequence, an Indian squaw was old at thirty.

The Potawatomi, Father De Smet said, were especially favored by Heaven, being exempt from many of the more barbarous practices of the savages; they received the missionaries with good grace and kept them amongst them, and were less addicted to evil customs introduced by the pale-faces than were the other tribes —thus they were open to instruction. The church became in more than location the centre of the village. There the savages went for Mass, for public prayers and instruction morning and evening. On Sundays they sang High Mass to Mother Duchesne's delight. Their old pagan litany to the Great Spirit, "O our Father, make our hearts like Thy Heart, as good as Thine, as strong as Thine," was a promising foundation for devotion to the Sacred Heart, which appealed strongly to them—their minds were open to truth and their hearts to piety.

> "Father and God, how far above
> All human thought Thy wondrous love!
> How strange the path by which Thy Hand
> Would lead the tribes of this bleak land
> From darkness, crime and misery
> To live and reign in bliss with Thee."

Mother Duchesne rejoiced to be at last in this land of promise. She had hoped to work as well as to pray for her mission, but little by little the rigor of the winter in the wild woods, the poor food that she shared with the Indians when they had no game, no vegetables and no eggs to bring to the convent, her infirmities, her advanced age—all combined to rob her little by little of the labor she had appointed as her share. She seemed to understand the savages when they spoke of the Great Spirit, but their heart language was the only one she knew. Latin alone had come easily to her—English she had never mastered—and Potawatomi was still harder. The sign of the cross, for instance, is *"Olinosowinig Weosimit, ipi Welkwissimit, ipi Menojuwepisit Mennito—Ape iw nooilug."* Thus she was debarred from teaching catechism save when she could make use of an interpreter. Yet she was not disturbed, for she had changed under the chiselling of Christ and her zeal had become like unto His. The work she loved would be better done by others, and she could say: "We have desired the cross and not honor, poverty and not ease, the Will of God and not success. If the work of God undergoes contradiction, we have from this the precious advantage of being in a situation that can unite us more closely to Christ."

At this time she wrote to a priest:

S.C.J.M. FEBRUARY 20, 1842.

Dear Reverend Father:

I was transferred from St. Louis to Florissant where I heard only of its threatened suppression. Then as a result of prayers and representations that house was kept as a noviceship. I was sent back to St. Louis, where I led an active life in utter nothingness. For a long time I was ill. The arrival of Father De Smet from the tribe of the Flatheads, after his journey of three months across the Rockies, brought me back to life. He gave me the hope that we should have a mission there in two years, and he ardently implored our Mother Provincial to send us here to a tribe lately come from Michigan.

If I only knew, as you do, how to profit by suffering,

I could say, as you do, that I am happy. I have need to be tried, and God has made me pass along hard ways although He has brought me to the savages—the object of my desires. Here I still suffer because I do nothing.

"I do nothing here"—this privation of work, this thought that she was utterly useless, was one of the greatest trials of her life, one of the hardest tests of her faith. The Indian mission had ever been the goal of her hopes. For this she thought she had been sent to America. When about to sail in 1818, she sent to Mother Barat a letter in which she gave the story of her vocation for the instruction and salvation of savages; it was her only self-vindication—her proof that God wanted her to go to the Indians. It ran as follows:

S.C.J.M.   PARIS, 1818.

Very Reverend Mother:

I have often spoken to you of my vocation to teach savages and infidels, but the different facts on which I rested my hope of having God on my side were scattered, and so had not the same force that they would have when combined in one picture. I have decided, after a Holy Communion offered for this intention, to leave you this sketch, for I know only too well how fearful and apprehensive you must feel in confiding to me this important work, especially since we shall be at such a vast distance from those who have given to us their spirit; and from you in whom that spirit has been concentrated only that you might share it with all your daughters. But if God has shown His Will in my vocation, if it is He Who provides the means to accomplish it, then there is reason to hope that He will uphold His own work though confided to those who are weak, undeserving and incapable of success.

My first admiration for the life of the missionary

came when I heard the conversation of a good Jesuit who had evangelized Louisiana and who told us stories of the Indians. I was then only eight or ten years of age, yet I thought missionaries fortunate and envied them their work without being astonished by its dangers, for at the same time I was reading the lives of the martyrs in which I took a keen interest. The good Jesuit Father was extraordinary confessor in the Convent in which I was a pupil; I went several times to Confession to him, and I loved his familiar and simple manner of speaking—a manner he had used with the savages.

From that time, the names of Propaganda, Foreign Missions, of priests destined for them, of religious in far-away lands, made my heart thrill. When at eighteen years of age I was about to enter religion the wish to take part in the Apostolate made me choose the Visitation where children are educated rather than the Order of Carmel that I loved much. My Community was animated by the spirit of the Jesuits from whose Constitutions they boasted that their own had been drawn. The library was enriched with nearly all the works of Jesuit authors, because at the time of the Suppression, three who had been members of the Society of Jesus were in hiding in the house of our chaplain, and when they died they left their library to the Convent. During the entire two years of my noviceship I read only Rodriguez without ever tiring of it, and when we assembled after Vespers, I cited as examples the Jesuit Saints, telling the stories of their lives one after another. That of St. Francis Xavier touched me the most, and in his life I best loved the incidents of the Socoto holding their arms out to him on the bank, his ardor in the garden of Goa, his shedding of tears of consolation on the desolate Islands of Moro, his crying out when there was question of labor: "Yet more, O Lord, yet more!" And finally his touching appeals to the academies of Europe to send him missionaries. How often did I not say to him in my impatience: "Great Saint, why do you not call *me?* I should obey." He is the Saint of my heart.

My devotion to St. Regis began at about the same time, as I conversed one day with a nun whose patron he was. I often prayed before his relic. His labors, more hidden than those of St. Xavier, were more like those I should be able to undertake, and for love of him I taught the poor. When the Revolution drove us out of our monastery, I found that my father had a book of devotions containing the prayer of St. Francis Xavier for the conversion of infidels. During the twenty-four years since I discovered it I have recited it almost daily as well as the prayers of the first Jesuit Saints for missionaries. I said them before the pictures of Regis and Xavier in the parish church of Grannes. There the names of these saints were added to the litany, and as La Louvesc was near by, pictures of its patron were common in all the houses of that part of the country where St. Francis Regis was invoked as "Holy Father." At this same time I made the acquaintance of two Jesuits; one of them who sometimes heard my Confession made me promise to go on pilgrimage to La Louvesc. I did so on the very day on which this holy Jesuit died. There resulted such peace that I felt assured he had carried to Heaven my desire to return to religion. When I had taken only the first steps by leaving my family and going back to Grenoble so as to join some nuns if it should be possible, he had written to me: "You have done that for which God will reward you," and four years before the signing of the Concordat he announced to me the return of religion in France according to a prediction made by Venerable Benedict Labre when passing through Vivarais on his way to Rome.

I was constant in my appeal to St. Regis and in the hope that he would come to my aid and I made in his honor a vow to be fulfilled if I should be enabled to return to Ste. Marie within a year. At the same time I made several attempts and all went so quickly that in six months—instead of the expected year—I found myself on my mountain side.

The Vicar General who then ruled the diocese and whom I consulted in all I undertook answered my first letter with the words: "The Finger of God is here." And he upheld me in the contradictions I met with. So too did a saintly priest who had established devotion to the Sacred Heart in the hospital of which he was chaplain and who never failed to have each year a public novena to St. Francis Xavier.

After my admission into the Society of the Sacred Heart I spoke even more of the harvests in foreign lands —but vaguely—and in admiration rather than in the hope of seeing my desires carried out. Finally on the 10th of January, 1806, when I was in the children's dormitory meditating on the detachment of the Magi, I conceived the longing to imitate them. I felt my overstrong attachment for Ste. Marie d'en Haut disappear, and I determined to offer myself for the instruction of the idolaters of China or other countries. On the 23rd of the same month, I wrote to you, Reverend Mother, on this subject, and you answered: "This is just what I have been expecting from you."

I made the same request to Father Varin, and in an inspired tone he replied: "If I am allowed to read aright in the Heart of Our Lord, I see written there in large letters that you are destined to cause It to be honored in far-distant lands." I still have your answer, but Father Varin's letter as well as that of Mgr. Brocheve containing the words "the Finger of God is here" were destroyed at the order of one of my confessors. Soon after that, Father Varin came to Grenoble and reminded me of my letter. I asked him to allow me to be the first to go to infidel lands. He answered, "I do allow you." I replied, "Then, Father, bless me for that work." He did so, extending his hands farther than usual.

My longings increased when after several years of trial, disappointments and faults, I saw in my mission a necessary means of expiation for me, and of purity of conscience. I desired to be free from all occasions of sin, and this, added to my wish to save souls, made me pray with much ardor on the two Holy Thursday nights of 1805 and 1806. I believe that my petition was granted for I seemed to hear someone speaking in low tones within me or beside me saying: "Why do you doubt?" On Assumption Day, I heard, "It will be." On great feasts and on those of Apostles the longing almost always increased after Communion when, finding myself in tears, I would say, "Why is this? I have read nothing, said nothing, heard nothing which could have called forth these thoughts," and then I would realize at once that it was the feast of an Apostle. To fight against this longing I would avoid reading anything that might call it up. I tried to rid myself of any financial help on which I might have founded a hope of success, but all efforts were useless, and one day after Communion I decided to write to the Vicar General then at Rome to ask him to find out from the Pope whether I should stifle or follow my yearnings—you know the fate of this letter.

When you called me to Paris, I at first felt regret because I thought that you wanted to take from me all opportunity of going further. Yet, so great was my longing for the peace of soul that comes from indifference that I had even hoped the Holy Father would decide that I should think no more of my desires. Still, during my journey to Paris, I was overcome by the thought that God might make use of my stay in that city to bring definite results from your negotiations with Bishop Du Bourg.

I resolved to make a novena of Communions in the Chapel of our Lady at St. Sulpice before drawing up my petition. During this novena I prayed most earnestly to our Lady both there and before her statue at St. Thomas', at Montmartre, at the Carmelites and in the Chapel of the Foreign Missions, trying to become indifferent. But at once whatever indifference had been mine disappeared, and I found myself longing to brave human respect, blame and coolness, provided that noth-

ing would be wanting to my contribution to the cause I
desired. When I saw Father Varin so opposed to it I
went sorrowfully to St. Sulpice and said to our Lady:
"Are you going to disappoint me? The more I implore
you, the more my longings increase, and yet you see how
my views are being thwarted." I had scarcely finished
speaking when I heard in my heart the words: "My
child, you have not taken things as you should." And I
understood that I had counted too much on my request
instead of trusting all to my Superior. Then I grew
calmer, I renewed my desires, and our Lady made me a
promise about the future. In order to gain merit, I
asked Father Varin's permission to make a vow to consecrate myself to the instruction of infidels—under
obedience, but, as far as I myself was concerned, to refuse nothing. He consented, but fearing that he might
change his mind I pronounced this vow almost at once.
This promise it is that prevents me to-day from turning
aside from the burden of (Superiorship) for which I
feel quite unfit.

On St. Xavier's day I went to Mass at the Chapel
of the Foreign Missions. These words of the Epistle:
"How can they know the truth if no one instructs them,
and how will they be instructed if no one is sent to
them?" pierced my very soul. In spite of myself I shed
abundant tears and did not know where to hide. To
prevent this occurring again, I thought I would not
return there in the afternoon, but somehow, I found
myself locked out of our house. Inclination led me to
the shrine which incloses the relic of St. Francis Xavier.
I was the nearest to it, as well as to the Blessed Sacrament, which was then being brought to the chapel, and I
felt my hopes rise then and during all the novena that I
made to know the Will of God.

I have always forgotten to tell you, Reverend
Mother, what happened at Grenoble when they were
trying to take Ste. Marie away from us, and when
Father Enfantin and M. de Janson thought that we
should have to give it up. Sick at heart, I resolved to

abandon that dear house, to see it destroyed, to know that others were laughing at my expense. I began to make my spiritual reading in Deuteronomy and I opened at different passages which touched me deeply, especially these: "When the Lord Thy God shall have brought thee into the land and shall have given thee houses full of riches which thou didst not set up, cisterns which thou didst not dig, vineyards and olive yards which thou didst not plant—take heed lest thy heart be lifted up. . . . He hath fed thee with manna in the wilderness." A torrent of consolation flowed into my soul; I felt assured that God would confirm the gift of the house of Ste. Marie. As I found no explanation for "olive yard" I interpreted it as "gentle," as "filled with spiritual sweetness at the thought of the missions." Ah, dear Mother, "olive yards" is explained by the sweetness of seeing my longings accomplished and by the excellence of the fruits of Louisiana as foretold by my good Jesuit. I need meditate only on: "Let not your heart be lifted up" in my high destiny. I say well "Not to ask, O Lord," while each time I add "Not so hath He treated all nations." "He hath done great things to me."

You already know how I found at Grenoble two pictures of the Blessed Virgin—the Conception and Our Lady of Sorrows. They were neither pretty nor clean, but remembering that Father Enfantin owed his conversion to having shown reverence to pictures such as these, I felt drawn to honor them so as to obtain my desire to go to foreign countries. Soon after that I found a painting of St. Francis Regis so hideous and soiled that my first impulse was to burn it, but filled with the thought that always occupied me, and overcome with tender love for the Saint, I promised to keep it for his sake and to make him honored by savages if he would only obtain for me the grace to go to them.

So as to keep my promise I am taking with me this dear picture which I regard as my shield, and the vow that I have made to consecrate to him the house in St. Louis I look upon as that which will make my hope

come true. I have also told you that a few days before
the visit of Bishop Du Bourg I saw him in a dream telling me to be calm. As I had not been thinking of him
the evening before, I thought this a sign that he was
coming that very day, but he came only several days
later. On the Feast of the Ascension my desires were
stirred up early in the morning by words which seemed
to take hold of me as I entered the choir: "Go, teach all
nations." They produced an almost constant emotion
and a bitterness sweeter than any pleasure. I
longed to repeat my request, but I said, "I have
exhausted every means—it is for You, O my God, now
to act." Mgr. Du Bourg came the next day, and what
was my astonishment and delight when in addressing
the novices he told them that he had been particularly
struck the day before by the words: "Go, teach all nations!" I realized that God had given us the same
thought that we might fulfil like vocations.

There remains for me only to tell you that a pain in
my side from which I had suffered for several years and
which was sometimes so intense that I was tempted to
apply some remedy, suddenly disappeared when I heard
that Father Barat had begun to treat with the Bishop of
Louisiana. That morning, without knowing this, I had
offered my Communion for him and his missionaries.
I must also tell you that the vow to consecrate to St.
Regis the foundation in Louisiana was scarcely made
when Father Barat wrote to me eagerly telling me to
choose that holy Saint as patron of that house.

Mother, how good God is!

The goodness of God that had filled Mother Duchesne with joyful gratitude in 1818 was even more her
delight in 1842—in her union with Him lay her happiness. At Ste. Marie, in Paris, at Florissant and St.
Louis, she had given nights to prayer because the days
were not long enough for more than the devoted service
she had been allowed to render. Now that that devoted

service was no longer asked, she fled—like the arrow from the bow—to the prayer she so loved. She spent four hours of the morning and as many in the afternoon in the Sugar Creek Mission Chapel. On Sundays she took her light lunch at the church door that she might not be too long away. The Indians watched her with love and with awe and called her: "the woman who prays always." They would steal up gently in their deerskin moccasins to touch her habit as she knelt at prayer. In the meantime, Mother Galitzin, having paid long visits to the southern houses, had taken Mother Hardey, probably by way of Cincinnati, to New York where they founded a convent on Houston Street and where Mother Galitzin remained for nearly a year, awaiting the arrival of a new colony from France. There too, she learned that Mother Audé had died in Rome in 1842.

This news, together with the tidings that Mother Galitzin would visit Sugar Creek, reached the Indian mission only shortly before she arrived. She found the religious in their rough log-cabin which boasted of but one room on the ground floor and a garret. On Palm Sunday Mother Galitzin was touched almost to tears by the fervor with which numbers of Indians approached the Holy Table. The silence of Sugar Creek charmed her; the Indians spoke in low tones, the children played almost without a word, and even the parade formed in her honor was silent. Only on Sunday did the village resound, and then with hymns and canticles. The Mother Visitor learned from the Jesuits of their delight in the progress of the school for girls, and in the habits of industry, economy and cleanliness, which with piety had been instilled into the village this last year and to which the Government inspectors gave unstinted praise.

The Room at St. Charles in Which Mother Duchesne Died

Mother Galitzin noted with distress that Mother Duchesne was failing fast, and her opinion coincided with that of Bishop Kenrick, who visited the mission in July, 1842. It was decided to send the dear Mother away from the Indian village where she had hoped to die. She received her last obedience for St. Charles with characteristic words: "God knows the reason of this recall, and that is enough."

CHAPTER VI

Transfigured

CHAPTER VI

TRANSFIGURED—1842-1851

*"The men who met him rounded on their heel
And wondered after him, because his face
Shone like the countenance of a priest of old
Against the flame about a sacrifice
Kindled by fire from Heaven, so glad was he."*

A. E.

"God knows the reason of the recall, that is enough."
So said Mother Duchesne as Bishop Kenrick took her
back to Missouri after about one year at the Indian
mission, where she would have chosen to remain to the
end. As a postscript to the story of her vocation which
she had sent to Mother Barat in 1818, Mother Philippine had added these significant lines: "Of all the graces
that I most appreciate, I single out that of belonging to
the Society of the Sacred Heart of Jesus, and of being
allowed to share in extending it. Nothing in the whole
world could weigh for an instant against the love that
binds me to it. At this moment I feel all that I owe to
the Society and I shall try to live by its spirit and to
make it and our rules appreciated. My consolation will
be to renew frequently the sacred vows binding me to it,
thus to draw ever closer the bonds which in spite of distance will by God's mercy endure."

As she turned away from the Potawatomi Mission,
Mother Duchesne showed that, dear to her as her voca-

359

tion to the Indians had been, far dearer was the call of the Society to come home to a life hidden in God. She did not inquire into the Divine motive for her withdrawal from Sugar Creek, but to those who may look back through the vista of long years upon events hidden from her, it may be possible reverently to guess what these reasons were. At St. Charles, whence had sprung Florissant, Grand Côteau, St. Michael's, St. Louis, New York, she could best make the interest of each of these houses her own. St. Ferdinand's existence was a prolonged death agony. The southern convents and that of St. Louis needed prayer in prosperity no less than in adversity, even Bayou La Fourche might still profit from the example of a noble failure. St. Charles too, as the first mission, was the link between America and the Mother House—it was well that that link should be silently guarded by her who had forged it. St. Charles, through vicissitudes, hardships and threats of suppression, was to live on; in a few short years Sugar Creek would be no longer an Indian camp, but the nucleus of an American town, and the savages would have moved on, leaving merely the memory of the name, Potawatomi Creek.

To few has it been granted, as to Mother Duchesne, to perform each and all of the corporal and spiritual works of mercy. She had fed the hungry, given drink to the thirsty and clothed the naked in her childhood days, at Grenoble, during the Terror, and at Florissant. The indigent of Dauphiny and the poor Jesuits at St. Stanislaus Seminary, Missouri, she had harbored and cared for. Captives she had visited at Ste. Marie, and there—as at Paris, Florissant, St. Louis, and wherever she had been—the sick had been her first thought. It had even been hers to bury the dead—her mother at Grannes and her father at Grenoble. In spite of the poverty and privations of the Missouri houses, not a single religious died at St. Charles, Florissant or St. Louis until 1833, but with Mother Octavie Berthold, Mother Duchesne buried her own dead youth and the vigor of her riper years. She had ever admonished the erring, counselled the doubtful, strengthened the afflicted. There remained to her now to instruct the ignorant, to encourage and console, to suffer silently, to pray for the living and the dead.

The year after her return to St. Charles from Sugar Creek she was thought to have regained enough strength to take a little class in the parish school. The brick convent is on the side of a hill, so that in front the basement is partly above ground, and in two rooms just across from the kitchen the classes of the parochial school were held. The children of St. Charles who knew nothing but French were confided to Mother Duchesne, who taught them to read, to write and to sew. Her most important lesson, however, was the catechism, which she continued to teach even when, in 1848 and 1849, she had become too weak and infirm to spend the greater part of the day with the little girls. She would try to be in her place in the school before the appointed hour so that she might not disturb the young religious through whose classroom she had to pass to go to her corner.

Content though she was in this humble labor, she did not hesitate to offer herself for more when in 1846 an occasion presented itself. Four years previously the noviceship had been transferred by Mother Galitzin to a new house at McSherrystown, Pennsylvania, and in this change Mother Duchesne read the impending suppression of Florissant. In 1843 Mother Galitzin returned to America as Vicar, and visited the convents of Missouri on her way south. A great change had come about in the soul of this Mother; during a retreat made in France she had seen in its true light what her attitude to the saintly Foundress had been. Humbly she acknowledged her fault and earnestly she set herself to repair it, solemnly offering her life as a holocaust for the welfare of the Society which she so truly loved. In this spirit she gladly returned to America.

> *"His overthrow heaped happiness upon him,*
> *For then and not till then he felt himself*
> *And knew the blessedness of being little."*

From St. Louis Mother Galitzin went to New Orleans, and at St. Michael's God took her at her word. The yellow fever was at its height. Heedless of warning, she devoted herself to its victims. Struck down by fever, she endured a long agony and died strongly, generously, as she had lived, and confident that her sacrifice had been accepted and that the past was repaired.

Mother Galitzin was succeeded as Vicar of the South and West by Mother Cutts, who, in 1846, determined to suppress the convent at Florissant. Then it was that Mother Duchesne asserted herself—offering to take charge of that threatened house if she might have with her only one Sister who knew both English and French. She thought that thus they could carry on the parochial school and take care of the Church of St. Ferdinand and of its pastor. Mother Cutts was so much touched that she hesitated to say "No," but reminded Mother Duchesne that she was nearly eighty years of age. The dear old Mother replied that the Duchesnes all lived long, that her health had so much improved that she still had some years of life, that she asked neither money nor help, and finally that the climate of Florissant would make it worth while to keep a house there. But, before leaving St. Charles, Mother Cutts was obliged to tell Mother Duchesne that it had been decided in France that Florissant was to be for her another Ste. Marie d'en Haut—the house must be closed. In silent sorrow Mother Philippine returned to her little class in the basement of St. Charles. It was a relief to her when, in 1847, she heard that the Sisters of Loretto at the Foot of the Cross had taken up at Florissant the work so dear to her heart.

Her love for the "instruction of the ignorant"— for Christian education—made the threatened suppression of St. Charles another great trial. So certain had it been that this house was to be closed that the few boarders were sent home and Mother Duchesne was taken to St. Louis. Her prayers and intercession prevailed, and after a few weeks word came that Mother Barat had determined to prolong the existence of the convent of St. Charles, which was one day to be enshrined in the heart of the Society by its association with the Venerable Mother who returned there in joy.

It was her work in these last years to counsel, to encourage, and console. She had a ready sympathy for those in need. With the Mothers and Sisters whom she had left on the frontiers of the Society, at the outpost of the Indian Mission at Sugar Creek, or, after 1848, at St. Mary's, Kansas, she could best sympathize, for, while she envied their lot, she knew by experience that Father De Smet's words were true: "To come to America, to teach in a college or to be a missionary to the whites is child's play in comparison to the Indian Mission. I see so many difficulties in this work, that did I not know that our Divine Lord is all powerful, I should regard the enterprise (the mission to the peaceful Potawatomi) as a great folly." On the feast of St. Anthony in one of these last years, Mother Duchesne wrote to a religious of another order:

My very dear Mother:

I thank you with all my heart for having given us news of yourself. I realized the danger of your situation in the midst of the storm while we trembled even under shelter. I have confidence that Divine Providence will always sustain you. You do God's work upon earth in consoling the afflicted and unhappy. The orphans will be your support in trial because he who gives alms prays without words. I renew my gratitude for all your kindness to me, and I beg the Heart of Jesus to be your reward,

PHILIPPINE DUCHESNE.

To one of her former daughters she wrote:

My dear Sister:

I cannot tell you what pleasure your letter gave me. I shall love having the letters you promise to write when you have time—I do not say strength because I am convinced that will not be wanting to you to carry all the crosses that God will be pleased to send you. This is not impossible when one has meditated on the mystery of the cross, the blood-stained garment of Our Lord, and the necessity of doing penance in order to enter Heaven. Your penance has been neither long enough nor in proportion to your debts. Be ready for work without rest, for prayer without consolation, for infirmity without solace. Thus you will be really a spouse of the Sacred Heart.

Ask Mother Thiéffry to let you read the verses

written by Father Varin at the end of his Notes of Retreat which I have just sent back to her. In C.J.M.,

PHILIPPINE.

P. S. Tell Mother Regis that I think as she does. I do not know what good education has done for me, but when I remember how I enjoyed it, how highly I thought of it, and how little it has served me, I take pleasure in thinking that in Heaven all sciences will be annihilated. There we shall say only one eternal "Amen" and "Holy, Holy Lord."

On August 7, 1842, she wrote to Mother Boilvin:

My dear Sister:

Several days ago I sent Mother Mathilde two letters for France. I enclose others, but I hope to limit my correspondence more and more, especially that with France.

I have heard that you are suffering, and my loving interest in your health makes me fear and guess that you have been doing more than your strength allows. You have always needed to be careful of your voice, and longer hours of sleep are a necessity for you. Be then humble and simple enough to acknowledge your needs and to allow yourself to be cared for.

My last letter will have told you that I have left the Indians. I cannot forget them, although I am now surrounded by all that edifies and fills me with gratitude. The Sisters whom I had not known before, as well as those whose kindness I had already tried, are full of attentions for me.

I left our community of Sugar Creek in good health, but Fathers Verreydt and Hoecken were not well. Pray for the welfare of all and for the good of the poor tribes who surround them. Our little house of five rooms has been completed. Several Indian children have learned to read, knit and make lace; some knew already how to sew and prefer that kind of work. They are beginning to settle down, and as they are intelligent, one may hope that if we persevere in praying and in caring for them, they will make progress in virtue and learning.

Mother Gonzaga Boilvin was sent to the new house at McSherrystown, Pennsylvania, to be Superior and Mistress of Novices; and Mother Duchesne wrote of her sympathy:

My dear Mother:

Your letter came yesterday and I began at once the novena you asked for. To-day I received Holy Communion for the same intention. I knew nothing of the illness of Mother C, nor of your having replaced her. I am not surprised at your astonishment and am still less so at your sorrow. But after all, God has wished this blow to fall upon you. His Will is expressed by the orders of Superiors. In the urgent need of replacing the poor Mothers, your inclination is thwarted which only proves that nothing on your part gave you the position you now hold—small as you are. You should then bend beneath the yoke of your two burdens of Superior and Mistress of Novices.

If humility is always good, generous humility is better. Obedience does not destine you to be an Alexis or a Benedict Labre, but rather to imitate the courage of St. de Chantal and of St. Theresa. The former did not hesitate to find out whether St. Francis de Sales had made his meditation or not. The latter did not shrink from teaching her method of prayer to her Bishop or from directing monks and her own brother, a renowned man of the world. And they were both Saints! I hope that you will be one too in your new post no less than you might have been in the lowliest employment. I shall pray often for you and for your large religious family. Those whom you have left will do likewise.

Mother Duchesne's gift of consolation and encouragement was not confined to the religious of her own Order, to the old children of Florissant and of St. Louis—many of whom venerated her and sought her advice—but as in former days, priests, especially missionaries, came to tell her their disappointments, their hopes and their plans. One of those who best appreciated her was Father De Smet, who never failed to visit her when he was in Missouri. In her he found a ready listener when he spoke of the Far West. She was still more interested to hear of the Indians themselves, and of their picturesque manner of speaking. "Father, Father," one of them had said, "when the snow will have disappeared from these hills we shall think of your return; when the plants begin to spring forth we shall set out to meet you." Another chief had assembled the tribe and exhorted them: "Be prompt at our Father's lodge at the first sound of the bell; be quiet when you are there. Open your ears to hear and your hearts to hold fast all the words that he says to you." Mother Duchesne loved these visits of the missionary, of whom it has been well said: "There is in the pursuit of his life's calling a divine variety and a consecration. Now he is teaching his boys how to work and how to play, now in the criminal's cell bringing to the unfortunate some ray of hope, some evidence of Divine Mercy; or again, he is insistently directing some rare soul along the mystic way that brings it among the elect of God." That he considered Mother Duchesne one of these rare souls one cannot doubt as one reads his words: "Never did I leave her without feeling that I had been conversing with a saint. I have always regarded this Mother as the greatest protector of the Missions. For several years she offered two Communions a week and daily prayers for the conversion of the Indians whom she dearly loved."

She wrote to a missionary, probably Father De Smet:

S.C.J.M.   ST. CHARLES, APRIL 16, 1843.

Reverend Father:

I hear that you are back in St. Louis, but as the season is far advanced I fear that we shall not see you at St. Charles. However, in spite of my longing to hear details of your important mission, I rather dread the sad impression that your visit would cause me, for I have just seen all my wishes frustrated and my hopes destroyed. Perhaps you already know that our Mother General has recalled me from Sugar Creek. While there I had a presentiment that it would not be for long. In my happiest dreams I was always in the Rocky Mountains, and I prayed without ceasing for you and for the success of your Mission. I have continued to do so during your journey through the United States, and I shall go on doing so as long as I live.

While I was among the savages I received from France a box containing objects for them: medals, pens, small boxes, etc. The agent of the Potawatomi is supposed to furnish the last-named articles and I wonder whether these would be useful to you—if they are not they can stay in our house in St. Louis. As to money, this convent is so poor just now that we can offer you only some lace for an altar cloth. I am glad to have colored paper for flowers. Mrs. Chouteau told us that Father Point can make artificial flowers and that he will be helped by the ladies of Westport. If you want any more of this paper, Mother Aloysia, the Assistant at St. Louis, can give it and will supply you with models.

Believe, Reverend Father, in the earnest petitions that I always address to God that He Himself may uphold you, and that He may console you by conversions which will be the fruit of the labors. Deign to give me some share in the merits which you and the happy companions of your work must be gaining.

Priests often appealed to Mother Duchesne to intercede for them in behalf of the needs of their mission or church. At the end of a letter in which she has begged for help in repairing the Church of St. Ferdinand at Florissant she says: "Mrs. St. Cyr, who came to make her home near the church, has died the death of the predestined. Her son is married, and her little daughter, Adeline, is now Superior of our house near Philadelphia."

To Father De La Croix she wrote in August, 1842:

I live in solitude and am able to employ all my time in going over the past and in preparing for death; but I cannot put away the thought of the Indians, and in my ambition I fly to the Rockies. I can only adore the designs of God in depriving me of the object of my desires.

Later she wrote again to Father De La Croix:

Your letter pleased me because, far from being bored by those I have written, you tell me to write again.

Father Van Assche has repaired his church at St. Ferdinand. You, my kind Father, guided our first steps in our mission. We shall never forget what you have done for us; I have the greatest reason to be grateful for your having offered the Holy Sacrifice for me. Give me again a share in it, for my eighty-one years make me think that death must be near.

Again she begs for the needs of the Church of St. Ferdinand:

S.C.J.M.   FEBRUARY 10, 1850.

Dear Reverend Father:

We have had a visit from Father Van Assche, the curé of St. Ferdinand. He has at last had the church re-roofed, but he wants a bell. He told me that you were hoping to get him one from Flanders, and he needs it badly to call his scattered parishioners. Despite my repugnance, he insists that I should interpret his wishes.

We are no longer at St. Ferdinand; the Sisters of Loretto of Kentucky have taken our place there, and they are also among the Osages under the direction of the Jesuits. Our religious, with whom I went to the Potawatomi, have changed their abode with the tribe and are now at Kaw River, where the Government has had schools built for both girls and boys, and has erected a church.

After alluding to the fire and the plague of cholera from which St. Louis had just suffered, she adds:

I am now in my eighty-first year, I have spent thirty-one in America where I have done very little for the Glory of Our Master. Pray for me, and I beg you to say a Mass to obtain for me a good death.

My Superior is Mother St. Cyr whom you met at St. Ferdinand's and at the Opelousas. Bless us both for the love of the Heart of Jesus.

The missions were still Mother Duchesne's dearest thought. Once when Mother Cutts had returned from a visit to the convent among the Indians she asked for volunteers. A Sister exclaimed impulsively: "It would be only the love of God that would make me go there."

"Well," Mother Cutts answered, "for the love of God you will go." When the Sister accepted the mission generously, Mother Duchesne's joy was unbounded. She made a spiritual bouquet for this new missionary, and taking both her hands told her how happy she was.

Mother Duchesne's favorite reading was "The Annals of the Propagation of the Faith," and when she read them aloud in the refectory, she forgot to stop and seemed strangely insensible to signal or bell.

The spiritual works of mercy: "To forgive all injuries" and "To bear wrongs patiently" were in these years to consist chiefly in patient endurance of the ills of life and in sweet oblivion to apparent slights and forgetfulness which needs must come. Her physical suffering increased—walking became more and more painful. She would drag herself from place to place— upstairs to the community room with her bundle of wool which she was carding, or with cope or quilt she was making, or downstairs to the parish school—as long as she might. Her hands had never become immune to cold, and so as to hide from delicate eyes her chilblains and wounds she wore mittens which were made of odd pieces of cloth. Towards the end, her eyesight grew so dim that her sewing, once beautiful, became coarser and coarser, and finally was forbidden her. Her mental suffering was great—for a time her memory seemed weakening and she sincerely thought that her last sacrifice was to be that of her mind. God, however, accepted the generous thought for the actuality—her strong intellect never dimmed. Her heart suffering was the greatest of all. To the young and active it often seems strange that the old suffer so much in seeing those whom they love slipping away into the eternity to which they know themselves to be hastening. Yet, it is certainly true that to the old the death of friends is the keenest of sorrows. Mother Duchesne now learned of the death of Sister Lamarre, who had come with her in 1818 and whose end came at Florissant in 1844 as she listened to the organ on which she had asked someone to play. In 1847, Mother Gonzaga Boilvin died at St. Vincent, Canada. Bishop Rosati had also gone to his reward, and had been succeeded by his coadjutor, Bishop Kenrick. This prelate discovered the poverty of St. Charles when he asked that the communion-rail of the religious be moved further back so that they would be less exposed to the view of the public in the church of St. Charles Borromeo into which the convent chapel opened. When the Superior answered that she wished this no less than did His Lordship, but that the house could not afford to have the work done, the kind Bishop himself saw that the change was made.

Mother Duchesne sought in her sufferings no alleviation such as her advanced age might seem to have justified. Her room, though to her convenient since it was next to the chapel, was very small. Its furniture consisted of a cot, a chair into which she had fastened a piece of rawhide as a seat, and a worm-eaten box which held her treasures—instruments of penance and letters received from her loved Mother Barat. Two or three old pictures hung on the wall, and in the corner were a few books of devotion. One of these—an Office-book worn beyond use—was removed and another put in its place. She remonstrated on learning that the old one had been burned, saying that she might have used it to teach Latin to the little ones. Until the end of her life she observed strictly every fast day, allowing herself no meat and taking only a little coffee in the morning and a cup of tisane at night.

Her greatest suffering was that which she had not imposed on herself, but which God in His inscrutable Providence allowed. Since she had first heard from Mother Barat in 1804, the letters of this sainted Mother, which had been her joy and her consolation, had come to her frequently. Both at Ste. Marie and all through the thirty years in America they arrived as regularly as the primitive post would allow. Then towards the end came a strange silence. For two or three years she received not a line from the Mother whom she venerated and loved with all the ardor of her warm nature. That letters were written and lost is more than probable. Mails were still irregular in the forties. Moreover, the Foundress, in her love for poverty, intrusted letters— especially those not addressed to superiors and therefore not urgent—to travellers. The absent-mindedness of amateur letter-carriers is proverbial—especially if they are men; so Mother Barat's letters to Mother Duchesne may have been lost. The Superior General would naturally write seldom to one whom she loved when that one was now no longer in authority.

One thing is certain—Mother Duchesne, fearing that the dearth of letters spoke of the displeasure of the Mother whom she loved, relapsed into a silence which did not inspire Mother Barat to write. Thus the heart of Mother Duchesne tasted a sorrow she had never before known—that of apparent rejection by those one loves best. Yet there was no bitterness in her grief. She might have whispered the complaint which St. Bernard puts upon the lips of the just man whose soul is left in darkness and desolation: "Lo, these many years I have been careful to lead a mortified life. I have applied myself with diligence to spiritual reading, I have resisted my passions, I have watched, I have been constant in prayer, I 'have recounted my years in the bitterness' of my soul. As far as was possible to me, I have, I think, lived without reproach. I have been obedient, going out and coming in at the word of authority. Far from coveting my neighbor's goods, I have rather given him my own and myself with them. In the sweat of my brow have I eaten my bread. What am I now, but according to the Prophet, as 'the heifer taught to love to tread out the corn' ". Yet no such complaint escaped her. Meanwhile, Mother Barat was uneasy about her loved Philippine. At that very time she sent to the house of St. Vincent in Canada, Mother Amélie Jouve, Mother Duchesne's own niece to whom her dying sister Aloysia, had said: "Amélie, you will replace me." St. Charles is hundreds of miles south of Canada, yet so great was the holy Foundress' solicitude for her grand old missionary, that she told Mother Jouve to go first to Missouri.

It was on September 14, 1847, that Mother Jouve arrived at St. Charles, whence she hastened to write:

This letter will show you that I am with my holy Aunt. I can say like St. Anthony: "I have seen Paul in the desert". I have seen a great saint who is nearing the end of her life. She is under the obedience of Mother St. Cyr—one of the first pupils of Florissant. She feels the inaction to which she is reduced, for she is without any employment save that afforded her by her needle. They venerate her as a relic, but to my way of thinking it makes her sad to be only a relic. One could overlook it if one were enshrined in the reliquary of Heaven, but as long as the soul lives in its earthly dwelling it longs for occupation in its exile. Prayer is her only refuge and the greater part of her day passes before the Blessed Sacrament. She answers two or three Masses on her knees in the centre of the chapel without any support.

You would be touched by the destitution of St. Charles—one can imagine nothing poorer. Mother Duchesne's room is the sanctuary of Holy Poverty, and Benedict Labre would recognize her as his sister. I found her very feeble and her voice so faint that at times one has difficulty in hearing her. She received me as an angel from Heaven, and ecstatic happiness was depicted on her face as she read the letter from our Very Reverend Mother.

"What," the saintly old Mother murmured, "our Mother General still thinks of me, still cares for me, she has been so good as to send you to me?"

Mother Jouve tried to find out what she could do to give pleasure to Mother Duchesne. Her answer was that she would like the picture of St. Francis Regis, which had been left behind at Florissant, brought to St. Charles. This painting was the one given her by Bishop Du Bourg in 1819, that in which Heaven is seen opening to receive the Saint whom Mother Philippine loved as much now as when sixty years before she had gone to his shrine at La Louvesc. The second request was that Mother Regis Hamilton, her old child and co-worker, might return from Canada to St. Charles before Mother Duchesne should have followed St. Francis Regis to the Heaven that for her too seemed to be opening. In the name of the Mother General, Mother Jouve promised the fulfilment of both petitions. The Sisters of Loretto willingly gave the picture to Mgr. St. Cyr, who took it to St. Charles.

Shortly after Mother Jouve's return to Canada, Mother Duchesne wrote to her:

S.C.J.M. ST. CHARLES, OCTOBER 10, 1847.

Dearest Amélie:

I received your letter written from St.Louis. It was a great sorrow for me to see you leave me forever, for we can hope to meet again only in Heaven. So we must try to get there—both of us—though by very different paths; I, by my insignificance, and you by a work important in God's eyes—the education of youth. He has given you the talents needed for this, it is for you to make them yield the hundredfold. Let us never forget that the road to Heaven is that of suffering. Our Lord has called us to follow Him carrying the cross as He did. There is no choice—we must carry it if we are to be saved. You made a big step forward when you left France and much that you cared for. Now you must courageously persevere in your generous gift of yourself. Renounce lawful satisfactions, adapt yourself to characters of different nationalities, see God always in His creatures and live with them as children of one Father.

Immediately after your departure I made my retreat. God offered me nothing but crosses; ask Him that I may bear them well. I had great difficulty in reading your letter. I hope that in future you will use better ink. What you wrote me from Paris was almost illegible. *I* shall try not to deserve the same reproach.

A year later she wrote—again to her niece:

Give news of us to Mothers de Kersaint and Hamilton. I greet them in the Sacred Heart, as I do also Mother Roach and Sister Short. If Mother de Monestrol knew me, she would not travel far to see me. It is only you who have the courage to do that.

Her letter to Mother Amélie Jouve, written on the 30th of May, 1850, is characteristic:

We still have at St. Charles three Jesuit Fathers who on Sundays serve three parishes. These last two days we have had six Masses each morning, thanks to some visiting priests. One Mass was offered for my intention. I answered another kneeling between two altars on which the Holy Sacrifice was being offered by our greatest missionaries—Father De Smet, who has four times crossed the land separating us from the Pacific and who has visited all the tribes living in that territory, and Father Hoecken who is very gifted for Indian dialects of which he speaks eighteen or nineteen. He is stationed at the Mission where our Sisters are but he is longing to undertake fresh conquests for God. Think how well placed I was between these two saints, whose charity is so great that they often offer their Mass for me.

In a letter written in February, 1851, she speaks of the Golden Jubilee of her beloved Society. In ending she says: "I fear to be a burden to my Sisters as I have had several fainting spells which menace my old age. Mother St. Cyr suffers also. Pray for her and for us."

One of the Mothers, seeking to provide a little distraction for Mother Duchesne in her lonely suffering life, procured a peacock, which the dear Mother did not appreciate, for when it spread out its feathers and strutted she saw in it the personification of pride. She thanked the child who had brought the bird from her farm and asked whether there were any sheep there. The child understood, and brought a lamb, which symbolized what Mother Philippine had been striving to become ever since she had known Mother Barat. The lamb loved her also, followed her to the chapel, got in if it could, and then lay at her feet unperceived. She had become more lamblike herself. The children in disgrace were her favorites, and they found in her such a refuge that punishment became far too popular, and the most effective threat in the school grew to be: "If you do that, you may *not* go to Mother Duchesne."

So the years passed in waiting, in hidden suffering, in prayer; for Philippine was reaping the holy habit of years. It was not for nothing that she had long cherished the strong doctrine of her favorite ascetic writer, Father Guilloré—it was not in vain that she had learned what he calls "The sovereign felicity and the incomparable grandeur of being despised with Christ." This felicity and this grandeur were read on her radiant face one day when she was seen coming from the chapel with a heavenly expression on her countenance and about her head a halo of light.

CHAPTER VII

The Consummation

CHAPTER VII

The Consummation—1851-1852

"Ah, God is good, Who writes His glory plain
Above thee and about thee, at thy side—
Bids thee look upward from that blinding pain;
And ere thy longing tires,
Kindles His sudden fires.
Look, and let all thy soul be satisfied!"

ROBERT HUGH BENSON.

As the year 1851 wore on, Mother Duchesne grew weaker. Little by little aid which she had been able to give was abandoned: she no longer supervised the morning study in the boarding school; her little bent figure was sometimes seen in the garden, but she was not allowed, as formerly, to gather up the fruit that fell from the trees. Her eyesight gradually weakened and she could no longer make use of her needle even when it had been threaded by the willing hands of the children. Yet though little light reached her eyes from without, they were luminous, and they seemed to read one's very heart.

On October 14, 1851, she wrote to Mother Amélie Jouve: "I am growing very old. My memory is going, and my strength diminishes more and more. Perhaps this will be the last letter from me. I count on your prayers and those of your good daughters to whom I recommend myself."

Her Superior added the following postscript:

I hope, dear Mother, that you will excuse my silence which is due only to lack of time. The weakness of our holy Mother Duchesne causes us anxiety, but her fervor and regularity encourage us in the practice of virtue. Pray for her, pray for us all.

EMELIE ST. CYR.

A little later the journal of the house of St. Charles notes: "Our holy and venerated Mother Duchesne's declining days seemed to have acquired renewed animation and vigor from the sight of her loved and devoted daughter, Mother Regis Hamilton, who has arrived with Mother Gallway."

In her gratitude, Mother Duchesne wrote to Mother Amélie Jouve: "How happy I am to be able to give the name of Mother to my dear Regis." This referred to the fact that Mother Hamilton has just been named Superior of St. Charles. She made use of every opportunity to try to repay by loving care all that Mother Duchesne had done for her and her sister in years gone by. She slept in the same little cell with this valiant Mother, and tried to foresee and to supply her every need, as she wrote:

I am at St. Charles with my holy Mother Duchesne, who, instead of saying her "*Nunc Dimittis*," shows renewed vigor. When on my arrival I found her scarcely able to walk and with a voice so feeble that she could hardly make herself heard, I was sadder than I can say. I care for her, but not as I should wish, for she still has the idea that she must do penance and that everything is too good for her. As a result, we sometimes quarrel; at one time I win, at another I lose.

During these last years of life only one work of mercy remained to Mother Philippine—"To pray for the living and the dead." The needs of the Church, of the Missions, of those afflicted by war, plague or disaster were ever before her, as her letters bear witness. With pleasure she noted that President Taylor had ordered that the First Friday of August, 1849, be set aside for public prayer and humiliation to draw down the mercy of God on a land devastated by plague. Her prayer embraced the whole world, "The state of Europe lies heavy on my heart," she wrote, "but France is foremost in the good cause, and like Charlemagne of old, re-establishes the Holy Father in his temporal possessions. How greatly we need the aid of Heaven to repress this passion for anarchy and division." When Mother Duchesne was leaving the Mother House in 1818, Mother Barat gave her a small silver statue of our Lady of the Pillar. This image owes its origin to the legend that the Apostle St. James was granted a vision of the Mother of God who appeared seated on the top of a pillar of jasper. She asked him to build a chapel in her honor on the bank of the Ebro in Spain, and the column of jasper is preserved even to-day in the great seventeenth-century church which evolved from the tiny shrine erected by the Apostle. Mother Philippine prized her little statue, not only as the parting gift of her revered Mother Foundress, but because it represented a Mother even more dear to her heart. It was to remain with her to the end, years after her death it was to find its way back to France, and it may be seen to-day among the treasures and souvenirs in the Mother House of the Society in Rome.

Philippine's greatest devotion all through her life had been to the Holy Sacrifice and so it was to the end.

As her sight had grown dim and she feared that her memory was no longer reliable, she read aloud from her Office-book with its very large type the responses for Mass. That Office-book was her constant companion, for even after she had been anointed in August, 1852, she was still in her stall for the canonical hours, uniting her faint voice and her valiant spirit to the rest of the choir. The same Office-book bears witness to this day to the zeal of her prayer. Its flyleaves are covered with the intentions for which she heard Mass, received Holy Communion, and recited certain prayers on each day of the week. The Church, the Missions, travellers, sinners, the Souls in Purgatory, her loved Mother Barat, the Society, the Vicariate, the house of St. Charles—each had its place in her calendar.

The same old Office-book also testifies to her poverty. "At the Inn of Divine Providence," said Venerable Félix De Andreis, "one fares well"; and Mother Duchesne was to the end of her journey the poor pilgrim of Christ. She inserted additional leaflets, scraps that no one else could have used and an old envelope with the postmark, "New York, 10¢," on which slips she copied prayers or wrote out resolutions. There one may read a promise written in English with French spelling: "I *firmely* resolve henceforth to lead a *penitente* and mortified life," and again:

> "*N'aimer que Toi,—C'est mon plus doux plaisir.*
> *Vivre pour Toi,—C'est mon unique vie;*
> *Souffrir pour Toi,—C'est mon plus grand désir;*
> *Mourir pour Toi,—C'est ma plus forte envie.*"

On one page are the words, "*Fiat Voluntas Tua,*" and the traces of tears.

On the 17th of August, 1852, Mother Duchesne wrote a last farewell to Mother Barat:

Very Reverend and dear Mother:

According to all appearances this is the last time that I shall write to you. Yesterday I received the Last Sacraments, but perhaps God wants me to wait longer for the joy of seeing Him. The wandering of mind that I experienced came merely from high fever. I do not know when my end will be, but I come again to beg your forgiveness and to assure you of my profound veneration.

She kept up until the sixteenth of November, when she was forbidden to go to her stall for Office. The next morning she wished to rise as usual for Mass and Holy Communion, but this being refused, she obeyed with childlike simplicity, saying only: "But why will you deprive me of the graces of this beautiful day?" She thought it would be her last, but it was another blessing that was to beautify it for her. That very afternoon Mother Cutts took to St. Charles Mother Anna du Rousier, who had come to North America as Visitor and was on her way to found the first house of the Society of the Sacred Heart in South America. The Mother Visitatrix brought Mother Duchesne a last blessing from her loved Mother Barat, and in return she asked the prayers of the dying missionary and her benediction on the work that lay before her in the great southland. Mothers du Rousier and Cutts were obliged to hurry back to St. Louis without even spending one night in St. Charles. Of the blessing she had received there, Mother Cutts afterwards said: "Oh, I seem to feel still the cross that she traced on my forehead. I trust to that cross to bring me happiness, and I shall try to love it ever more and more."

That evening, Mother Duchesne noticed that the last bell had rung and that her old daughter and young Superior still remained near her cot: "Mother Regis," she murmured, "if you do not go to rest, I will get up." Mother Hamilton lay down, but hearing Mother Duchesne coughing, rose to give her a drink. Once midnight had come the dying Mother refused to take a drop of water and break the fast for the morning's Communion. At eight o'clock she observed that a fire had been lit in her room. "You think only of the things of this world," she whispered; "it would be very much better if you recited a Pater and an Ave for the good of my soul." She was assured that the community were praying for her in an adjoining room.

"Oh," she said softly, "how happy I am to die in this house where charity reigns."

The Infirmarian asked her to pray that she too might soon die. To this the dear Mother replied with some of her wonted vehemence: "Indeed I shall not. What would Reverend Mother do if everyone in the house should die?"

At ten o'clock Father Verhaegen heard Mother Duchesne's last Confession, gave her Extreme Unction again, for she had not been continuously ill since her anointing in August, and brought her Holy Viaticum. It was her last Communion Day, November 18, 1852.

After some moments of thanksgiving Mother Regis suggested the ejaculation: "Jesus, Mary, Joseph, I give you my heart, my soul and my life." Eagerly Mother Duchesne repeated the prayer some twenty times and then added: "Oh, yes—my life—generously. Come, Lord Jesus, do not delay. Come, come quickly.

The Convent in St. Charles As It Is To-day

Oh, what happiness to die in this holy house! Oh, what charity in my Mothers and Sisters!"

When the Angelus rang at the noon-day, Philippine Duchesne had, in truth, given to God her heart, her soul and her life. Her body was laid in the tiny parlor near her cell and a few of the many who revered her went there to pray for her whom they loved. A daguerreotype was taken of her as she lay there in marblelike peace, "in case," so said her community, "she may one day be canonized." And to the Mother House they wrote: "She was to the end a model of obedience, love of poverty, humility."

On the 20th, the funeral Mass was said in the Church of St. Charles Borromeo, for the convent chapel adjoining it could not contain all who wished to be present. Then she was laid to rest in the little cemetery on the hill behind the convent, whence through the leafless trees could be seen the Valley of Florissant, her "Valley Forge," and the turbid tawny Missouri flowing from the west where Sugar Creek nestled, down, down towards St. Michael's—past St. Michael's out to the sea—measureless as the love that had bound her to the Mother House and to the Foundress, St. Madeleine Sophie.

Father Verhaegen turned away from the view and followed the religious down the slope past the gnarled and angular pear-tree which, it was said, François Duquette had planted, and which had been grafted by Mother Duchesne and was to live on through the years, bearing abundant fruit.

As Father Verhaegen saw the nuns enter the chapel to say the *"De Profundis,"* he went on to the presbytery to write in the Parish Burial Register what he had done. He was generally brief—but it was not only because he had known Mother Duchesne for twenty-five years in

Florissant, in St. Louis, in the Indian camp, in the obscurity and oblivion of St. Charles—it was not only that he had known her long and under varying circumstances—that he wrote:

On the 20th day of November, 1852, I, the undersigned, buried the mortal remains of Madame Philippine Duchesne, professed religious of the Society of the Sacred Heart, aged 83 years.

Madame Duchesne was a native of France, and came to the United States of America with a small number of religious of the Society of the Sacred Heart in 1818. She may be considered as the foundress of all the houses of the Sacred Heart in the United States. Eminent in all the virtues of religious life, but especially in humility, she sweetly and calmly departed this life in the odor of sanctity on the 18th day of November, 1852.

P. J. VERHAEGEN, S. J.

Three weeks later the great missionary, Father De Smet, wrote: "You should publish a beautiful biography of Mother Duchesne. The dry announcement of her death in that paper 'The Shepherd of the Valley' truly vexed me. No greater Saint ever died in Missouri, nor perhaps in the whole Union."

AFTERWORD

AFTERWORD

"When the high heart we magnify,
When the sure vision celebrate,
And worship greatness passing by—
Ourselves are great."

JOHN DRINKWATER.

Mother Duchesne had said: "You will see that when I am dead, everything will progress." Her thought must have sprung from "the highest degree of the hardest grace—humility"; for it has proven true.

She must rejoice to-day in the fruits of her work. Her dearest love was the Church, which has never ceased to keep pace with the young Republic, "exulting as a giant to run its course." Within the Church the work of education has waxed ever stronger. Convents of the Sacred Heart, founded directly by Mother Duchesne or taking their rise from those she brought into being, have had their little share in the great cause of furthering the interests of the Kingdom of Christ.

The result of the labor, the prayer and the suffering of Venerable Philippine Duchesne is not confined to the United States, nor even to the borderlands of Canada and Mexico. When in 1818 she stopped at the convent of Poitiers on her way to Bordeaux for America, she was asked to speak to the boarding school on the mission to which she was going. Among the children who listened was Anna du Rousier, who felt herself fired with the desire to follow the missionary so soon to embark.

391

Thirty-four years separated her from her desire. In 1852, in her visit to St. Charles, she felt once more the inspiration of example. At Poitiers Mother Duchesne had been—like Elias—a flame of ardent impetuous fire. Now the embers burned low, and in their glow Mother du Rousier kindled the torch of zeal that she was to carry to South America.

Mother Aloysia Hardey, the foundess of the older houses of the eastern vicariate, had been a child at Grand Côteau, where she had known Mother Duchesne, and where as a novice she was trained by those who owed their formation to Venerable Philippine. Another child of Grand Côteau was to carry devotion to the Sacred Heart to more remote shores, for Mother Suzanna Boudreau led a little colony of religious to New Zealand, and died, as Mother Duchesne had thought she herself would die, a fortnight after her arrival in the promised land. The foundation which she made in Oceania lives on and has spread out into an extensive vicariate. A third child who received her education in Grand Côteau, Mother Mary Moran, in 1883, made the first foundation in the Republic of Mexico.

In the works of zeal initiated by Mother Duchesne there have been developments of which she never could have dreamed. Academies have matured into colleges and normal schools, elementary schools have expanded to receive great numbers of children, the work of retreats has branched out while its trunk has been strengthened by high organization. The Society has come in close contact with the princely pagans of Japan and the infidel Mussulmans of Egypt, and recently has had the privilege of carrying a humble apostolate to China.

Yet the work dearest of all to Mother Duchesne was

that for Indians—the work for which she longed to come to America—yet after all, not the work for which the Society of the Sacred Heart had been founded. This is why this love of her heart has not been furthered with the advance of years. True, the Society has come frequently in touch with Indians in South America and Mexico in schools and retreats, as it has also instructed colored children—the second love of her heart; but it was not for these two races that the little Society was destined; consequently work with them has always given place to more pressing needs in other fields. But, even here, Mother Duchesne's ardently desired mission still lives.

Some years ago, a young American girl knelt at the feet of Pope Leo XIII, and implored His Holiness to send to the United States missionary nuns who would help to care for the millions of negroes and the thousands of Indians in need of spiritual help. The Pope looked at the kneeling figure before him, and as if inspired said: "My dear child, why do you not become a missionary yourself?" It was the decisive moment for Katherine Drexel, who only needed the word of the Vicar of Christ to assure her that such was her vocation. Returning to her country, she founded the Order of the Sisters of the Blessed Sacrament, whose great and beautiful work is the care of the Catholic Negroes and Indians in the United States of America. Her home had been on the outskirts of the Convent of the Sacred Heart, Eden Hall, and in her frequent visits there, and at her daily Mass in the convent chapel, she had felt the longing to devote herself to Christ's little ones—a longing and love that she shared with Mother Duchesne.

Venerable Philippine Duchesne's work lives after her, and Bishop Du Bourg's words to her ring with prophecy: "We must clear the field before we can cultivate it—you and I will pass our lives in this ungrateful task. Our successors will reap the benefit in this world —let us be satisfied to reap it in the next."

On the 24th of May, the Feast of the Ascension, 1865, the Holy Foundress followed her dear Philippine to Heaven. Forty-four years later, after having studied her life and her virtues, examined the miracles worked at her intercession in the New World as well as the Old, and noted that the Society which she had founded was still imbued with her spirit, Pope Pius X, of holy memory, declared Madeleine Sophie Barat Blessed. In the Holy Year of Jubilee, 1925, Pope Pius XI raised her to Sainthood.

Bishop Du Bourg encouraged Mother Duchesne to seek her reward and success only in the life to come. We may not look behind the veil that hides that life; we cannot conceive the happiness that radiates Heaven, but we can be glad for her and hope that since her Cause has been introduced in Rome she may show her power with God by signal miracles, and that the Church may set its seal of approbation upon her life and death.

END

INDEX

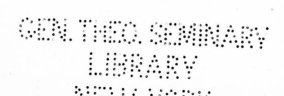